W9-AQM-662

PHILIP KAPPEL

By John P. Marquand

Timothy Dexter
Revisited

Timothy Dexter Revisited

by JOHN P. MARQUAND

Illustrated by Philip Kappel

921

LITTLE, BROWN AND COMPANY
Boston · Toronto

C L

LEE COUNTY LIBRARY
SANFORD, N. C.

COPYRIGHT 1925, BY J. P. MARQUAND

COPYRIGHT 1953, © 1960 BY JOHN P. MARQUAND

ALL RIGHTS RESERVED. NO PART OF THIS BOOK MAY BE REPRO-
DUCED IN ANY FORM WITHOUT PERMISSION IN WRITING FROM THE
PUBLISHER, EXCEPT BY A REVIEWER WHO MAY QUOTE BRIEF PAS-
SAGES IN A REVIEW TO BE PRINTED IN A MAGAZINE OR NEWSPAPER.

LIBRARY OF CONGRESS CATALOG CARD NO. 60–9335

FIRST EDITION

Published simultaneously in Canada
by Little, Brown & Company (Canada) Limited

PRINTED IN THE UNITED STATES OF AMERICA

Contents

Contents

Timothy Dexter Revisited

The Palace of the Late Lord Timothy Dexter of Newburyport, Mass., as Viewed from a Dentist's Chair

IN AUGUST 1957, I was seized one day with a violent toothache. When toward afternoon the pain in my lower jaw showed no sign of abating, I telephoned a Newburyport dentist, Dr. Sullivan, whose dental parlor is in his dwelling on High Street in that city. It was indeed fortunate that I did so in time, as all doctors and dentists — or almost all — customarily leave the city of Newburyport in August for vacations in cooler and more salubrious areas. Actually Dr. Sullivan, when I called, was on the point of packing his family into his car to pursue this conventional tactic. It was kind of him to have delayed his trip for nearly an hour while we together faced a rather eloquent example of physical disintegration.

I pointed out to Dr. Sullivan that I was invariably a coward in a dentist's chair. I told him that I realized how anxious he must be to start on his vacation, but, even so, I did hope that he would spend enough time to give me a massive dose of Novocain and to allow it opportunity to work so that the extraction would be as agreeable and painless as possible. Dr. Sullivan, I am pleased to report, was kind, considerate and cooperative. He told me to rest quietly in the dental chair until my lips, tongue and the left side of my face were numb, and while we both awaited this result we spoke of the Newburyport we had once known in our childhood, of the recent demise of various prominent citizens, of the hideous increase of motor traffic on High Street, and of the general disintegration of the town since our youth. We also agreed, both of us being broad-minded, that everything, even Newburyport, looks better at that stage of one's development than in later years and that it could be that we now saw it with jaundiced eyes. We conversed until the numbness in my tongue made speech markedly difficult. Then I looked through the left-hand window of the extraction room and observed, from the functional chair in which I reclined, that Dr. Sullivan's house was contiguous to the grounds of the old Lord Timothy Dexter dwelling on High Street. Neither building nor grounds were in a condition of which the late Lord Timothy Dexter would have approved, but then too, neither was Newburyport.

As this book is designed to explain, at least superficially, something of the extraordinary career of Lord Timothy Dexter and of the bizarre but often beautiful historical and social climate which permitted such an extraordinary individual to burgeon and to bloom, it is needful to state here that Lord Dexter occupied the house and grounds next to Dr. Sullivan's office at the turn of the eighteenth century. One might also add that Mr. Dexter (1747–1806), a sort of overgrown Horatio Alger hero, but who deviated

from the pattern in many, many ways, has become a part
of Newburyport folklore and historically has the reputation of being one of the greatest eccentrics so far produced
in America. Though some figures of the present, both local
and national, are daily contending for the honor, compared with Dexter they are pallid mediocrities.

The Novocain was working and Dr. Sullivan was growing restive. Perhaps only an instinctive desire to postpone
my approaching ordeal sharpened my interest in the Dexter
house and grounds. These both were in poor shape compared with what they had been in my childhood or even
a decade ago. Of course the majestic fence, and the arch
exhibiting the wooden figures of our first three Presidents,
and the numerous columns about the lawn that had supported historical and mythological personages, executed by
a local carver of ships' figureheads, had all disappeared long
before living memory. So, too, had Lord Dexter's glass
summerhouse that had once been built above his tomb. The
dwelling itself, an early example of local architecture derived from the English Georgian, which developed into a
style that is now termed Federalist, had doubtless been
bowdlerized and overembellished by Dexter after he had
purchased it and turned it into an American palace. Unfortunately subsequent owners, some possibly more affluent
than Dexter himself, including the Corliss (steam-turbine)
family, and Madame Tingley, daughter of a Newburyport
entrepreneur and Theosophy's Purple Mother, had added
their own well-intentioned improvements, throwing rooms
together, installing hardwood floors, tampering with paneling and adding Victorian piazzas. With all these changes,
it is impossible now to tell where Dexter left off and ex-

actly where his successors began. Thus the interior of the house, or more accurately, mansion, with its three stories and cupola, though built in 1771 by a gentleman whom a Newburyport writer has termed "a merchant prince," is now more Edwardian than pre-Revolutionary. Its spaciousness remains and some of its majestic proportions — too majestic perhaps, because Newburyport merchant princes of this early period appear to have had as great a desire to impress as their successors of a later century.

Unfortunately, to anyone enlightened by modern historical reconstructions, many rooms of the old house lack the authenticity which one might anticipate. The third

story, now reached by a narrow stairway not designed by
the original architect, contains some rooms which one suspects were once used by Madame Tingley's followers, since
one still bares traces of gymnastic appliances that may have
been used for semi-Oriental physical exercise. Only the interior of the cupola has definitely remained unchanged,
with its beautiful old glasswork and simple window seats on
which Lord Dexter, himself, may once have sat, if he cared
to look from High Street across the Merrimack River.
And on the way up to the cupola one can still see in the
attics the imposing wood framing of the mansion, hand
hewn and pegged; and here is the smell of old wood and antiquity, the clear, untainted atmosphere of the past.

The grounds outside, as well as the exterior of the house
itself, formerly presented a fine and disciplined appearance.
The house was spotless white; its fence, fronting High
Street, though not the ornate Dexter fence, was in keeping
with the façade; the lawns were mowed; there were horses
and later automobiles in the commodious stable, and there
was a flower garden whose bordered walks stretched toward the orchards and hayfields which Dexter himself has
mentioned. There were many shade trees on the lawns,
magnificent specimens, especially the silver and the copper
beeches and the umbrella trees, and several of these might
very well have been set out by Lord Dexter's gardeners; and
the garden plan itself bore traces of his supervision. The
weathervane upon the cupola, an immense American
eagle, carved to Dexter's order, looked down upon a well-
kept demesne, an ample piece of land that extended from
High Street to Low Street. But now the place had changed,
viewed from the dentist's chair.

The Dexter property had been "let go," to use a New England expression. Its previous owner, after trying in vain to find a purchaser for an estate unfitted by its size and appointments for present practicality, had finally sold it piecemeal. Part of the High Street frontage had been purchased as the site for a Baptist Church, and why should the Baptists continue mowing lawns and trimming shrubbery until at least their edifice was built? The house had been purchased by a young antique dealer, who was not only an avid reader of Tolstoy but who also had excellent ideas regarding its artistic restoration. However, even Tolstoy himself could not have done everything at once, and a great deal did need to be done. The house demanded a coat of paint, for instance, like many other houses along Newburyport's once famous street. The grass on most of its lawn was now so high that it was difficult to perceive the line of the terrace which may have marked the edge of the Dexter garden and the site of the Dexter summerhouse and tomb, to which, Lord Dexter has told us, he occasionally retired to smoke his pipe and read a few good songs. The eagle himself had left the cupola — at least temporarily. His wings and head were becoming cracked and he needed a general overhaul after a century and a half of Massachusetts weather.

"I think," Dr. Sullivan said, "you are as ready now for the extraction as you ever will be. Open, please."

The illusion of sadness that had come over me as I gazed at the desuetude of the Dexter place was increased rather than dispelled now that my jaw was open and my molar was in Dr. Sullivan's competent grasp. Thirty years ago it had been easier to appreciate many aspects of Newburyport's golden past than it is at present. Frankly, the last thirty years had dealt with Newburyport as roughly as they had with me, from a physical point of view. Newburyport was suffering from its own ulcerated molars. It was no longer the separate community which the social anthropologist, W. Lloyd Warner, has classified so successfully in his "Yankee City" series. The static social barriers, the eccentricities of the older town — at least a good many of them — had disappeared beneath a five-o'clock shadow of mediocrity that was now creeping over it. Newburyport was no longer the classic example of Yankee isolation that had delighted observers, including myself, once. Assisted by superhighways and fin-tailed motor cars, the advance guard of suburbia was now approaching. Acres of split-level ranch types were appearing on developments being given the resounding names of "Worcester Heights" or "Sandy Acres," or sometimes no names at all. The streets were thronged now with individuals who cared nothing for the past of Newburyport and who were utterly ignorant of the gradations of status of its elder citizens and families. Newburyport, after its years of self-sufficiency, after its glorious hiatuses of ingenuity and initiative, was at last becoming a bedroom town, and a successful one at that, judging from the playpens on the lawns of Worcester Heights and from the increasing overcrowding of its schools. The motor traffic in Newburyport, which had once been tolerable, was now appalling, as I sat and opened wider for Dr. Sullivan.

"It seems to want to stay there, doesn't it?" Dr. Sullivan said.

This, I imagine, might be termed a dentists' cliché. A

truck roared by on High Street. I was shaken by its vibra-
tion and I had a fleeting thought of what such shaking
would have done to the wine in the Dexter cellar. In order
to free my mind as much as possible from my ordeal, I
gazed through tear-dimmed eyes at Timothy Dexter's
former home, and recited to myself a verse from the ode
that had been composed for him by Jonathan Plummer, his
poet laureate.

> His house is filled with sweet perfumes,
> Rich furniture doth fill his rooms,
> Inside and out it is adorn'd
> And on the top an eagle's form'd.

"I think we're beginning to get it now," Dr. Sullivan
said.

I, too, was beginning to get it. Modern America, with its
immediacies, including extraction, had made the past of
Newburyport more remote than ever. There is, of course,
always a sonic and physical barrier between the past and
the present. No generation can wholly understand another,
but the slender liaison which had existed in my youth was
broken now. A thicker, less definable curtain had fallen
between me and the past of Newburyport, between me and
my ancestors who had helped to make that past. It was
not an iron curtain, nor a bamboo curtain; it was a plastic,
spun-glass curtain through which one viewed old shapes
dimly. There were distortions; there were blurs, and sometimes voids. What had life been like when Lord Timothy
Dexter had existed just outside Dr. Sullivan's window?

I felt a twinge in spite of the Novocain.

"Here it is," Dr. Sullivan said, "and I think it's a boy."

It was, I am sure, another dentists' cliché, but I could not answer because I was hemorrhaging, as they say in the medical profession. I was still thinking of the new curtain that had fallen between past and present. I was thinking of ancient values, including the eagle that needed repair. I had tried once to estimate these values, thirty years ago, and now that I was hemorrhaging I knew that my estimation had been naïve. The question was still there. What had Newburyport been like when Lord Timothy Dexter walked its streets followed by his, presumably, Mexican hairless dog? Why had people put up with him? What was life like when no trucks roared down High Street? I could remember in my infancy the horse-drawn age, but now the opaque plastic curtain had dropped down. I did not know the answers, and Dr. Sullivan was leaving for his vacation.

"Keep this piece of cotton in your mouth," Dr. Sullivan said, "and bite down on it. It will control the hemorrhage."

"Will it be all right," I asked Dr. Sullivan, "if I have a drink when I return home?"

"Yes," he said, "a drink is indicated," which I fear is another dental cliché, but I was thinking that Lord Timothy Dexter, under such circumstances, would have taken rum, not Scotch — rum, perhaps, from the old Caldwell distillery in Newburyport, an institution which was nearly as venerable as the old town itself and, like the old town, had fallen upon different, if not evil, days.

The Catalogued Dust Heaps of a Venerable New England Community

NEWBURYPORT is an excellently documented town. In fact, it is doubtful whether any town in the country has a better or more carefully indexed local history than the late John J. Currier's substantial volumes that deal with Newbury and Newburyport. Here one can find superbly regimented facts that start with the town's first settlers on Parker River in 1636. It is regrettable that the pages of Currier's history end with the unenlightened era of the early nineteenth-hundreds, but even so, until very recently the Currier volumes could have served as guidebooks, because most of the old landmarks still stood as he described them.

But the Currier volumes are not the only historian's tribute to Newburyport. There is also Coffin's *History of Newbury*. If not always based on Currier's solid factual foundation, a perusal of the Coffin opus reveals many interesting facts. One discovers here that in the year 1793 a codfish weighing ninety-eight pounds was sold in Newburyport. He (or possibly she) was five feet and a half in length, his girth at the thickest place three feet, four inches. A year later we learn that Newburyport passed two laws, one prohibiting any person from smoking any pipe or cigar in any street, lane or alley in the town, the second imposing a fine of two shillings on the owner of "every duck or goose, gander or drake found in Frog Pond." As of now this last regulation appears to have been more effective than the other. Frog Pond, with its mall, is still extant and has a Bulfinch courthouse standing on its bank. Ducks, geese and ganders are a rarity upon its waters.[1] But on State and Pleasant Streets even middle-aged women in shorts and halters may now be observed smoking filtered cigarettes on any summer's day or night.

There is also the *History of Newburyport, From the Earliest Settlement of the Country to the present time, with a biographical appendix,* by Mrs. E. Vale Smith, published in 1854. This is written in narrative form. Most of it is refreshingly lively and some of its prose rises to an apex of "fine writing." Describing the great fire of Newburyport in the year 1811, which may still be the greatest crisis Newburyport has faced to date, Mrs. Smith writes: "Gathering clouds of smoke obscured the bright, clear moon, which shone out upon the origin of the fire, as if willing to lend its aid to expose the concealed perpetrators." It may be that Mrs. Smith lacked the accuracy of John J. Currier, since it would seem, from other sources, that the fire started in a stable and that internal combustion was responsible, but then, there always have been subversive elements in Newburyport.

[1] Since this was written a change has occurred. The civic authorities have established some Peking ducks in the Frog Pond and have given them a floating house on the roof of which is written: "Be kind to us. We are your friends.—MR. and MRS. DUCK."

The Story of Byfield, by John Louis Ewell, D.D., is another compendium of fact and gossip, but for readability the best of them is *The Reminiscences of a Nonagenarian,* by Sarah Anna Emery, published by William H. Huse & Company, 42 State Street, Newburyport, in 1879. This curious work exhibits a liveliness which still has charm. Despite eighty years' rest in secondhand bookstores, one can still read the Emery volume with the bemused admiration that one experiences on perusing Cotton Mather's earlier *Magnalia Christi Americana.* Both have a comparable accuracy, and, like the *Magnalia,* Mrs. Emery's reminiscences are largely a patchwork of hearsay, gossip, and unsubstantiated facts gathered during a long and active life from her mother, grandmother, and other old inhabitants.

It would be easy to mention several other works of reminiscence that include at least partly life in Newburyport, and these are supported by numerous journals, account books, and letters removed from Newburyport attics; but better than all of these annals and manuscripts, because they have an immediacy which time has not erased, are the daily newspapers of the town. A nearly complete file of these still exists in the old Newburyport Public Library, which occupies the great Nathaniel Tracy mansion on State Street. The mansion, in which General Lafayette and other dignitaries, including Aaron Burr, were formerly entertained, would now be practically unrecognizable to any of these gentlemen because of the golden oak alterations installed there. The papers represent their time far better than the Tracy house ever will again.

The extensive bibliography of Newburyport, outlined here only in a casual manner, extends almost, if not quite, into the present. In the days of the great depression a well-trained team of investigators, headed by W. Lloyd Warner, now of the University of Chicago, descended upon Newburyport equipped with institutional funds and remained there, some of them, for several years. Their purpose was to examine the mores and ambitions of a community on the northeast seaboard. Newburyport was selected for this honor because it was, at that time, an independent entity whose population largely derived a living from farming or from small neighborhood industries. Today the results of this research are available in five volumes with a greater wordage than the Currier history, and the last of them has only recently been published, under the title *The Living and the Dead*.

The Yankee City Series is, unfortunately, written primarily for social scientists who, like our medical profession, persist in coining a language all their own, and indulge too often in sentence and paragraph structures that verge on the unliterary.

Although the Yankee City Series began to be printed in the nineteen-forties, its studies, from the point of view of modern Newburyport, are as dated in many respects as those of Mrs. Emery or of Mrs. Smith, for the town has changed more in the last two decades, socially and materially, than in all its previous history. The Newburyport society which so interested the Warner researchers, though outlines of it are still extant, has been altered in many areas beyond recognition. High Street is not the same High Street that Mr. Warner scrutinized, nor is Newburyport any longer an isolated community. If Mr. Warner were to continue further with his Yankee City, another volume

might be a very different social saga. When he studied the
town, he encountered habits formed by a puritanical and
also a considerably sophisticated past; and much of the
Newburyport that Mr. Warner examined was socially
extant in the greatest days of Lord Timothy Dexter —
far more than exists at present. Yet only the other day,
while sitting in the Dalton Club, built in the 1760's, once
the residence of the Honorable Tristram Dalton, later
occupied by Newburyport's jurist, Theophilus Parsons,
and still one of the finest dwellings in the city, a member
made a sad remark. He made it while looking from the
front parlor of the Dalton House at the site of the old
Wolfe Tavern, now demolished and replaced by a plastic-
tiled lubricatorium.

"Why is it," he asked, "that there are no quaint old
characters in Newburyport any longer?"

It was one of those interesting questions that one can
still hear in the Dalton Club on a Friday or Saturday afternoon, and one that has an easy answer. The truth was that
the gentleman who asked it was turning into a quaint old
character himself. In fact, all of us in the room, except for
a few young interlopers, were in the process of becoming
quaint old characters. A little more time was all that was
needed. Newburyport was still turning out its most famous
product. Perhaps the town has not changed so much as I
think it has, in spite of its supermarkets and parking
meters.

There have always been quaint characters in every Newburyport generation, but most of them have their counterparts in dozens of other salty Yankee communities. In my
very early childhood, for example, Newburyport still had

a town crier, and with my own eyes I saw him in Market Street ringing his bell. As late as the twenties there was a Poet of Newburyport who gave himself this title and who could readily be found at a quick-lunch counter, willing to recite from his works if you gave him a cup of coffee. It is a pity they have never reached printed form, for I can remember only snatches of them. One was a lyric describing the wanderings of a couple in Newburyport, a bit of which went:

> Arm in arm the lovers went
> Down Monroe and up Kent.

He also had composed an ode to Plum Island at the mouth of the Merrimack River, a poem which he could recite with appropriate gestures.

> Plum Island is the place to go, away from summer heat;
> You take the cars at Market Square and go down Merri-
> mack Street.
> The people of Haverhill and Amesbury and all the country
> around
> While looking for a cooling spot — *Plum Island* they have
> found.

Newburyport gossip has always treasured individual exploits. Anecdotes abound regarding the town's most famous politician, and there are many local raconteurs who can resurrect very early tales of characters who would be in their middle hundreds if they were still living. There is the story of a Newburyporter known as Mousetrap Jones, who, when troubled by a mouse, would go to a local hardware store and buy a mousetrap, which he would re-turn when the mouse was caught. There is the tale of a

Newburyport druggist whose soda fountain had a leaky sarsaparilla tap, which compelled him to place a glass beneath it in order to collect the slowly dripping sirup. It is said that once when two Newburyport schoolteachers visited his store, he offered them each a glass of sarsaparilla, to find that the sarsaparilla spigot had only leaked enough for a single drink, but he handled the occasion prudently by mixing one beverage and saying:

"Your turn next time, Miss Smith."

Remarks along these lines are valued in Newburyport. It still retains the tradition of the small town that was once obliged to furnish its own entertainment, but these examples are pallid compared to legends of its more distant past. An abrasive quality of manners has developed which tends to rub off rough edges and which encourages conformity. Newburyport, even if it wished, could not play host today to anyone of the stature of Lord Timothy Dexter. What is more arresting than the personality of Lord Dexter himself is how a town the size of Newburyport, considerably smaller in his day than it is at present, could have been able to produce him. That it could do so implies the existence of a different genius and a different culture. Timothy Dexter is a final product of a blooming that has been called the Federalist Period of New England, which is not a bad term for it, either, since the era started roughly with the conclusion of the Revolutionary War and ended with the advent of Jeffersonian democracy.

It is only natural that the name of Dexter should appear frequently in Newburyport's bibliography. Currier has given him a chapter of his own, and Mrs. Smith and Mrs. Emery a page or two. A native of Newburyport, Samuel

Lorenzo Knapp, born in 1783, published in the last year of
his life, 1838, a sketch of Timothy Dexter which is a work
of importance, if only because Mr. Knapp in his boyhood
had seen Dexter and the Dexter palace; and he had spent
his childhood and youth in this Federalist period, which was
still vividly imprinted on his memory in 1838. Mr. Knapp
received his secondary education in Newburyport, graduated from Dartmouth College in 1804 and, like John
Quincy Adams, read law in Newburyport with Theophilus
Parsons; he opened a law office in Newburyport in 1809,
married a Boston girl, and served in the Massachusetts General Court from 1812 until 1816, when he was imprisoned
for debt in the Newburyport jail. His chief claim to fame,
aside from his writing, was his association with Daniel
Webster in the defense of two men accused of robbery near
the Merrimack Bridge.

His life of Dexter is second-rate, from a literary standpoint, but second-rate writing sometimes reflects the attitudes of a period more accurately than literature. The
Knapp opus has portentous gingerbread literary trimmings. Its sentences are interlarded with irritating quotes
and scholarly condescensions. Knapp refers to Dexter's
Newburyport as "the sweet village." "It will be seen," he
tells us, "by those who take the trouble to think upon the
subject, that there are more singular and eccentric characters to be found in small places than in large; in the
latter it is hard to attract notice."

Unfortunately, the Knapp life of Dexter is full of in-
accuracies, not that any life of this peculiar man can be
exact. He admits that Lord Timothy Dexter and most of
what was related to him had passed from his mind "as one

of those dreams in the course of our lives, that make a
strong impression for a time, and then sink from the memory, perhaps never to return." He could not get all his
recollections straight when he came to sorting them out
more than thirty years after the death of Timothy Dexter.

William Cleaves Todd is another Dexter biographer. His
terse sketch of Lord Dexter has a schoolmasterly lucidity,
as have his notes on Samuel Lorenzo Knapp. This might
be expected, since for ten years he was principal of the
Female High School in Newburyport, said to be the first of
its kind in the country. He is still remembered for his
philanthropies — fifteen thousand dollars for the support
of the Reading Room of the Newburyport Public Library
and fifty thousand dollars for the Newburyport Hospital.
His view of Lord Dexter, who was dead before Mr. Todd
was born, is uniformly dim. He explodes the myth of
Dexter's great wealth by pointing out that he left a comparatively small estate. The real Dexter, he believes,
amassed his property by prudence, industry and business
sagacity. Toward the close of his life, his vanity, ignorance
and drunken habits made him eccentric and he amused
himself by telling stories of how he acquired his money that
eventually began to be believed. Mr. Todd's inquiry omits
one vital fact. Lord Dexter may have been eccentric and
untruthful, but he had a vivid imagination. Even behind
the Todd strictures there are evidences of genius, and hints
of a remarkable individual. No one today can tell exactly
when or whether Lord Dexter was laughing at his audience,
or where eccentricity ended with him and senility began.

Mr. Todd lays an unerring finger on several of Knapp's
erroneous statements regarding Dexter's boyhood and

youth and regarding the exact date when Timothy Dexter first arrived in Newburyport, but Mr. Todd did not clear up all the Knapp discrepancies. In this respect, to round out the Dexter bibliography, I must mention a book that I wrote on Lord Dexter in 1925, when both Newburyport and I were younger and more naïve than we are at present. The volume *Lord Timothy Dexter of Newburyport, Mass.* has fortunately been out of print for the last twenty years. It embarrasses me to pick it up again because it has the faults and not the virtues of the literary renaissance of the twenties. We are all, except on rare occasions, imprisoned in our age, and subjected to fleeting fashions — Lord Dexter, Knapp, William Cleaves Todd, Mrs. Smith and Mrs. Emery, and I am with them.

There is only one thing I can say in favor of this out-of-print book. It did contain a few new facts abouts its subject. Apparently I was the first student of Dexter who had made a complete search of the files of the Newburyport *Impartial Herald*, which are virtually complete for the years of his residence. It occurred to me that anyone as exuberant as this man would have been certain to have sent many communications to the editor. I found that I was right, and I was able to collect a significant number of pieces of Dexter's writings not previously unearthed. These discoveries of new source material are, I am afraid, my only contribution toward unraveling the Dexter myth.

Aside from these communications and advertisements, plus a few outside witticisms and satiric poems in the *Impartial Herald*, there are only two other bits of original source material regarding Lord Dexter: his own book, *A Pickle for the Knowing Ones,* and broadsides with the

verses of Jonathan Plummer, the preacher and fish vendor
whom Dexter finally employed as his Poet Laureate. Timothy Dexter's more sober and literate contemporaries have
paid scant attention to him. Perhaps his name is mentioned
in some diaries or correspondence of the time—but in my
superficial investigations I have not found a trace. Somewhere, in some Newburyport attic, there may still be unknown Dexter material, but this possibility grows daily
dimmer. Newburyport's women have always been hard on
original historical material. With every spring houseclean-
ing they have made new inroads into attics, annually
burning or throwing into the dustbin old letters, old deeds,
diaries, ships' logs, and maps. Further, the old families have
been leaving Newburyport quite steadily and death cuts
down on continuity. As the houses on High Street are sold,
their documents go with the wind. Our rare book dealer,
Robert W. Lull, once did his best to preserve them, but
now he is gone, and no successor has entirely inherited his
persistence.

   We must do, I am afraid, with what we have, and I no
longer feel great distress that there is so little. I have learned
something I should have learned long ago—that few individuals are important in themselves. The environment
that produced and tolerated Dexter is far more interesting
than the man.

III

"Mars Came Fored — Joupeter Stud By Holding the Candel — I Was to Be One Grate Man" — from Personal Reminiscence by Timothy Dexter

TIMOTHY DEXTER, born in the town of Malden, Massachusetts, in 1747, was the son of a farmer and a member of one of those customarily large Colonial families in which infant mortality was effectively combated by speed of reproduction. In spite of his later foibles, he came of excellent stock. His parents and his brothers and sisters were hardworking, sober people living in a puritan community that was inured to heavy labor and hardships. Malden, though near to Massachusetts Bay's capital, Boston, was not a suburb of that city. And for that matter, Boston was not a city at all from a modern standpoint, only a small town on a peninsula connected with the mainland by a narrow isthmus that barely stood above tide level. Nevertheless in Dexter's childhood it was a leading community in North America. But, aside from buildings on the waterfront and the beginnings of a slight housing congestion in the North End, most of Boston had a highly rural aspect, though not so marked as the village of Malden with its rocky fields, most of which were not hospitable to agriculture. Malden, like other New England villages, was almost a frontier town, enjoying its frugal way of life under the stern Church government of the period. But young Timothy, who spent his childhood and early youth there, must have been fond of the place and of his family, since in his will he left a handsome sum to the Malden church and mentioned two of his brothers. Any child who could live to the age of nine in the Colonial New England climate, through winters far more severe than they are at present, in a house heated only by a kitchen fireplace, was bound to be hardy and healthy. Dexter himself eventually wrote a few reminiscent words regarding his birth and childhood, and now is the time to quote them:

> I was born when grat powers Rouled — I was borne in 1747, Janeuarey 22; on this day, in the morning A grat snow storme — the sines in the seventh house wives; mars Came fored — Joupeter stud by holding the Candel — I was to be one grate man.

This, we discover on examining other samples of Dexter's work, is not an exaggerated example of his literary style and spelling. The passage is unusual only for its punctuation, which may have been supplied by a friendly printer. It is, among other things, an interesting commentary on the boy's early education. He could not have gone far in school, and perhaps, too, as a young child, he was not interested in learning, but he could write, which is more than can be said for many of his toilworn contemporaries. And actually the Dexter signature, which one can examine at the end of occasional deeds and other contracts, is done in a legible script. In fact, the penmanship, I honestly believe, is preferable to that now being taught to freer and more privileged children in our more progressive schools.

I have seen only one full page written entirely in Dexter's hand. This is a letter in the Newburyport Historical Society, dated 1787, when Mr. Dexter was forty years old. It is addressed to a man of affairs, referred to once as "your onner," which may make the recipient the Honorable Theophilus Parsons, of whose legal services Dexter often availed himself. Mr. Dexter writes asking for a paper made out to his son Samuel for a share in a land venture in the Midwest, since he has heard that officers and soldiers are on the Mississippi River. Financial details that follow mention the sum of one thousand dollars. It would be a very hard letter for a script expert to decipher, but coming from a man of Dexter's background, it is well composed and written. Although it is far from an Adams manuscript, not many artisans in those days could have expressed themselves so ably. He was decidedly not an illiterate in his social group.

Still, the man's spelling is hilarious and this, together with his style, explains why his book, *A Pickle for the Knowing Ones*, is in print whereas the works of Cotton and Increase Mather and the soundly constructed sermons of the Newburyport divines to whom Dexter listened are now out of all but specialized circulation. Dexter's ability to write this letter would not have signified much in Massachusetts fifty years ago. However, it is attaining a significance in the growing illiteracy of the present, now that surveys indicate that a large percentage of American high school students can scarcely laugh at Dexter's efforts. In fact, if present cultural trends continue for another fifty years, Dexter's writing may not be funny at all.

There is an extension of this autobiographical note by Dexter on his youth which shows that he lived the conventional life of the average lower-class boy.

> 1755 in may 9 Day my father put me with a farmer in malden in which I stayed six years and six months then to Chalston I stayed Leven months at Dressin of skins for briches & glovs — then went to boston there stayed till I was free — in fourteene days I went to Newbury Port with A bondel in my hand to A place all noue to me — I had sole my free Dom sout at the vandours — five shillings A yard starling in Roum of a guinea Cloth — I was angry — this money I began with Eight Dolors & 20 sents — I had faith by reading A book — I was to have this world's goods and be Come grate and be Amonkest grat men in the East and to give lite to the blind wherein my fellow mortels have bin Douped for many thousand years with untrouth.

Fully to understand this passage it is necessary to cast back into the social climate of Colonial America, where there were conventions and customs imported direct from England, which underwent only minor changes until well into the nineteenth century. If parents in Dexter's youth could not support their children, these children were customarily bound out to work, as Dexter was at the age of eight. Then, when a child had attained stature and intelligence, he was given the opportunity to learn a trade

Philip Kappel

and was bound out, for example, to a leather dresser in Charlestown, the starting point of Paul Revere's ride and the scene of the battle of Bunker Hill. When an apprentice had finished his time and had learned his trade, he was given a journeyman's recommendation by his employer, and also, under the usual terms of apprenticeship, a new suit of clothes, called a freedom suit, to which Dexter refers in this passage. In his case it was a good one, which proves that Dexter had been sober and diligent. In fact, all evi-

dence indicates that he was quiet and industrious for many
years after his arrival in Newburyport, and not conspicuous until he suddenly made a fortune. Indeed, if he had not
run into speculative luck, he would have ended like any
other of the thousands of mute inglorious eighteenth-century Miltons. Although he tells us that he had read a book
that made him feel that he would become great among
great men, this passage was hindsight, and written when
he owned a gold pen and sat in his Newburyport mansion.
It is a reasonable assumption that he had few premonitions
of greatness when he was a poor boy trying to get along.
What is more interesting today is why he chose Newburyport as a place to start in business, instead of continuing
his leather dressing at Boston.

In the light of modernity, this is hard to understand.
But one must remember that in the limited world of young
Timothy there were only a few harbor towns up and
down the Eastern seaboard, connected on land only by
wretched roads or trails and far more easily reached by
sea; and, though it seems incredible today, in 1767,[1] which
is about the year the young man left Boston, Newburyport
had the Colonial reputation of being a flourishing town
with alluring prospects. For some years a brisk commercial
center had been established at the mouth of the Merrimack
River. Shipbuilding, for which Newburyport was to grow

---

[1] It is difficult to determine the exact date of Timothy Dexter's arrival in Newburyport. From his own account he started for the town two weeks after completing
his apprenticeship as a leather dresser in Boston, presumably at the age of twenty or
twenty-one. J. J. Currier, who does not mention the source of the date, states categorically that he came to Newburyport in 1769. We know for a fact that he purchased a small lot of land on Prospect Street in 1770. Since he only had a small
sum of cash on his arrival in Newburyport, even the date of 1769 would appear a
trifle late.

famous, was expanding rapidly, and at the time of Timothy's arrival approximately seventy vessels were being completed by local shipwrights. Since these vessels were found and rigged by local artisans, the industry demanded a variety of skills besides carpentry, including all sorts of smithing and ropemaking, and the production of sea supplies down to ship's biscuits. Ingenious artisans were attracted to Newburyport in growing numbers, and the influx of talent rose until a year or so before the Jeffersonian Embargo and the Fire of 1811 that ruined the waterfront. Many intelligent Newburyporters honestly believed that the town had greater potentialities than Boston.

Before this could be disproved by the machine age, Newburyport's clock had stopped with the Fire; even today there are still citizens living who classify events as having occurred before and after the Fire; but it was long before this calamity that Dexter started for Newburyport. Because of a hard life, he was not to live to see the Fire — he died five years before this disaster. As Dexter traveled to Newburyport he was journeying toward an expanding community with a future and no past, the exact reverse of what it is today. He was right in going there. There was gold in Newburyport in those days, and he made his fortune there. Newburyport, although no one could have known it then, would hit the jackpot in the opening years of the Revolutionary War.

If the Newburyport of 1767 was new to Timothy Dexter, it was easier for him to comprehend its values than for any of us now living, if we could turn back the time machine two hundred years and see the sights that Dexter

saw on his arrival. Because of industrial change, it is strange
for me to realize that I am in a far better position to accept
the life and thought of this aggressive and expanding
Colonial community than are my children or my grand-
children. It is strange to see oneself in the light of a surviving link between an improbable past and such an improbable present; and further, to believe that there will
be no such link existing when my generation is gone. I am
beginning to be, without my wish, one of the rare minority
who can recall the Newburyport of horse-and-buggy
days, when Newburyport still lived in the solitude that
Lord Dexter would have taken for granted.

When I was a child, the house in which our family lived,
purchased by my great-grandfather and eventually pre-
sided over by my great-aunt, Mary Russell Curzon, was
interchangeable with a Newburyport pre-Revolutionary
dwelling. True, it was built later than the time we are dis-
cussing—in 1780, to be exact—by the son of "King"
Hooper of Marblehead, as a duck-hunting lodge—but
rural life had not changed perceptibly in the thirteen
years' gap between the building of the house and 1767
Newburyport. In my childhood, when my great-aunt was
in command of all her faculties, Timothy Dexter would
have been at home in the routine of the household, with
the exception of its nonalcoholic proclivities. As far as I
can recall, there were only four concessions to a changing
world that separated us from Colonial New England, and
these were of a minor nature. The fireplace in the kitchen
had been closed and an iron stove, such as one can see in an
ancient mail-order catalogue, had been substituted. In the
cellar with its earth floor stood a rudimentary and balky

hot-air furnace, a piece of modernity which my great-aunt on the whole resented because, as she observed, the heat was not good for the stores of winter vegetables. She only agreed to hot-air heating at all because she had been told it would be good for her sister. Her father, who was a widely traveled man — as a youth he had sailed from Boston in the first Perkins ship to round the Horn and engage in the Northwest fur and China trade — had been impressed by the useful qualities of coal grates in London. He had diminished the fireplaces in the front parlor and the dining room by installing grates in which hard-coal fires burned around the clock in winter — enough, as my great-aunt said, to keep these rooms at a comfortable temperature. Besides, with feather beds it was a waste to heat the upper chambers.

On a cold winter's night she preferred to seal the little parlor as hermetically as possible — always drawing the sliding window shutters, not only to keep out the cold but because once in her younger days she had been startled to see the face of a man staring at her from the dark — and to sit before the anthracite grate over which a copper kettle was suspended, reading or doing what she called her "coarse" work by the light of a kerosene lamp — or coal oil, as she often called it. These three or four downstairs lamps, I honestly believe, were the house's greatest concession to modernity, unless one added the sulphur matches, for which Aunt Mary had little use. She preferred lighting her lamps from paper spills, which she made in the evening, when she could not induce her younger relations to make them. (I made one myself the other day, gaining the reluctant respect of a Park Avenue cocktail party.)

She had not forgotten how to use a flint and tinderbox, and she once produced one and operated it when I was five years old. Incidentally, I never saw the feat performed again until 1934, when I was in Mongolia near the Gobi Desert and gave a Camel cigarette to a camel-driver. He was no more adroit than my great-aunt had been, with flint and steel.

There was no plumbing, excepting a pump in the kitchen, the water from which was used for washing purposes only. The drinking water always came from a red hand-pump across the sandy road. Bathtubs were of tin, and the hot water for them was carried upstairs in spouted containers resembling those that now exist in Brown's Hotel in London. My aunt did not approve of coal-oil lamps, feeling that they might be upset and burn the house down. Like R. L. Stevenson's hero in *A Child's Garden of Verses*, we used yellow candlelight; a candle for each member of the family was ready, cleaned and waiting, on a shelf at the foot of the stairs. Whimsically, my aunt had names for many of the candlesticks. Her own she referred to as "Coddy," presented to her, she explained to me once, in her younger days, by her friend Mr. J. T. Codman from Boston, author of *Brook Farm Memoirs*.

The house was furnished with chairs, tables, beds and bureaus, hardly a piece of which was made after 1800 and most going back further — passed down by ancestors, whose portraits hung in the dining room and parlor and in the long room, with its open fireplace, which my aunt preferred to tend herself in winter. Her temper, occasionally violent, always flared when she discovered that the hired man had placed an improperly fitting backlog in the wood closet. She could lay an open fire herself as correctly as Mr. Whittier had done with words in his *Snow-bound*. In fact, she and the Quaker poet had been friends for many years.

Outdoors was as far from a modern setting as indoors. There was a well-stocked woodshed and a chopping block, where my great-aunt would still amuse herself by splitting white pine kindling. Once when she was living alone there, she told me, she had once gone to the shed to split wood and had inadvertently cut her leg above the knee. Since the house was far from town, my aunt walked back into the parlor, fetched down her workbasket from the cupboard beside the coal grate and stitched up the wound herself. Next to the woodshed was a workshop with a carpentry bench and tools such as one found on any properly conducted Newburyport place. Beyond was the barn with haymows, under which were stalls for the horses and stands for two or three cows. There was also space for sleighs, light carriages and a blue farm wagon. In the barn cellar, well warmed by manure, there were the pigs. My aunt was very fond of them and brought them a special treat of table scraps every day. She was averse to chickens. They were, she said, not only dirty, stupid creatures, but were constantly getting out of their pen and scratching up her garden. She would not have minded ducks, except that they kept getting into the river, where they were eaten by the snapping turtles. There was, of course, a cat. The one I remember best was named Bellamy. The cat was needed in the house to keep down the mice, and a barn cat was kept in the barn for rats. There was a dog, too, an ill-tempered Irish terrier named Mike, whom my great-aunt called, incorrectly from my observation of his habits, her hairy dove.

A tragic aspect of living is that one is seldom aware of the value of what is happening until a given event is over. It seems incredible to me that this conventional picture of rural life, backed by the dignity and continuity of centuries, should have either disappeared, or in the remotest parts of our country, be rapidly approaching extinction. There are a diminishing number of children today who appreciate the friendship of cows and horses or who know the peace that settles over a barn when the stock has been watered and its doors have been closed for the night. Very few under forty have acquired the skill of milking a cow. Almost no one, except the middle-aged and beyond, knows how to harness a horse, or has driven a light carriage. The memory of rutted lanes and wheels turning in sand, the rattle of wagons and the clopping of horses' hoofs is nearing inevitable extinction. Few individuals of thirty or younger have driven in a sleigh or have seen town streets plowed out by horses. They have not heard the sound of sleighbells, a necessary device to warn of the noiseless approach of a sleigh, except on the radio or in department stores at Christmas. It would be an educated guess that a sleigh has not appeared on the streets of Newburyport for more than a quarter of a century, and never will return now the highways are salted and sanded and plowed clean for motor traffic. The horse, since the dawn of history a means of locomotion and a farm necessity, has been metamorphosed into a plaything even on many Western cattle ranges. No one sees a yoke of oxen any more, except at a county fair. Hardly a soul is now alive, in New England at any rate, who is able to handle these patient creatures, and yet in my childhood there were oxen on many Newbury farms. Few boys can make a willow whistle; it takes a long search to find a top that can be spun by string. Candles are merely a table decoration, not bedside companions, except in time of hurricanes. It is superfluous to marshal any more such obvious facts. They are listed here for the sake of contrast, not as a lament for the good old days. Some aspects of them were damnably dull and uncomfortable even when examined through the glass of sentiment, but in the last few decades a sharp cleavage has occurred in continuity between generations.

There was no such gap in my childhood. My grandfather Marquand, for example, who often left his banking business in New York to visit Newburyport, had sailed to China as an apprentice seaman when he was seventeen, then as customary a thing for a young man to do as it was for my contemporaries to sell bonds. He died when I was seven, but I was old enough to ask him once about his sea experiences. He told me that he had been a sailor before the mast, like Richard Henry Dana, Jr., and that it might be just as well if I did not attempt to be one. He told my mother once of visiting one of his former shipmates at a sailors' home. The elderly man was dying of what was probably appendicitis.

"John," he said to my grandfather, "this comes from having chewed finecut tobacco. It gets inside you. Be sure always to chew plug, John."

Once my grandfather also talked to me seriously about the dangers of drink, because it was his belief that a weakness for alcoholic beverages was prevalent in the Marquand

side of the house. Whisky and rum, he said, had been a
temptation to him ever since he had been a teen-age boy in
Newburyport. Decanters and tumblers were on the sideboards of every town house, and every guest out of cour-
tesy was expected to avail himself. This hospitality, he told
me — and my Great-aunt Mary told me later — had been
too much for my great-grandfather, Joseph Marquand.
And there is still an amusing mock epitaph on him in
Currier's history, written by his witty contemporary, Mrs.
Hannah Gould:

> Here lies our kind Joe
> And a handsomer beau
> Ne'er danced with the handsomest lady.,
> He's had his last ball
> And he's now left the hall
> For a place that is narrow and shady.

He lies buried — and I only mention it because burial
grounds have always been an integral part of Newburyport — in the Hooper tomb in the New Hill, not the Old
Hill, burying ground, a locale now patronized only by
young lovers and juvenile delinquents. My grandfather had
him laid to rest there because he was shocked by the appearance of the Marquand family tomb, a monument which I
have never been able to discover.

"Your grandfather's family were impoverished by the
Fire," my Great-aunt Mary told me several times. "Their
wharf and warehouses and dwelling house, and their ship,
the *Washington*, all were burned. When you grow older,
never accept hospitality from sideboards."

There was nothing to drink in the house while my great-aunt was alive, and I can remember, after World War I, the surprise and horror on the face of her niece, Elizabeth Marquand, when I once said in New York that I was going to go across the street to drink a glass of beer.

"Don't forget," she said, "that drinking does run in the family."

These reminiscences are mentioned only to indicate the bridge over time that once existed. They successfully span an interval that permits acceptance of a past, for better or worse. This bridge is rudely shattered now, and attempts at reconstruction are poor substitutes for echoes.

I have heard the idea advanced recently that life is fuller than it used to be because of mobility that allows one to go anywhere merely in a matter of hours. Personally, as I think upon the careers of my Great-aunt Mary and of her father, a contemporary of Timothy Dexter, but doubtless not acquainted with him, I am not inclined to approve of this idea. Their lives were fully as rich as mine and better ordered by the very factors of time and place that limited them. My great-grandfather, Samuel Curzon, traveled as a representative of the Boston house of Perkins through many parts of the world. As a boy he was in the illicit trade with Spaniards on the beaches near San Francisco. He saw sea otter purchased from Indians off Vancouver Island. He was friendly with a Polynesian chief on the Island of Hawaii, who gave him a pearl for his bride-to-be, and he no doubt met Hu Kwa, the most famous of all the compradors, at the factories of Canton. He knew London well, and Spain and the Caribbean and South America. I have been to all the places he visited, not once but several times, and to more besides, but he had an advantage. He traveled so slowly that background was never a blur, whereas I have always gone by fast ship or by air. Judging from his letters and journals — those which Aunt Mary did not burn when she began to lose her memory — he was meticulous with detail, but his writing is frankly dull, considering his opportunities. He was a handsome man, redheaded and dashing in a distinctly Federalist way, judging from the crayon picture of him that hung in the little parlor. This was done by a false friend in Peru who later attempted to turn him over to the Inquisition. A sketch of the false friend is also in the family archives, underneath which my great-aunt has inscribed the word "Traitor."

There is still in the family a fire screen made from exquisitely embroidered boot tops which he wore when received by the Spanish Viceroy of Mexico, and an Inca mortar in the shape of a llama that he brought back from Peru, together with a magnificent filigree silver basket. There is a *bargueño,* a chest-on-chest, which he brought from Spain, inlaid with tortoise shell, ivory, mother-of-pearl, and silver — the silver was removed before my time. Now that we are on the subject, there is also his Spanish picture of John the Baptist, to which he refers as an art object of great value, with the suggestion that it could go up for sale, in case of straitened circumstances. Ancestors are not always right. The Vose Gallery in Boston, who cleaned the little picture last winter, has referred to it as amusing, and with no intrinsic value. The same is true of a beautifully woven light wool blanket which he also brought home from his travels, telling my great-aunt that it was a poncho. I have traveled myself in those regions, and like him I have observed the Andean Indians. It is not a poncho but a Mexican serape, and not a museum piece either, because it was turned down when offered to the Boston Museum of Fine Arts. The legend, I fear, that surrounds two slight Fragonard-like landscapes, painted upon copper and brought back by him from Spain, is equally incorrect. The family story is that a vessel on which he was supercargo was given a new copper bottom in a Spanish port. When the copper was subsequently removed, to everyone's surprise there were pictures on the copper sheathing. I cannot believe this, although I accept the story's spirit. These objects are of little value when taken separately, and most of them can be readily duplicated in many New England curio shops. But seen all together in the old house where he had left them and where they were tended ritually by his surviving daughter, they had a ghostly message, plus a glittering reality. They told their wordless tale of the sea and demonstrated better than words that the distant places from which they came were once physically and emotionally closer to Newburyport than they will ever be again.

My great-aunt's manner of life, too, her motivations and routines, were a living affirmation of an older culture. She was proud of her liberalism. Her sister had been a member of the Brook Farm community. She herself had been an abolitionist and had once sheltered a fugitive slave. In her time she had been acquainted with most of the Concord Transcendentalists. William Ellery Channing, the poet, had proposed to her. Thomas Wentworth Higginson of "Bleeding Kansas" had been in love with my grandmother, and my great-aunt had known him well. In fact,

I can remember him when I was a child of four or five, and
when he paid his last visit to our house. I recall distinctly
being led to meet him on the lawn by the riverbank, and
my reaction to him then was similar to my reaction now
toward the Daniel Chester French statue in the Lincoln
Memorial.

"Poor Mary," the Reverend Mr. Higginson said to some
younger members of the family, "how beautiful she was
once, how pitifully she has failed."

"Poor Wentworth," my aunt said, directly after his
departure, "it is pitiful to see someone who was once such
a figure of a man now broken physically and mentally by
age."

Like the Reverend Mr. Higginson, my Aunt Mary was
a Unitarian, and she also favored the school of medicine
known as homeopathy, but she was seldom obliged to make
a test of its benefits because she was seldom ill. As a girl
she must have often passed the three wooden images on
their arch before the Dexter mansion.[2]

The liberalism of her youth would have compared
favorably with that of Americans for Democratic Action;
her education was wholly Federalist. She owned a collection
of samplers sewn by various young ladies of the family,
some dating to the mid-eighteenth century, many exquisite and illumined with pious inscriptions. Her own,
which she made at the age of seven, was not up to the high
standards of the rest. Her alphabet had a rebellious un-
evenness that exhibited impatient stitching. She told me

[2] In 1872 Miss Curzon had been plagued by toothache. Finally, without con-
sulting her relatives, she drove to Newburyport and had all the teeth removed by
Dr. Kelly. At that time his extraction room was in the Dexter House — not next
door where Dr. Sullivan operates today.

once that she had always hated sewing tasks as a young girl, but when I knew her, her embroidery, or "fine work," as she called it, was excellent. She had most of the accomplishments of a Jane Austen heroine and she liked to tell how she had been obliged to read *Ivanhoe* behind the lid of her desk in school to avoid punishment because the Waverley novels were then regarded as trashy literature. Incidentally, as an indication of the change in literary taste, I once paid her great-great niece three dollars to read *Ivanhoe,* only to be told that its boredom was not worth the pay.

Her father insisted that all his children keep journals; and until her last days she always wrote in her diary. It is too late now to ask where she acquired her excellent education, but it was of a far higher quality than anything to be encountered now in an average public school. Her father's and mother's library, most of it from the Searles in Boston, was extensive, though eighteenth century.[3] She had read all of it in that indefinite leisure that was one of the chief advantages of her generation over mine, but had never lost touch with the present. She was a lifelong subscriber to *Littell's Living Age* and the *Atlantic Monthly.* She could read aloud tirelessly, if she was asked to do so in the evening, from Pepys' *Diary* or Gibbon, or from Scott if she was in a lighter mood. But what distinguished her from most people I have known was the variety of her resources and many skills that kept her from ever facing a dull moment. She had the disciplines of her generation and a deep guilt if she wasted time. Her methodical qual-

---

[3] The only books in this library that were censored were the works of Molière. Here many words were snipped out with scissors, making perusal difficult. I have been told that the relative who did this was a schoolmistress.

ities resembled those of Benjamin Franklin. She remained, in her eighties, a Federalist lady in her daily routine. I can recall her winter schedule better than her summer; her ingenious employment of time still impresses me.

She rose early, ate a frugal breakfast, tended her house plants and arranged the parlor. She said once that she always knew each morning that the earth had turned on its axis because the pictures were crooked on the wall. Next she took out her fine embroidery and worked on it until it was time to walk about the place and bring a few kitchen scraps to her pigs in the barn cellar. She would put on her bonnet, wrap herself in a heavy shawl, and take the ivory-headed cane that had belonged to her father. She was always at the road to meet the postman, who would arrive about eleven in the morning. Then it was time to go to her dropleaf desk and work on her correspondence. Like others of her time she was a gifted letter writer. After luncheon, which was at twelve, she moved into the unheated long room behind the parlor, where her hooked rug was on a stretcher. She would usually work on it until the light began to fail, and then again she put on her bonnet and shawl. It was time for a final walk around the place and time to fill her Nantucket lightship basket with pine cones and chips from the woodshed. With dusk it was time to light the lamps, draw the shutters, and see that the maid-of-all-work had trimmed the candlewicks. Then, directly before supper, it was time for making paper spills. After supper she recorded the day's events in her diary, the weather, the breaking of a limb from a tree, the condition of the ice on the river, the arrival of callers. Now that her day was officially over, it was time for backgammon or

dominoes, or reading. She always read until eleven and in-
spected the bar on the front door before she went upstairs
to her bed, on which she liked to say that she was born and
on which she desired that she should die. Her wish turned
out as she had hoped, in her eighty-seventh year.

I observed her days, with their clocklike program which
changed with the changing seasons, without much interest
at the time. It never occurred to me until decades later
that I had lived in a Federalist house that had survived
until my childhood, or that I had seen something of post-
Revolutionary America, as well as a life routine and a
serenity now impossible to imitate. I had observed the commonplace days in the culture of educated Newburyport at
the time of my great-grandfather, as expressed by his
spinster daughter.

I V

Dexter Takes the Road North
to Fame and Fortune

IT IS HARD to comprehend the essence of that time, unless one has experienced it. It is equally hard to make a translation of the Newburyport of Timothy Dexter unless one has heard the sleighbells, or seen the oxen or a schooner in the river, or heard conversations of the past. It is still harder, now that continuity is gone, and now that its silences are broken, to follow Timothy Dexter as he carried his bundle to Newburyport. Since he carried his bundle we may assume that he had walked the distance from Boston or Malden. He was young and tough, and walking was a conventional means of locomotion. Also, since he walked, we may assume that the season was spring or summer. Not knowing the exact date of his arrival, we may arbitrarily set the time into the end of May. With this assumption let us attempt to travel with Dexter to this new place, which was stranger to him than to us.

There is no doubt concerning the path taken by Timothy Dexter. It must have been the road from Boston along the coast to Maine, once an Indian trail and now a narrow and traffic-clogged motorway called Route 1A. In colonial times this track was dusty or muddy and in poor repair, but it was a main source of communication. From the earliest days of the colony it had wound over the land like the string of a loose necklace to which were attached the early settlements of Charlestown, Lynn, Salem, Ipswich, Newbury. These towns had been founded in the 1630's and so they and the road that served them were well over a century old in young Dexter's time, which would make them venerable. But progress moved more slowly then, when the upsurge of inventions and gadgets was still around the corner. Though the towns were well established, their populations had not increased by geometrical progression.

The land, on the whole, was poor, as is illustrated by the place names that have come down to us, such as "Heartbreak Hill," "Labor in Vain," or "Dogtown." Their populations, now that the French and Indian difficulties appeared to have been resolved, were already being decanted to the westward, and Massachusetts already was performing its historic function of being the purveyor of Yankee ingenuity to the hitherto untapped mid-sections of the continent. There was restiveness along Route 1A in those days. The catalogue of uncertainties and resentments and of heresies was being compiled which would lead to the war of the Revolution. The towns had grown but had not burst their boundaries, although they were beginning to move from coastal trade to commerce with the West Indies and the Baltic. In spite of the signs of a new prosperity, they still had an uninviting aspect. Their few gambrel-roofed dwellings and occasional examples of the early Georgian were outnumbered by houses of the clap-

boarded salt-box type with a single huge chimney and a
rear roof reaching nearly to the ground. Many farms along
the highway stood on the boundaries that still exist. Most
of the virgin forest had been cleared, making a conventional New England countryside with the same farmsteads
and tilled fields and stone walls that Lord Percy encountered a few years later on his march to Lexington and
Concord. The country on the Bay Road was more open
than at present, now that motor cars and tractors have replaced the horse and dairying is a large-scale industry instead of being, as it was in Dexter's time, a family affair.
Former fields and pastures are now being rapidly covered
by scrub growth and "home sites," until there is an illusion
of the jungle closing in, plus a sense of impending material
change.

At the time of young Dexter's walk the country was so
economically productive that its arable land was carefully
cleared straight to the fieldstone boundary walls. The
traffic on the road was negligible, mainly farm wagons, a
few individuals riding horseback, and more on foot, many
of whom were furtive and ragged because there was a large
vagrant population then, that comprised not only peddlers
or tinkers but restless misfits. The old Bay Road and its
neighboring lanes were frequently trod by the unsuccess-
ful, maladjusted fringe off to find their own Never-Never
Lands. There were on that road, traveling like Dexter,
runaway apprentices who could not endure the harsh
treatment meted out to them or who were too dull to learn
their trades, slaves — not many of them because the institution had not been economically successful north of
Boston — sailors and cabin boys who had jumped ship,

runaway farm boys and dispossessed farm families, and an occasional confused, diseased, and bibulous Indian, a few of whom still came from the back country with their birch-bark baskets and their moccasins. Dexter no doubt carried his food with him and slept out. Even in his early days, he was in a higher class than many of his fellow itinerants. He was a journeyman who, if asked by a local authority, could produce from his bundle his freedom papers. He was not one of the runaways, advertisements for whom appeared occasionally in the local press.

An Old Pelt Reward [we discover an employer writing]. Ran away a few days since an apprentice boy named Barnabas Redman, about 19½ years old, an ill-looking fellow of a forbidding countenance, clumsy in his address and deportment of a morose aspect, much pitted with small pox, bandy legged and ill bred, having had his origin in the American Army. Whoever will deliver said runaway to the subscriber in Elizabeth town shall have the above reward.

There were marshes on Dexter's right hand after he passed the Rowley Green. Then there were marshes right and left. The bare drumlin of Oldtown Hill, where one can still see the cellar hole of a first settler's hut, was in front of him, with the marshy banks of Parker River in the foreground and fishing boats resting on the mud flats. The bridge over the lower stream may not have been finished, but there was a ferry. He was now passing the lower green of Newbury, close to the settlers' first landing place. Along his route he must have seen several of the houses that are still standing, not as mellowed by time as they are now but uncompromising, with their clapboards, lean-to roofs and

wide chimneys. He would have seen many, whether he took the shore road or the older stage road farther inland, past the Dummer mansion, and over what is now Thurlow's Bridge and then to Four Rocks and to Newbury's upper green, where Morgan's riflemen were to stop on their way to Quebec in the Revolution.

The houses around the upper green were functional, framed of oak, clapboarded and insulated with clay and marsh grass, and finished inside with feather-edged paneling. Although one can be delighted now by their low-studded rooms, their gaping fireplaces, and the patina of the paneling, these houses, when stripped of reverence and sentiment, were no more beautiful than the "ranch-type" structures which have now become their counterparts.

They were considered drafty and uncomfortable by wealthy persons in Dexter's youth, and were the dwellings of the yeoman, artisan, and laboring classes. There were few great houses in Newburyport when Dexter finished his walk. High Street was mostly farm and grazing land, but the town was large enough already to have broken from the rural township of Newbury.

There is a rare print still extant that depicts the Newburyport of this period. It was done from the High Street ridge near State Street (called Fish Street at this Colonial moment), and State is still Newburyport's business street. A ropewalk stands on a field near our present Bartlett's Mall and Frog Pond. There are four churches, by far the most ambitious structures in the place. The print is not well drawn. A key gives the names of the chief landmarks, but the drawing is inaccurate in line and scale. Yet, granting its crudeness, one is confronted with a startlingly different town from the pretentious Newburyport of only fifty years later. The bareness of the place is what strikes one first. Instead of elm-shaded streets the artist indicates only a few saplings among the stark wooden buildings. In spite of the vacant ground around it, the town is close and compact. There was hardly a building on Salisbury Point across the river, and no trees to interfere with one's view of the rivermouth or of the Plum Island dunes and beaches. It is strange after a glance at this uncompromising print to recall that the captain of a British merchantman only a few years later mistook Newburyport on the Merrimack for Boston. But then, the handsomer and better-done view of the Boston waterfront executed about this time shows why there might be confusion. Boston was larger; but even

so, by present standards it was still in the small-town category.

If Newburyport was grim, bare and unshaded, with muddy streets and only gravel on its walks, there were some hints of a greater future. Faith in this future was exhibited by the fine house of the Honorable Tristram Dalton. It had been built only a few years previously, a gambrel-roofed structure with a façade that gave the illusion of marble blocks. Its woodwork is heavy, compared to the Federalist style, but its hallway and its staircase are splendid. Only a little further down Fish Street, on the opposite side, was the Tracy mansion, just being built by Mr. Patrick Tracy for his Harvard-educated son, Nathaniel. More in the country was the equally magnificent new dwelling of Mr. Tracy's son-in-law, Jonathan Jackson.

Dexter was later to acquire both those houses when the Tracy and Jackson families fell on evil days. The Wolfe Tavern was farther down Fish Street, and a Congregationalist meetinghouse, with butchers' stalls behind it, stood in Market Square, where Fish Street ended. Not far away, near what is now Water Street, were the town jail, the whipping post and stocks. Already an emotional conflict was developing between puritanism and a materialistic affluence that expressed itself in the growing number of warehouses, workshops, and grogshops near Market Square.

It is unfortunate that neither Mrs. Emery nor Mr. Currier made any study of off-color districts. A veil has usually been drawn over the lower social aspects of Bay Colony life. If the Newburyport waterfront was not different from others, there was a district near the docks,

with sailors' boardinghouses and apartments for women of easy virtue. These establishments must have been in the vicinity of Market Square among small shops and warehouses. The Square was then and still is the place toward which any stranger gravitates.

Somewhere in that neighborhood Dexter, a poor but sober and hardworking young man, a stranger and tired from his journey, must have found food and lodging paid for from the proceeds of the sale of his freedom suit. This action of his that had started him on the way to fortune lingered in his memory as an outstanding achievement, and the deed comes up again in a broadside encomium of Dexter published at his decease by his admirer, Jonathan Plummer, and sold at the same Market Square, where Dexter has now arrived.

He immediately mingled with the lower echelon and became lost in a world of artisan mediocrity. Not long after his arrival he established a shop, called "The Sign of the Glove," at the foot of Green Street in an old house which was standing until recently. There he sold the leather goods which he had learned to make: gloves, and moosehide breeches, then a popular item of Colonial apparel. There was nothing out of the ordinary about him in those days. He was an average citizen, converted, as he tells us, a churchgoer, an industrious man well down in the lower middle of the town's social strata. Unfortunately, no one will ever know the frustrations that made him attempt to be mobile upward. He might never have been mobile at all, except for a sudden, surprising turn of fortune that touched him some years after the Revolution.

"Mister printer," he wrote later in the *Impartial Herald*,

"my fortin has bin hard very hard that is I have had hard Noks on head 4 difrent times from A boy to this Day twice taken up for dead two beatings."

It might be that a knock on the head did it. We may leave him for a moment implanted in the levels of the society with which he had to cope, and consider these levels ourselves.

V

The Ancestor Worship and Status Strivings of a Colonial New England Metropolis

NOT SO LONG AGO Miss Elizabeth Cushing, who lived for a hundred years in the brick house built on High Street by her grandfather, told me that we should both remember with pride that we were descended from shipowners, not ship captains. This is a subtle distinction, and I mention it here not to bolster my own ego but to show that such gradations have been treasured in Newburyport until very recently. They flourished more vigorously in the days of Dexter; they denoted inevitably a rigid caste system.

As we have mentioned previously, in the early 1930's while the depression was gripping Newburyport, a town long inured to economic boom and bust, Mr. Lloyd Warner was impressed by its static system of rank. He actually classified the town socially by his own system: upper-upper, middle-upper, lower-upper; upper-middle, middle-middle, lower-middle; upper-lower, middle-lower, lower-lower. There was no doubt that these gradations embraced everything in town.

Once, Mr. Warner told me exactly where I belonged in his classification, according to the records kept by himself and his assistants. I was surprised by my reaction. It seemed to me that Mr. Warner should have known this sort of thing automatically, because, then, Newburyport was an orderly place where every inhabitant knew instinctively where he belonged in relation to everyone else, and he knew also that he was as good as anyone else, no matter where he belonged.

"It does me good to think," one of my maiden aunts once said in my childhood, "whenever I cross State Street, that I am descended from the Dudleys." And truly enough, in those days it did many maiden ladies and others a great deal of good indeed to think along those lines.

But let us not forget that the cleavages of Newburyport so beguiling to Mr. Warner were already well worn when he was adjusting his research methods. They were harsher in Dexter's day. Nobody in Newburyport, except some lower-lowers—and there must have been quite a lot of them—truly believed, when the Declaration of Independence was written, that it was a self-evident truth that all men were created equal.

In pre-Revolutionary and in Federalist Newburyport the word "gentlemen" was not merely a directive to the men's lavatory. Instead, it had a definite connotation. In the legal instruments of that period and almost to the middle of the nineteenth century persons referred to in contracts were as likely as not also given their social description. Thus, "John Doe, Gentleman," often sold and devised property to "John Brown, Yeoman." "Mister" before a name also had an honorific significance, but never so high as "Esquire." In Harvard College undergraduates coming from some farm or simple mercantile establishment, when on a college staircase, were directed to move away from the handrail upon encountering a student more happily situated socially.

What bewilders me, and perhaps may confuse a more earnest and intelligent student of American history and Americana, is exactly how the lines were drawn and what attributes of lineage and wealth were required to create a Colonial gentleman. In the South, with its slaveholding aristocracy, such a distinction must have been comparatively simple, but in Massachusetts a gentleman would seem to have been more a figment of imagination or a product of community acclaim. It was pointed out to me in my youth that among the early settlers of Massachusetts Bay there were only two families from England that could be classed as gentry. These were the Gookins and the Saltonstalls. This limiting assertion may be startling to many families of Boston, Salem, and elsewhere, who have been able to secure coats of arms. Mrs. Emery, in her *Reminiscences of a Nonagenarian,* found plenty, but it is doubtful whether the College of Heralds would have confirmed most of Newburyport's armory. It would seem that aristocracy was manufactured rather rapidly out of gold or West India goods on lines that have no present parallel. No one now covets such distinctions in the febrile, energetic manner of old Newburyport. Yet there existed a board of review here, as in other towns, since social rank could be accorded only with the consent of the nonsocial. It would have been unthinkable in Newburyport not to have put ministers like Dr. Spring, lawyers like Theophilus Parsons, and merchants like Mr. Nathaniel Tracy or Mr. Jackson among the upper-uppers. Their position was accepted by everyone. The town treated them with an obsequious respect, the echoes of which linger in the pages of Currier and Emery, and faint traces still persisted when Mr. Warner came to town.

There was an honest and rather pathetic desire in the eighteenth century for an enclave of local gentry, which arose in part from a need for leadership and partly because any town worth mentioning had its showcase of leading citizens. It is natural that this sort of social accolade, with its fragile qualities, should have sometimes exhibited ridiculous aspects. There were hideous pomposities in Dexter's Newburyport, like the kneeling of a messenger before Madame Atkins the daughter of Governor Joseph Dudley. The rubicund faces, protruding waistcoats, and the satins in local family portraits show with embarrassing clarity what many sitters thought of themselves. In the folk tales, names still crop up of citizens who were called by the lower-lowers "Lord" and "Duke." Newburyport was sometimes hoist by its own petard, and occasionally the local noblesse it tolerated appealed to the risibility of some sections of the community.

There was a place for every individual in Dexter's Newburyport and there was a group of citizens possessing talents and abilities that would now be impossible to duplicate. At the top of this hierarchy came the men of professional rank. The clergy held a leadership that was close to autocratic. With few exceptions they were the best educated among the citizenry, and usually were familiar with Latin, Greek and Hebrew. Ministers held the front rank in the social scale, but lawyers and town officers and elected mem-

bers of the General Court were in about the same position. The wealthy shipowner and the successful merchant, with their fine houses, their horses and servants, each year received greater recognition until finally they were rated higher, by the thoughtless, than many of the men of God. They were able to set a better table and to serve imported wines, and they could give the shopkeepers better patronage.

Yet, as Mr. Warner has discovered, money was never everything in Newburyport. Style, distinction, and less definable qualities had to go with it; and sometimes merely the memory of a famous ancestor or of a family's vanished affluence commanded Newburyport respect. When Messrs. Tracy and Jackson moved down from wealth to comparative penury, there was no difference in the treatment accorded them. There has always been a species of loyalty in this complex social scene. Thus teachers ranked with merchants, or at least the better schoolmasters. Then came a very discernible cleavage, which produced a boundary beyond which few seldom progressed. The wealthy farmer or artisan would not be received by either Mr. Jackson or Mr. Tracy, except in a business way. They would have been ill at ease if they had been, knowing that they did not belong in Mr. Jackson's house, and they would have been right. The house is still an eloquent example of Newburyport's aspirations.

It is exasperating that such scant records remain regarding Newburyport architects or builders. There is no record that I can find of who built the house for Mr. Jackson about 1771, when as a prosperous Bostonian he came to Newburyport. The house must have been a considerable monument when it was built. In spite of its massiveness, it is graceful. Some doubt has been expressed as to whether Dexter altered its roof or added the cupola,[1] but the result is a success. The general ground plan is all that need concern us now, since it is one followed with little variation in all prosperous Newburyport houses. The front door opened into a spacious hall that ran the length of the residence to the gardens in the back. On entering, one passed rooms to the right and left and faced a broad staircase leading to the master's chambers. Further along the hall on the right was the dining room, and on the left the

[1] The doubt about the cupola, raised by John Mead Howells in his book on Merrimack architecture, has been resolved. Mr. Kelson, the present owner of the Dexter house, has found a letter in the 1850 files of the Newburyport *Herald* by a correspondent who states that his father built the cupola to Mr. Dexter's order.

owner's library. Behind the dining room was an ell for the kitchen and other service rooms, with bedrooms above. Upstairs were the spacious masters' rooms and on the third floor more bedrooms — ample space for a large family and guests. In fact, for many years after Lord Dexter's demise, the house was a hotel. As for furnishings, it is only necessary to visit the American wing of an ambitious art museum to gaze at rooms of the pre-Revolutionary period and move their contents mentally to the Jackson house. Judging from what we know of Mr. Jackson, the house was done with a taste that did not spare expense. The gilded mirrors, the silver candelabra and the service in the dining room, like its mahogany, were mostly English, but there may have been American interpolations by Hurd and Revere of Boston, and there were already silversmiths in Newburyport, as well as good local cabinetmakers whose numbers and skills were growing constantly.

The main rooms were heated only by fireplaces, the service of which must have kept a manservant busy all day long in the winter. And despite all his efforts, the house must have been drafty, and dusky, too, at night, for candles, chandeliers, and sconces could not compete with hundred-watt bulbs. Yet aside from these drawbacks, Mr. Jackson's mansion was more handsomely and more comfortably appointed, and far more adequately staffed, than any house in modern Newburyport. It is a house that appeals to the imagination, in spite of all the wrongs that have been done it. It must have appealed far more poignantly to the imagination of Timothy Dexter. It would be surprising if he ever entered the house during Mr. Jackson's occupancy, but he could gaze at it as he walked down High Street, as the rustics coming to market did. It was an upper-upper house that compared favorably with its contemporaries anywhere in the colonies.

The houses of artisans and prosperous farmers were simpler, though many made an effort to follow the Jackson pattern. The living conditions of the poor were, of course, more primitive, and no doubt wretched, even for people inured to hard living. Dexter's shop at the Sign of the Glove, where he dwelt shortly after his arrival, if it followed Newburyport custom, would have been in the front of the house. It was the day when small stores or workshops were combined with the proprietor's dwelling. Behind came the living quarters; in a modern realtor's jargon, a large living-dining room, devoid of breakfast nook or hostess area, connected with sheds and storage space and sleeping quarters. A side door, with a narrow hall and stairs, gave access to this main room and to the chambers above it. Dexter's furnishings were far more humble than Mr. Jackson's. He was in the heart of town, a few steps from Market Square, with a view of warehouses and shipping from his front windows. There was no garden, no coach, and there were no colored slaves to go with the property — nothing but the cold east wind and the reek of hides; no gardens for pleasant strolling. Dexter was not a lower-lower, but the line between him and the upper-upper was sharp and deep. On the other hand, the demarcation between a glove and leather-breeches maker and the lower-lower was much more blurred. Market Square, with its butcher stalls, warehouses and wharves, was teeming with lower-lowers, and Dexter understood them and got on well with them all his life.

The lower-lowers were a varied group. There was no welfare, or unemployment compensation, or social security to cover them with a kindly uniformity. From evidence extant, the lower income brackets of Dexter's Newburyport were more like a crazy-quilt than an olive-drab blanket. Down river by the tidal flats, in the section of the town which was already called Joppa, Mrs. Emery writes of barefoot women carrying cod from the fishing boats to the drying stages. Trade had already produced a variety of interesting foreigners, and the wharves had a cosmopolitan appearance. There were a few Negroes, but not many. They were beginning to settle in a section of the town still known as Guinea. There were sailors from the West Indies and an occasional Indian from upriver; and now and then a French *voyageur*. These people, of course, had little to do with solid citizens. They came and went as their wishes might direct, but some of them stayed on and became local celebrities.

There was, for one, a Negro woman, Lucy Lancaster — known as "Black Luce," a descendant of African kings, who was excellent in a sickroom and who later became part of Dexter's ménage. Perhaps the most outstanding product of the eccentric population was Madam Hooper, believed to be highly versed in witchcraft. She came to town with a handsome wardrobe and with a story, true or false, that she was the widow of a British officer who had fallen with General Wolfe on the Plains of Abraham. She was well educated and conducted a Dame School for some years. She was an expert with pistol and sabre. Her teeth were double all the way around. She eventually gave up schooling for necromancy and became less and less careful with her dress, wearing her antiquated costumes until they were in tatters. The witch legend still hung heavily over Newburyport and Newbury, where one or two cattle-killing and child-torturing old women had been unearthed by the testimony of neurotic children. One, in fact, had gone to Boston for trial, but she did not hang on Boston Common like some less fortunate old ladies. Instead, her sentence was commuted by Governor Bradstreet, and she returned to her home, where she lived to the end of her days, tolerated though feared by the superstitious. This was a time when horseshoes were nailed over the doors of many dwellings and when thought was given to the evil eye. Madam Hooper fitted perfectly into this picture. She sold love philters, told fortunes, and had a hen as a familiar.

Mr. Knapp, a "true beau" as Mrs. Emery calls him in her *Reminiscences,* leaves us an account of his visit to a neighborhood in Newbury called Dogtown, to which he once rode on horseback, with a friend. His description of this place is interesting because it shows an extreme example of rural poverty and because the neighborhood is still known as Dogtown; and its people are still called Dogtowners and are proud of their ancient name. Ten thousand prayers, Mr. Knapp remarks, have arisen from the altars of Newburyport for the heathen who walk in darkness, "but who ever heard a single aspiration to heaven for a blessing on the colony of Dogtown?" Things are different now. Dogtown houses are freshly painted, and multitoned motorcars stand in well-tended yards, but a little of the old spirit of

quarrelsome collision returns of a Friday or Saturday night.
Let us examine the Knapp decription. It is worth quoting
at length, because it illumines one facet of life in Dexter's
Newburyport:

> The travellers entered a dreary looking tract of neglected
> land, evidently thought by the owners too poor for cultiva-
> tion. A few wretched huts were scattered over the barren
> spot, among brush and weeds, with smoke issuing from
> every part of the roofs of the cabins. The horses . . . were
> here and there browsing upon thistles, wire grass and black-
> berry vines, looking full of misery. The crows were cawing
> over their heads, with whetted beaks, impatient for their
> natural rights, the possession of their carcasses, when the
> few sands of the wretched jades had run through the hour-
> glass of their existence. The ominous croakings seemed evi-
> dently to occupy the minds of the woebegone steeds.
> Among the bushes were seen the women gathering whortle-
> berries, black berries, and various wild herbs, such as
> thorough-wax, pennyroyal, white weed, mullein, five-
> fingers, yellow dock, scullcap, with other herbs half domes-
> ticated, as saffron, hyssop, and balm. The herbs and berries
> were for the next day's market. On looking into the cabins
> we found an abundance of children, but not any men ex-
> cepting one or two decrepit old fellows, past service; the
> others, we understood, had gone mackerelling. The children
> of both sexes were without hats, bonnets or shoes, and had
> but a scanty rag to cover them. The outer layer of their
> hair was bleached to a brown flax color, of whatever natural
> hue it might have been originally. Their feet felt nothing
> but the sharpest thorns; they scoffed at the brier and com-
> plained not of stonecrushes. These children were as agile as
> young goats of the mountains, and but a little more intel-

ligent. They were unacquainted with misery, for they were above the ills of life. Among the children were seen a few stunted swine, squealing around the hovels. They were the most sensitive of all the crew. There were also a few barn-fowl, the only well-fed creatures we saw, for they were revelling on clouds of grasshoppers. To make up the group there were several cows of Pharaoh's lean kine, with a bell hanging between their horns to direct the ear of the heath-born urchins who looked after the cows straying from the neighboring cabins; we did not see any spinning wheel, loom, or instrument of husbandry. There was, however, one branch of manufacture carried on even here; it was that of distillation. A few small stills were then in operation, for making tansy water, mint drops and similar essences. We bought there several bottles of rosewater of a most exquisite flavor. It was distilled from the leaves of the Eglantine. This species of the wild rose abounds in that region, and by long usage is the property of the herb women and never gathered by the owners of the pastures in which it grows. The friend of the writer, more fond of drawing landscapes than of shooting the wild pigeons, then plentiful there and all around, sketched a view of Dog-Town and adorned it with some figures of these weird sisters, over a still, drawing the alcohol from herbs, as was practised at Bagdad some nine hundred years before it was known on the Newbury borders. The sketch was graphic; the smoke of the alembic arose curling around the heads of the females watching the process; an old tattered remnant of a petticoat was thrown over their heads to keep off a scorching sun of the last of August. The figures were all to the life. The writer re-marked that in some distant day, the picture might be read in the heraldry of some family, as the priestess of Nature, interrogating her mother to disclose her secrets.

For relief from this gloomy if picturesque impression of the environs of Newburyport we can draw on Mrs. Emery. Like Mr. Knapp's, this quotation, too, is rather long, but were it to be paraphrased, much of its beauty would be lost. Here we find a hustle and bustle around Market Square comparable to the opening scene of an Edwardian musical comedy. And the anecdote with which the passage ends, dealing with labor difficulties in a Newburyport ironworks, forms a marked contrast to the efficiencies of modern labor.

At that time every vessel placed upon the stocks was wholly completed and equipped for sea before it sailed over the bar. This brought a multiplicity of business to the town. Along the wharves stretched lofty warehouses crowded with merchandise. Carts and drays rattled up and down, incoming and outgoing vessels came and went, the merry songs and "heave ho's" of the sailors, blended with the cheery tones and hearty jests of the stevedores, carts from the interior unloaded and loaded — at every turn was bustle, industry and activity. Here with the spacious sail and rigging lofts, pump and block makers' shops, and ship chandlers stores, was every thing that pertained to maritime trade. . . . Maj. Joshua Greenleaf did most of the ship iron work at his large smithy on Liberty street. Mr. Gordon had a similar establishment at Bellevilleport. This gentleman was somewhat economical in his household. At that period cheese was a customary appendage of the dinner table, being considered an accessory to digestion. Mr. Gordon employed several workmen. One day a large cheese was placed on the table; after the meat had been disposed of, Mr. Gordon took a knife to cut the cheese; turning it over, he exclaimed, "this is a good cheese, a pretty cheese, too

good to spoil!" and laying down the knife, he rose and
called his men to their work. That afternoon a large anchor
was to be forged, the fire was kindled, the iron heated.

"That is a good heat!" exultantly exclaimed the master.

"A good heat," with one voice responded the men.

"A grand heat," reiterated the master.

"A grand heat," again responded the men.

"Then why don't you strike?" impatiently demanded
the master.

"Is it a good heat?" queried the foreman.

"Yes, yes, strike, strike I tell ye," hurriedly ordered the
master in a quick authoritative tone. "Strike, strike."

"Don't you think it is too good a heat to spoil?" quietly
returned the foreman, while not an arm was uplifted.

The hint was taken; the cheese brought with a loaf of
brown bread. The luncheon eaten and well washed down
with grog, the anchor was forged with a will.

This has been an attempt to give a view of the social life
of Newburyport, as it existed about the time of the Revolutionary War. It is one that might apply equally well to
a number of other New England towns. Newburyport was
not fully matured, but there were the beginnings of individuality. What has been put down here is impressionistic
and more hearsay than history, but it may be that gossip
and half-truths are occasionally effective. In the end there
are no common denominators that one can employ to express the cold, the silence and isolation that surrounded this
Newburyport. This isolation created a self-sufficiency
which the quantity production of farms and factories has
now made inconceivable to a modern. In history and in
costume fiction or the theater there can never be such a

thing as a perfect piece of period reconstruction. Writers may attempt it, and so, too, may the management of Williamsburg, and Mr. du Pont in his breathtaking museum of American antiquities. But the essence is always lost; in the end the dead past will always bury its dead.

Timothy Dexter Embarks on a Sensible Marriage

NOW THAT WE are on the subject of death, one must remember that the grim reaper paid more calls on New England communities than he does at present. When he knocked on the doors of early Newburyport there were no physicians with penicillin or other therapeutic gadgets ready to frustrate his efforts. There was only the haziest understanding of epidemics, no knowledge of what caused typhoid or plague or a host of minor diseases.[1] High infant mortality was taken for granted, and if in early or middle life one were taken with a consumption or a fever or flux, cupping and bleeding seldom cured it, nor did the concoctions of the herb women. The pine coffin and its black crape might as well have been prepared immediately. Then, plus disease, the occupational hazards of the average New-

---

[1] Plague and yellow fever wrought havoc on Newburyport on several occasions. There is an account of one peculiar disease that arrived in 1735 called "throat distemper" that may have been diphtheria. At the time this disease was attributed to the appearance of immense numbers of large caterpillars. They could swim like dogs and "cart and carriage wheels would be died green from the numbers they crushed in their progress." The disease appeared in September and by February 81 persons were buried from Federal Street alone. But smallpox was the most dreaded of all these visitations. At one time smokehouses were established on all roads entering the town, and travelers were obliged to submit to washings with vinegar and smoking of their clothes.

buryport male were higher then than now, largely because
of shipwreck. Nearly every winter there were several small
vessels unable to claw away from Plum Island or Hampton
in a northeast gale. One had to take these tragedies as they
came, like our motor accidents of the present.

Death in early Newburyport broke up as many homes as
easy divorce does at present, and it was a grimmer but just
as efficient agent for social upset. At this time Newburyport had a large crop of widows and widowers, most of
them seeking some new sort of security. Remarriage by the
surviving party occurred almost immediately after a more
or less statutory period of mourning.

It is a tribute to the abilities of Timothy Dexter that he
found himself in an economic position to marry about a
year after he had set up his leather shop. In this brief interval he earned a reputation for industry, and had saved
enough money to purchase a small piece of real estate. As
a young man, he must have been good-looking too. Even
the print done of him in his later years and widely sold in
Newburyport, although it partly caricatured his eccentricity, shows a handsome face with good features and a
humorous, good-natured mouth. In these early days he was
considered a steady man with a good trade. At least a Newburyport widow by the name of Elizabeth Frothingham
made this estimate, since she married Timothy Dexter at
the end of May, 1770. She had four children (Benjamin,
Gilman, John and Betty), hostages that might have caused
young Dexter to look carefully into her financial background.[2] She was obviously well-to-do in a moderate way,

[2] The four little Frothinghams were grown up and gone by the time Dexter had
made his fortune. We know nothing about his relations with them, because no further
allusion to them is made by Dexter or by his biographers.

PHILIP KAPPEL

and besides, she was a relative of Governor Gilman of New Hampshire, a connection which may have put her, in the Warner scale, somewhere among the uppers. She was sober, industrious, and an excellent seamstress. The circumstances in which Mr. Frothingham left her included the old dwelling house which we have attempted to describe, and which became the Sign of the Glove. Since there was no place to go in those days for a wedding trip, Dexter must have moved immediately to the Frothingham dwelling, and there with his wife and stepchildren he sat out the Revolutionary War and the several years ensuing, and two more children were added: Samuel, in 1772, and Nancy, in 1776. These arrivals inevitably stimulated the profit motive, causing Dexter, according to one source, to become versed in the new art of making Morocco leather. At the same time on the same premises Mrs. Dexter set up what was termed a huckster's business, which probably means that Madam Dexter sold odds and ends, dry goods and notions, and swapped and bartered with passers-by. The old house was a good site for a store, close to the wharves and the market, and no doubt the corner was a busier place than now.

The fog of the past, which is often thicker than the fog of battle, obscures the details of the Dexters' early married

life, as it has the lives of most of our ancestors. At best they could not have been a very interesting couple, while they conformed like all their neighbors to the confining limits of their station. Except for the rumor that Madam Dexter was a good seamstress, kept store and had a short temper, nothing is heard of her until Dexter made his money. Yet, in the light of subsequent events, something was wrong with their married life. During the years of the Revolutionary War, there were more than the usual conjugal quarrels and frustrations at the Sign of the Glove. But nothing so overt as to appear in town or the parish records — simply an underlying friction and malaise that burgeoned at a later time. Since no one has ever fully understood the character of Timothy Dexter, the mental picture his wife made of him before her marriage doubtless was highly incorrect. Their relationship had always been in imbalance and was seldom mutually rewarding — not that such things mattered then in the way they do now.

Although few historians and biographers embroider on it, marriage in eighteenth-century America was a vastly different institution from marriage of the present. With a few lurid exceptions, the institution was irrevocable, to be broken only by the decease of one or the other party. The equality demanded in a modern marriage lay in the distant future. When a couple married in Dexter's Newburyport, obedience by a woman in all major matters was expected automatically. Pious resignation was taken for granted; little girls were often given the Christian name of Submit; and only a few years previously female scolds were ducked in village ponds. The property of a wife was managed by the husband, since women were supposed to possess no business ability. It was a man's world and one that made meaner male natures tyrannical, but there was nothing much a woman could do about it. No sympathetic judges sat on Colonial benches ready to listen to tales of cruel and abusive treatment. Under certain circumstances separation was judicially and socially condoned, but divorce as an institution was so frowned on by the clergy and the community that it could be considered as nonexistent as a solution for domestic difficulty.

This state of affairs made for a more static and perhaps more satisfactory society than now exists, and it does not imply that women could not control a situation or from their submissive station make things disagreeable for their husbands. Madam Dexter was a connection of the Gilmans of New Hampshire, and there is no reason why she should have forgotten it. Her late husband, Mr. Frothingham, had left her comfortably off and, now that he was gone, probably began to possess more endearing qualities than Dexter the tanner. It could easily have been that her cultivation and appearance were superior to Dexter's. At least Dexter must have heard a great deal about the Gilmans and he must have met his wife's family in New Hampshire, since the registry of deeds has records of sales of parcels of land in that state by Dexter, land which may have belonged to his wife. It is hardly conceivable that the Gilmans could wholly have approved of Dexter. The superiority of Madam Dexter, in breeding and wealth, possibly caused Dexter great bitterness, since from the beginning of his days he was sensitive regarding his position. Much of this is sheer speculation, but in those years at the Sign of the Glove something, somewhere, had engendered discontent. Something was encouraging the fantastic side of Dexter's temperament. Samuel Knapp tells us only that in those days the Dexters "went on, good, quiet, tidy, honest folk, blessed with children to labor for, as well as themselves." There must have been more to the picture.

In April 1776 the first pronouncement by Timothy Dexter that I was able to discover appears in the local newsprint. At the Sign of the Glove, he informs his readers, he offers for sale "good Deer, Sheep and Moose skins. Likewise

Deer, Sheep and Moose Breeches, and a quantity of good Blubber." The blubber is the first indication we have of Dexter's branching out in trade. The advertisement in itself is commonplace, and devoid of the spelling and originality of diction for which Dexter was later famous. The kindly printer must have helped him, as he did on other occasions, a species of assistance needed by many other citizens.

There is another more arresting public mention of Dexter in this same year. In the town election he was voted to an office called Informer of Deer. This was a sinecure in the small and fairly thickly populated area of Newburyport. In fact, Mrs. E. Vale Smith makes the following statement: "No deer," she says, "were ever known to have been seen in Newburyport after its incorporation." Still, public office was a distinction then that made this position more than a local joke. It is a first indication that he was making an impression and that he was respected by certain elements. Small as this beginning was, in those days when the Colonies were fighting a desperate war against Great Britain, it is significant that Dexter's humor and loquaciousness had begun to attract notice, setting him on his way to becoming a character in a town which was full of characters.

Anyone who is curious can easily visit the site of the Sign of the Glove. It is on the corner of Green and Merrimack Streets, not far from the police station. The neighborhood, once called Broadway, though less aggressive or original than formerly, has not changed much for better or for worse since the years when the Glove sign swung above the Dexter door. Unfortunately, few if any land-

marks remain in the vicinity that can be used as a basis for reconstructing the Revolutionary scene. What old houses remain are concealed by more modern and inartistic façades. To the right, diagonally down the street, is a view of Market Square, now not much more than a bus stop and wholly inadequate parking space. The old meetinghouse that stood there during the Revolution was pulled down without much regret toward the end of Dexter's lifetime. The city fire station, with its open doors and motorized equipment, stands near a very old excavation known as Watt's cellar. On the banks of the river a few decaying warehouses and other small commercial buildings of seafaring days stand neglected, with gaps between them once filled by establishments that dealt in marine supplies. The wharves are mostly gone except for an occasional piling visible at low tide in the river's noisome black mud.

There is no shipping left worthy of the name — no lumber schooners from Maine, no coal barges, nor tugs that in my childhood used to tow the coal upstream. The only craft on the river are a flock of motorboats and very few of their hulls are of local construction. In outline the Newburyport waterfront still resembles an engraving done of it from the opposite shore of the river a hundred years ago, but it is now like a ghost town in the West. The river itself is sadly useless. Its waters, made dark and malodorous by the waste from the upriver manufacturing cities of Haverhill, Lawrence, Lowell, Nashua and Manchester, are so contaminated that hardly a self-respecting fish ventures to approach them, except in times of greatest emergency; and boys only swim off the riverbanks on rare occasions and generally afterwards regret the experiment. It has been said, and it is believable, that a cubic centimeter of water from the Merrimack is more germ-laden and noxious than the water of any river except the Ganges. Having visited the Ganges, I should prefer bathing in it in a group of the most sickly pilgrims to venturing into the Merrimack.

The great runs of fish, so abundant in Dexter's day as to furnish an important source of food supply for the rich and poor — the salmon, the herring, the alewives and the sturgeon — naturally have vanished, leaving a once magnificent river a startling example of unnecessary pollution, the worst perhaps of any existing in the nation. Suitable disposal plants could control this commercial pollution, and even the industrial debacle of the thirties enabled a few fish to return temporarily. One hundred million dollars would cleanse the river, a small sum compared with the moneys annually spent by our Interior Department for needlessly irrigating uninhabited sections of the West, but our rulers are not interested in this improvement. No appropriation for the pollution control of the Merrimack seems ever to be included in Congress's Rivers and Harbors Bill, which customarily embraces every project that everyone else has forgotten. But it is time to cease this melancholy digression. It has only been indulged in to make a single point.[3]

The unclean waters of the Merrimack have pushed the sea so far away from the Sign of the Glove that one is scarcely conscious of the nearness of the ocean unless one crosses Merrimack Street and stands on the riverbank. Then it is possible to see the dunes at the mouth of the river with its comparatively modern jetties. The harbor entrance may have shifted somewhat since Dexter's time, because northeast storms have twisted and turned the channel. At low tide on a windy day, one can observe the impediment that in spite of the jetties has now made Newburyport a difficult and often dangerous harbor for even small craft to enter. Surf frequently breaks on the Merrimack sandbar at low tide, and this bar, though less formidable in Newburyport's shipping days, at that time plagued mariners, who were compelled to wait for a favorable tide and wind before entering or leaving the harbor. Now that there is no longer

---

[3] The pollution of the Merrimack River has been increasing to its present state only over the past fifty years. As a child I can remember being taken to the riverbank to watch the sturgeon jump, although the run of salmon had ceased long before, because of the construction of industrial dams upstream. My father, who graduated in the class of 1889 from Harvard, told me that once during his college years he went up the Merrimack aboard a tugboat. He remembered that the captain stopped just above the Chain Bridge, where the water began to be fresh, to take drinking water from the river, a custom that had always been the practice of captains of sailing vessels. Such an attempt now would be a most unpleasant form of suicide.

carrying trade or shipbuilding in Newburyport, the river and the chilly waters of the Atlantic have lost their earlier significance. It was a different situation in Dexter's lifetime. There would have been no Newburyport without the sea or the river. They were the sources of its wealth and of all that remains of its originality and beauty.

V I I

When the Streets Were Paved
with Gold

WHEN DEXTER ADVERTISED his breeches and his blubber, there was a rash of excitement just outside his door. Money has never poured into Newburyport as quickly or as easily as at the start of the Colonial rebellion. A very short time after the Battle of Lexington, Newburyport became a boom town because of a maritime activity known as privateering. Shipwrights and merchants had quickly discovered the beauty of this new profession. All that was really necessary in early war days was to secure a permit from the Bay Colony and later from the Continental Congress (and a permit was sometimes overlooked) to arm and equip any ship in the harbor to prey on British commerce that was plentiful off the coast.

In the dawn of the fight for freedom it scarcely mattered what sort of vessel was fitted out, because of the quantities of unprotected English shipping. Any brig, sloop, or schooner, given a few guns and an enthusiastic crew, might, after a few days' cruise, return with one or more British merchantmen as prizes. For a surprisingly long period the British merchant fleet appeared to be unaware

of the extent and seriousness of the Colonial insurrection, and this unawareness was shared by the Admiralty. What is left of Newburyport privateering records shows that one vessel with a burthen of only twenty tons, aptly called the *Game Cock*, cast off from a local wharf. Shipowners, as this lucrative business continued, were generally happy to protect themselves partially from loss by selling public shares in the outgoing vessel. The division of prize money according to agreement was sufficient to give substantial sums to officers and crews, but the owner's share might reach enormous figures.

Privateering has been often called "licensed piracy," a phrase that is nearly correct. Its popularity sprang less

from patriotic drives than from the profit motive. However, the enthusiasts who sailed from Newburyport, with
a parson's prayer to cheer them on, could share the happy
feeling that they were doing the Right Thing. The names
of their ships echo this ardor. In fact, listing a few is about
the best means left to illustrate the euphoric spirit of Revolutionary Newburyport — the *Washington*, the *Yankee
Hero*, the *Hawk*, the *Civil Usage*, the *Independence*, the
Satisfaction, the *Defiance*, the *Revenge*, the *Retaliation*,
the *Thorn*, the *Sky Rocket*, the *Success*, the *Shark*, the
Hannibal, the *Hornet*. These are only a few of the vessels
listed in Mr. Currier's compilation of American privateers.
There is another category of a softer and more sentimental
nature — the *Fancy*, the *Gloriosa*, the *Hope*, the *Virgin*,
the *Peacock*, the *Friendship*, the *Betsy*, the *Charming
Nancy*. In spite of their resounding titles, their combined
tonnage was probably less than the Gloucester fishing fleet
when Mr. Kipling wrote *Captains Courageous*, but they
were large enough and spry enough to achieve spectacular
success. In fact, it soon became obvious that nearly any
conceivable good fortune might occur, and tales of sudden
wealth did not need to be exaggerated along the waterfront
or in the town bistros. (There were no package stores in
those days, unless some warehouse selling rum, strong waters, and Madeira, by the pipe, keg, or hogshead, may be
considered in that category.)

For example, one morning Newburyport awoke to see
a British merchantman hove to off the bar, and Mr. Offin
Boardman, after whom Boardman Street must have been
named, got together two whaleboats full of local boys and
rowed out to her. The unfortunate British captain was

under the impression that he had just made Boston harbor and that Captain Boardman was the pilot, coming to take him in. We can imagine the Britisher's surprise, and the joy of the Newburyport locals, when they collected a small fortune without firing a shot. I have never understood why this exploit, though bold and lucky, has been thought heroic by local chroniclers. Indeed, in my childhood the Newburyport *Herald* published a column of verses by a romanticist, beginning, "Have you ever heard the story of the British ship, the *Friends?*" I have forgotten the rest, but generations of little Newburyport boys and girls have heard the tale with varying degrees of interest.

The episode offered visual proof that anything could happen, and new proofs were quickly added. Strange ships kept coming over the bar, singly or in groups, sent home by the privateers, or sailing under their escort. These gifts from the sea were greeted with huzzas or prayers of thanksgiving, according to temperaments along the waterfront, for the spirit of Newburyport was made up of contradictory combinations of holier-than-thou right-living mingled with acquisitive materialism and heavy drinking. There was every excuse for Newburyport not to have maintained its emotional balance at this especial time.

A large part of the privateering record is lost — much of it no doubt destroyed by shipowners who did not want facts made public, but it is still possible, beside the ship *Friends,* to catalogue many other examples of extraordinary good fortune. Captain John O'Brien, one of our best fire-eating seadogs, captured three brigs, a ship, and a schooner the very first time he embarked upon this novel activity. There is small wonder Captain O'Brien's services were much sought after by shipowners, and no wonder, either, that some men in moderate circumstances grew rich overnight. Anybody with the money could buy a share or two in the latest ships being fitted. There is no record that Dexter made any such investments, but we may assume he did, in moderation, since the jolly "Heave-ho-ings" of Mrs. Emery sounded just outside the Sign of the Glove. Captain William Russell, commanding the *General Ward,* took only a light swivel and sixteen men to sea, but returned with a schooner and two brigs. The *Hawk* sent back an English merchantman from Oporto, loaded with wine and carrying a large sum of currency. This brief list of happy happen-

ings is perhaps enough to explain why certain memories
linger on in Newburyport. There is still an echo, though
now it is dying, dying, to a muted point where Alfred,
Lord Tennyson himself would scarce be able to perceive it.

Nathaniel Tracy, Esq., one of the most successful privateer owners, young at that time, and opulent and widely
traveled, whose State Street mansion is now the Newburyport Public Library, lived in those early Revolutionary days
a life that would amaze the present Friends of the Library.
His fine house was furnished in the most modern eighteenth-century manner and was tended by Negro servants
in livery, and he could afford the costs, just as his brother-
in-law and partner, Mr. Jonathan Jackson, could easily
afford a similar establishment. Later historians give an
eloquently startling tally of the gains of Newburyport
privateering and also the subsequent losses. But no one was
thinking of loss, at the moment. The vessels sent out by
the Tracy-Jackson partnership alone captured one hundred and twenty sail, which brought with their cargoes
three million nine hundred and fifty thousand dollars
gross.

Although the memories of this time have grown dim
because of the hideous repercussions of two world wars,
they were vivid in my childhood, in the household of my
Great-aunt Mary. She could point out tangible evidences
of the period, which still make it a personal family matter.
The portrait of Daniel Marquand, the first of my ancestors
to come to America, in 1732, together with his stern-
visaged wife, the widow of a Captain Brown, hung in the
old house. The old gentleman—he was alive at the beginning of the Revolutionary War, but too old to have had

much to do with the family business — wears his own hair, presumably in a queue, although this is not visible, since this is a front-face portrait. The face, good-natured and florid, has a faintly foreign, Latin appearance, explained by his Norman-French antecedents. He wears an expansive red waistcoat, and there is a family rumor (to be distrusted, like all family rumors) that when he ordered this waistcoat he insisted that there should be no false backing but red cloth all the way around. It is said (another family rumor) that he left St. Peter Port in Guernsey in 1732, taking his own ships with him, and that he was accompanied by a nephew. For some reason never now to be known, he was, like Lord Dexter, sold on the possibilities and future of Newburyport, and thus settled there, whereas his nephew was more impressed by the port of New York. After the 1811 Fire, it is said that Daniel Marquand's son, Joseph, my own great-great-grandfather, whose property was almost entirely wiped out in the holocaust, sent his silver to his Marquand cousins in New York, where it might be more advantageously disposed of. True or false, vague as the connection is, we and the New York Marquands still call each other cousins.

Joseph Marquand made privateering money in the War of the Revolution, and, contrary to recklessness and gambling traits discernible in some of his descendants, and unlike Messrs. Tracy and Jackson, he was far-sighted enough to stop operations before it was too late. There are a few indices still left that point to his prosperity, which must have been considerable, but never at the multi-million-dollar level attained by Tracy and Jackson. It is a pity that there is no portrait of him left. His picture, if one existed, was burned in the Fire of 1811, along with his gambrel-roofed dwelling that stood near Water Street, close to the head of Marquand's Wharf, also destroyed along with his three-hundred-ton ship *Washington;* and after the Fire there was no money left to defray the extravagance of a portrait.

At the opening of the Revolution he was rich enough to contribute two vessels to Arnold's unfortunate Kennebec expedition. A tall clock made in London and still in the family came from the Marquand house, and four beautiful French Chippendale chairs of the darkest San Domingo mahogany — a wood which age has made nearly as brittle as porcelain—and also a pair of silver candle-snuffers. These items are said to have been the property of the Governor General of Canada and were on their way across the ocean when the ship carrying them was taken by a Marquand privateer. I doubt whether any of these pieces are of the 1776 period, but there is no doubt that Joseph Marquand's house was partially furnished by the Governor General's possessions, and the community once took pride in this sort of nautical pilfering. For example, Mrs. Emery mentions the Governor General episode and adorns it with another bit of gossip. It seems that along with the other goods aboard the ship was a fine library. Madam Marquand, evidently a kindly lady (though I believe she was said by young John Quincy Adams to be pretentious), knowing a young man in Newburyport who was interested in reading, invited him to occupy the library each evening and ordered extra armfuls of wood to be placed there for light and heat. It being a period exclusively of candle- and firelight, the young gentleman almost lost his sight because he availed himself so freely of this invitation.

There is a further legend regarding Mr. Joseph Marquand — and he should not be called "Captain" Marquand, because he was a shipowner and not a ship's captain. This one has a ring of authenticity, or at least the pietistic quality dear to former Newburyport citizens. The event occurred at the height of the privateering boom after Mr. Marquand had already been enriched by the trade. There are two versions of this legend. The first is that he was called from his countinghouse to the head of Marquand Wharf to see two new fine prizes being escorted by one of his vessels into the harbor. When he saw them, he is supposed to have spoken as follows: "Lord, stay Thy hand; Thy servant hath enough." The other version is more theatrical. In this, he is rowed out to view the prizes, and on this occasion his privateer captain presented him with a handsome and massive silver bowl taken from one of the ships. After gazing at it, he tossed it into the river, repeating the same words. Needless to say, to round out the anecdote, retribution soon followed. The Lord stayed His hand, and things went very badly afterwards. The Marquand privateer, *America*, disappeared with all hands, and finally the Newburyport Fire destroyed almost all of Joseph Marquand's property. It may be added that the prayer has in the main been answered ever since, in that no member of the family has been permitted to accumulate and keep any substantial sum of money.

This piece of folklore shows how fashions of thought can change from generation to generation, leaving an accumulation of intellectual debris and broken shards of ideas that cannot be wholly reconciled by any historical archeologist. Thus the speech of my great-great-grandfather's is a reflection of a certain facet of the latter eighteenth-century

New England mind. To a modern it has a schizophrenic quality, an unreconciled split between God and privateering, but it is doubtful whether this contradiction disturbed many of Joseph Marquand's contemporaries. It is as archaic as a speech attributed to the late capitalist, Mr. Baer, during a nationwide coal strike in 1902. God Almighty, Mr. Baer announced, in His wisdom, had seen fit to endow a number of persons with the natural resources of the United States of America, and those persons, so endowed by God, would always attempt to deserve His trust. Today this early twentieth-century mind is becoming as difficult to analyze as that of a century earlier.

One cannot hear the voices of the men in the Stuart and Copley portraits. My great-great-grandfather, although he existed, is nothing more now than a shadow. He was a liberal, a member of the Democratic Party when most of Newburyport was violently Federalist. And he must have had a high temper. Disliking the political views expressed by his minister from the pulpit, he resigned from the congregation, and his stinging letter still exists among the archives of the First Religious Society of Newburyport.[1] After his impoverishment by the Fire, he lived temporarily in a Federalist brick house on High Street near State, now the McKinney Funeral Parlor. He was made Collector of the Port, and here, except for a few receipted bills and a

Newburyport, 29 April, 1814
[1] To the Clerk of the First Religious Society in Newburyport:
Sir, Joseph Marquand, being aggrieved at Mr. Andrews Pulpit being a Vehickle of Slander on the 22nd February and 4th of July annually against the Government of the United States, wishes to withdraw his name from the Books of the First Religious Society in Newburyport, and does hereby give notice that he is no longer a member of said Society.

Jos Marquand

Waterford glass decanter bearing his initials, our record
ends.

It is fascinating, and futile, to imagine what Newburyport was like in its privateering splendor. It had a quality
of piracy, blockade-running and smuggling that lingers in
legend around the town of Nassau in the Bahama Islands.
Nassau, like Newburyport, has had two great moments,
though both of a later vintage. In the Civil War, Nassau
was the center of blockade-running. As in privateering, the
risk of the trade was high, but the profits were enormous.

Captains and crews were paid fantastic sums for running assorted supplies into Wilmington and Charleston, and the rash of prosperity had the same contagion that once existed in Newburyport. One still hears tales of drunken captains, who, having completed a successful round trip through the patrols of the United States Navy, sat on balconies above Bay Street with bags of shillings beside them, throwing handfuls of silver between beverages to the crowds. Then came Nassau's rum-running days during United States Prohibition. As one of Nassau's politicians once told me, even the choir singers in the Anglican Church would make ventures in cases of champagne.

In Newburyport, local merchants, whose lucrative West India trade was being cut off by the war, made gains out of privateering exceeding their previous profits. Their houses became filled with elaborate odds and ends from British prizes. The shipyards and attendant industries were working overtime; and though the money in its larger sense remained at the top, there was still a wide distribution of the wealth through the prize crews; and the rich were spending freely, patronizing silversmiths, clockmakers, chaisemakers, cabinetmakers, and itinerant artists. Prosperity encouraged forms of ostentation that would have been impossible a decade earlier and created a set of *nouveaux riches*. This sudden injection of easy money started Newburyport in its abrupt rise from a plain Colonial sea town to a community with sophistications, prejudices and arrogances, and a taste for gracious living that was recognized respectfully along the North Atlantic Coast. It may also be assumed that the insistent shipping demands of this brief halcyon period gave an impetus to shipbuilding that made Newburyport shipwrights famous all through the days of sail. Finally, this hectic interim, despite the depression that marched on its heels, engendered an optimism that remained with Newburyport for many subsequent decades. There was a dynamic quality in Dexter's Newburyport when there were so few other centers that demanded skills and initiative.

Perhaps some of the shrewder merchants, my ancestor among them when he petitioned Providence for less generosity, had a premonition that things could not go indefinitely as they were going. Some people must have begun asking what had become of British sea power. They were to find out, because eventually an efficient task force, abetted by British privateers, appeared off the coast and brought virtual annihilation to the improvised sea forces of the Colonies. Thousands of men and boys who had manned the Yankee ships ended in British prison hulks; shipping on the Massachusetts coast approached zero and the wharves and yards were as deserted as they were to be later under the Jeffersonian Embargo.

It appears, if one reads between the lines of Currier, or scans the advertisements of the Newburyport *Impartial Herald,* that a considerable number of prosperous individuals engaged in mercantile pursuits retrenched before it was too late. This was not true, however, of two of Newburyport's richest citizens whom we have mentioned. Such painful things began to happen to Mr. Nathaniel Tracy that they eclipsed the smaller embarrassments of others. Mr. Tracy and his partner, during the Revolutionary War, were the chief owners of twenty-four cruising ships mounting three hundred and forty guns and carrying two

thousand eight hundred men. Twenty-three of these privateering vessels were lost by the time peace was signed,
and these were only part of the firm's interests. During this
same period, Mr. Tracy was chief owner of one hundred
and ten merchant vessels, valued with their cargoes at
$2,733,000 — a figure that gives, along with the Tracy and
Jackson privateering gains, an unexaggerated picture of
Newburyport's prosperity. Only thirteen of these ships remained when the war was ended, the rest having been
either captured or lost at sea. By peace the firm of Tracy
and Jackson was faced with ruin.

Newburyport has always been a fertile field for financial
loss. In fact, one might term it failure-prone, if one were
to call the roll of its generations of speculators. The sea,
and the town's location on the rather insalubrious edge of
the North American Continent, always encouraged extreme financial risks; but there have been few Newburyport crashes as stupendous as this one, and its effect upon
the whole economy was very great. Courageous efforts were
made by the firm to recoup. In fact, Mr. Jackson in 1784
even sailed to England seeking for loans. Nothing could
bring back the good old days. Mr. Tracy eventually sold
the High Street mansion, as he did his Cambridge house on
Brattle Street, and moved into the country to the Spencer
Pierce house, where I was once shown his initials scratched
on a windowpane in the low-studded parlor. The window,
if my recollection does not fail, looked across the fields and
marshes of the old farm toward the harbor; and the legend
was that the straitened merchant stood there often, looking
out to sea. Mr. Jackson kept his High Street house somewhat longer, but he, too, eventually sold, to a Captain

Thomas. The Jacksons and the Tracys, together with the Higginsons and Lowells, and some other Essex County families, eventually moved to Boston, where many of them married Cabots and where their descendants still reside. It is ironical that Timothy Dexter, the leather dresser, was to obtain a position in the immediate future that would enable him to purchase both the Tracy and the Jackson mansions.

The sudden Newburyport overturn was economic and not social. In spite of the Declaration of Independence, the Revolution, as viewed by the more prosperous shipowners of the Eastern seaboard, was to their thinking more a war to protect the American carrying trade against the commercial pressures of London than to uphold the rights of man. But in the North a depression had appeared that in many respects surpassed the great depression of our 1930's. The flimsy federated government offered no great hopes for a firm political future. The fishing trade, on which towns like Newburyport were dependent for their manufactured and West India goods, was virtually destroyed. The farmers in the Berkshires were in open rebellion, and financial uncertainty and speculation had brought on inflationary extravagances not yet quite equaled by our present. The *nouveau riche* classes lived in a riot of luxury, although even by 1786 the exports of Massachusetts were only one fourth of what they had been earlier. "Travellers," Mr. Morison states, "commented on the vulgar display of the profiteers and the reckless spending of farmers and mechanics" — some of whom even bought silk stockings, when unemployment was enormous, and wages and the prices of produce alarmingly depressed.

This drama, so calculated to horrify or gladden the

modern social economist, was played against a very different backdrop from the present. There were acute examples of poverty, but one doubts whether many inhabitants, including unemployed sailors, shipwrights and artisans, went hungry, because there was an abundance in the countryside difficult to imagine today — flights of passenger pigeons, of shore birds and wild fowl in numbers that would now be astounding. The flats of the Merrimack and Parker Rivers abounded with clams not yet contaminated by industrial waste nor attacked by the small green crabs that have now moved in from the South. The Atlantic waters were colder then, so that cod could be taken in quantity off the coast. There were huge schools of mackerel in the summer, and the clear waters of the Merrimack were hospitable to the spawning fish from the ocean. Lobsters three feet long were not a rarity. There was no reason for anyone with a spade, a shotgun or a fishhook to starve in Newburyport. This primitive frontier plenty must be the reason why one encounters less desperation in the newspapers of that period. The situation would be very different now, with scarcely a fish in the river, hardly an edible clam, the cod moving even beyond the Grand Banks, and a dozen gunners for each migratory fowl. The ecology of Newburyport has undergone vast change. Ironically enough, the deer that would seem to have been rare in Timothy Dexter's time are nearly the only creatures that show promise of survival.

The Continental Federation was splitting at the seams, and the conflict between local and federal government was more acute than it was on the eve of the War Between the States. It is now intellectually possible to believe that dur-

ing the chaos following the Revolution many sensible individuals were convinced that a future government of the
United States should be patterned along the lines of mon-
archy. As many observers have pointed out, only a miracle
brought order and created the Constitution. When economic and political stability finally began to be apparent,
Massachusetts emerged from the upheaval as a section of
the country controlled by the old vested minority that
commanded brains, ability and arrogance incommensurate
with its size.

V I I I

A Most Distinguished Visitor

I T IS BEWILDERING, as things are in Newburyport today, to understand how the town could have developed resources that have furnished the basis of several of the largest fortunes in Massachusetts. Today it is becoming a bypassed community. Its connection by rail to the outer world grows yearly more tenuous. The last half of the Newburyport Turnpike, a stage road financed by Newburyport investors in the last years of Timothy Dexter's life as a rapid means of communication with Boston, has become a subordinate artery. The main motor road now skirts the town, using a new bridge farther up the Merrimack. The river itself is scarcely navigable at its mouth. The early editions of Blount's *Coast Pilot*, a work first published in Newburyport, stated that there were seven feet over the bar at the river's mouth, at mean low water. This was precarious enough for vessels of any tonnage, but now the depth is closer to five than seven, and commercially the town is almost closed from the ocean.

The Merrimack River, rising at Lake Winnipesaukee in New Hampshire, is the key to the riddle. In a roadless continent it was a main thoroughfare. It was once the watery warpath for marauding Indian bands that committed depredations as close to the river mouth as West Newbury and one of which had the bad fortune to capture Mrs. Hannah Dustin of Haverhill, the lady who tomahawked ten braves in their sleep. Today anyone with a modest amount of anthropological knowledge can discover the camp sites of these vanished people along the riverbank and, in fact, at one point in my memory this past almost, though not quite, touches the present. My Great-aunt Mary told me once that when she was a very little girl playing by the landing near the mouth of the Artichoke River, a tributary to the Merrimack, she was startled by the appearance of five or six birch-bark canoes filled with Indians, a sight which caused her to run screaming to the house. Her father, who was not at sea at that moment, came to the riverbank and conversed with the group. According to my Great-aunt, the Indians said that they were following their ancient custom of journeying from Winnipesaukee to obtain sea water for religious rites. Her father gave them a measure of corn, and the Indians camped on Emery's point across from the Curzon house. This digression shows how history can compress itself and why auras of several pasts still linger over Newburyport.

The river once tapped the virgin forests of the back country with their immense stands of white pine and white oak, and the size and quality of these trees can still be seen in the floor boards and the framings of old houses. This plentiful lumber, which could be floated readily downstream, formed the basis of a shipbuilding industry that grew to such proportions, in the last days of Timothy Dexter, that the lower Merrimack became a chief shipbuilding center in the United States.

Shipbuilding gave Newburyport a complex industrial aspect with its ropewalks, sail lofts, and ironmasters' forges capable of turning out all ships' hardware, from nails to anchors. These and allied industries demanded an aggressive commerce that brought into being an elaborate community requiring a variety of individual creative skills. Such diversities attracted not only an ordinary laboring class but highly skilled artisans, imaginative and daring entrepreneurs, and outstanding representatives of the professions, including the clergy, medicine, and the law. Privateering had educated some of the ablest and most daring captains and crews in the new nation. The necessity for speed imposed by privateering had also produced a new and radical school of ship designers. The shipwrights who in the time of the depression had been obliged to turn a hand to anything, had developed new levels of versatility, and the same was true with local smiths and sail- and ropemakers. Other talents were untapped and waiting. Like Timothy Dexter himself, they needed only impetus, which came primarily with the adoption of the Constitution of the United States of America, but came also because of the financial genius of the politically aristocratic young artillery officer and former member of General Washington's staff, Alexander Hamilton, that remarkable immigrant from a sugar island in the Caribbean.

During the literary flowering of the Roosevelt era, when it was the fashion for all works of fiction, drama, or history to teach a lesson of social significance, a school of villains was created with Alexander Hamilton as its prototype. It is futile, though interesting, to speculate on what finally might have happened to the Hamilton ideology

had his life not been ended well before its prime by Aaron
Burr's bullet. His ideas on democracy might have mellowed
had he lived into the early adolescence of his infant nation.
As it was, he died an arch Federalist, a political species now
as extinct as the eighteenth-century mind, but roughly
resembling an extremely conservative modern Republican
infected by the extreme aristocratic beliefs once prevalent
in the ante-bellum South. Hamilton had an undeviating
dread of what he termed "the mob," as opposed to the
Jeffersonian belief in the general rightness of citizenry. His
distrust of broad civil franchise was shared by many of
his classically educated contemporaries, particularly those
with accumulated wealth, and admittedly there was cause
for alarm during the French Revolution. It was the Hamiltonian belief that strong steps should be taken by the new
Republic to prevent the mob's seizing power and to con-
centrate the handling of affairs within the grasp of the
informed and privileged.

These theories have aroused the ire of our New Deal
literati. Thomas Jefferson, in mythology, is the hero, and
Alexander Hamilton his antithesis, but one may question
whether our generation treats Alexander Hamilton with
the respect he deserves. When he became Secretary of the
Treasury, he found fiscal affairs in a state of chaos, compared to which the nightmare of our present creeping
inflation is the dawn of a hopeful tomorrow. During the
war, currencies had been issued irresponsibly by the various Colonies as well as by the Continental Congress. In
the post-bellum years it was usually necessary to resort to
the British pound or to barter in order to conclude any
reasonable business transaction. The Continental currency

had inflated itself to such a degree that the phrase "not worth a Continental" was still a term of derision in my childhood. Very few people at the time of the framing of the Constitution had faith in this wartime currency, but some merchants had collected it, including Messrs. Russell and Hancock of Boston; and lesser traders followed their example in buying up Continentals, including Timothy Dexter in Newburyport.

Samuel Knapp tells us that Timothy Dexter, during his residence in Boston, received advice from Messrs. Russell and Hancock. This is an obvious error. Dexter resided in Boston some years before the Revolution, apprenticed to a leather dresser, and even had he lived there later, residents of Beacon Hill would not have received him, or offered financial tips. No one can tell what induced Timothy Dexter, during the post-Revolution uncertainties, to acquire a considerable amount of Continental money at a few cents to the dollar. There could have been hardly anyone in Newburyport, except possibly Theophilus Parsons, who might have possessed advance knowledge of Mr. Hamilton's fiscal plans, and this jurist, although Dexter was his client, moved in circles beyond the Sign of the Glove. Regarding Timothy Dexter's investment, one can only advance the theory that brains and ability have often been minor adjuncts where skill with money is concerned and that the Midas touch has always defied explanation and social barriers.

Even a superficial examination of Hamilton's plan for centralizing national credit and for assuming state debts, and of his successful forging of that plan into laws eventually passed by a reluctant Congress, shows the man's extraordinary brilliance and sagacity. In spite of his dislike of many of Mr. Jefferson's theories, Mr. Hamilton had a politician's instinct for compromise. It appears that after a long conversation, the master of Monticello gave his support to the Hamilton plan in return for Hamilton's supporting the Jeffersonian idea of establishing the nation's capital on the banks of the Potomac. This temporary alliance of two of the best minds of the age overcame the jealousies and wranglings that always surround measures of taxation. According to the Hamilton prescription, a national tax measure was passed, with laws for the establishment of a national banking system and a Federal assumption of state debts incurred throughout the war. Conservative though Hamilton may have been, few Americans have performed a greater service to their country than he by his financial reconstruction. Daniel Webster himself has saluted the achievements with an eloquence out of style at present. The defender of Dartmouth College tells us that the rock of credit was tapped and that a healing stream of gold poured forth, subdividing into a million rivulets, spreading to the deepest roots of society. That healing stream of gold is now, for better or worse, underground at Fort Knox. Even so, vestiges of the Hamiltonian order remain, and the gold did trickle downward far enough to touch the palm of a tanner of Newburyport.

Continental notes, previously worth a few cents to the dollar, now, backed by taxation and a gold reserve, became redeemable at par, and almost overnight Timothy Dexter became wealthy because he had not been a bear on the United States. He became affluent exactly when many of the rich of Newburyport grew poorer. It is unfortunate that no one knows the exact amount of Dexter's

fortune. There can be little doubt, though, that the sum
was smaller than supposed, since Newburyporters up to
the present day have been prone to exaggerate the financial
totals of their neighbors — a tendency that has caused
many of the richest members of the community to live
in an exaggeratedly modest manner. If the quick acquisition of a few thousands of dollars has always caused a stir
in State Street and Market Square, a dollar also went
further in Dexter's day than now. Whatever his gains,
they were enough to shatter Dexter's sense of values as
well as his pedestrian personality. They made him a golden
legend in his lifetime, endowed him with a reputation for
keenness in all business ventures, and moved him suddenly
from the Sign of the Glove and his leather trade into the
Tracy mansion on State Street. The man in the street has
always loved tales of rags to riches. In Dexter's day people were still close to the true story, told by the Reverend
Cotton Mather in his *Magnalia,* of William Phips, who
found Spanish gold near a Bahama reef. But such events
occurred so seldom that they were easily sublimated into
folklore, along with the tales of the buried treasure of
Captain Kidd, and now Dexter was placed on these same
heights. No one can blame him for nervous maladjust-
ment.

On October 30, 1789, President George Washington
stopped briefly in Newburyport during his tour of the
new nation. Details of the welcome accorded him have
been copiously reported in the Newburyport *Impartial
Herald* and by Mr. Currier, Mrs. Emery, and others. The
arrangements were on an elaborate scale that fitted the
greatness of the occasion. The President traveled in his

private coach and might have preferred to stay in it,
inured though he was to a lifetime of rough journeys. Instead he descended as the vehicle neared the juncture of
State and High Streets and mounted a horse, whereupon
the town's local militia marched to meet him, and with
them all distinguished gentlemen of the neighborhood. As
he moved toward State Street, the local artillery fired the
federal salute. Then as soon as the cannon smoke lifted,
a company of especially trained young men sang the following ode, composed for the occasion:

> He comes! He comes! The HERO comes!
> Sound, sound your Trumpets, beat, beat your Drums;
> From Port to Port let Cannons roar
> He's welcome to New England's shore.
> Welcome, welcome, welcome, welcome,
> Welcome to New England's shore!

> Prepare! Prepare! your songs prepare,
> Loud, loudly rend the echoing air;
> From Pole to Pole his praise resound,
> For Virtue is with glory crown'd.
> Virtue, virtue, virtue, virtue
> Virtue is with Glory crowned.

When the lines of the first verse called for beating drums or roaring cannon, the words were literally punctuated by drum ruffles and cannon shot. "And to the vocal," says one historian, "was joined all the instrumental music in both choruses." It is hard to envisage this complicated scene, but its impact was such that General Washington, who had faced other extraordinary demonstrations of affection and respect, was moved to tears.

Following the song a procession marched up the street, made up of all the social orders of the town. Following the musicians marched the selectmen, the marshal and the high sheriff. Then came the ministers, the physicians, the lawyers, the magistrates, the town officers, and the Marine Society. Behind the Marine Society were tradesmen, manufacturers, ships' captains, sailors, and finally schoolmasters with their scholars. Upon approaching the President, the parade divided its ranks to right and left, allowing the honored guest to pass through. Then they joined ranks again and followed him. The teachers, we are told, led four hundred and twenty scholars, each bearing his quill pen.

But the President's reception was only beginning. Followed by this stratified parade, he proceeded down State Street attended by his entourage, consisting of six servants and his private secretary, Colonel Lear, whose wedding ceremony the President witnessed personally some days later, at Portsmouth, New Hampshire. He halted at the entrance of the Tracy mansion, where a group of the town's most distinguished gentlemen presented him with an address of welcome. The Honorable Jonathan Jackson, the privateer entrepreneur, who was residing at the Tracy mansion at the time, was there to greet the President, and presumably Mr. Nathaniel Tracy, living then in Newbury, was also present. Also in the group were the Honorable Benjamin Greenleaf, Esq., the Honorable Jonathan Greenleaf, Esq., Colonel Edward Wigglesworth, and Micajah Sawyer, Esq., all on the committee. There is some uncertainty as to who prepared or who delivered the welcoming address. According to town records it was written by Theophilus Parsons, Esq., but others believe that the work was done by the youthful John Quincy Adams, who was then reading law in the jurist's office. Mr. Adams mentions the speech in his diary but makes no claim. Frankly, upon perusing it today one can understand why neither Parsons nor Adams quarreled over the authorship. Its sentences were executed in the perfect periodic style of the eighteenth century, but there was small novelty in its content.

"Sir," the address began: "When, by the unanimous sufferages of your countrymen, you were called to preside over their public councils, the citizens of the town of Newbury-port participated in the general joy, that arose from anticipating an administration conducted by the man, to whose wisdom and valor they owed their liberties."

The rest was in the same vein, enhanced by one happy simile. The citizens of Newburyport saw the General now, the speaker said, "entwining the Olive with the Laurel and, in peace, giving security and happiness to a people whom in war you covered with glory."

"Long, sir," the address ended, "may you continue the orderment and support of these states and may the period be late when you shall be called to receive a reward adequate to your virtue, which it is not in the power of your country to bestow."

This solemn hope combining the here and the hereafter, so characteristic of the era, was partially realized in that the General had a decade left of life. General Washington made a gracious response which one hopes was written by Colonel Lear, but in those days Presidents of the United States seldom employed ghost writers.

"In visiting the town of Newburyport," he said, "I have obeyed a favorite inclination, and I am much gratified by the indulgence. In expressing a sincere wish for its prosperity, and the happiness of its inhabitants, I do justice to my own sentiments and their merit."

When the hospitable front door of the Tracy mansion closed behind him, he was able to sit down to a well-cooked meal in the company of the town's first gentlemen, but his day was not over yet. Early in the evening he received another address, from the First Presbytery of the Eastward, then in session in Newburyport, who also expressed the wish that "Free grace may confer on you as the reward of all your great labors the unfading laurels of an everlasting crown."

The President made an answering address composed on an equally high level.

"The affectionate welcome which you are pleased to

give me," he began, "to the eastern parts of the Union would leave me without excuse, did I fail to acknowledge the sensibility which it awakens and to express the most sincere return that a grateful sense of your goodness can suggest."

The President continued in this vein for five or six more minutes, but still his evening was not finished. A *feu-de-joie* was fired by several companies of militia, the price for the gunpowder having been paid by the town, and in the evening some fireworks and excellent rockets were "played off" opposite the mansion. "Much praise is due to the citizens of Newburyport and others assembled on the occasion," says the *Essex Journal and New Hampshire Packet,* "for their orderly behavior through the day and evening."

General Washington, as we know from his letters and journals so unfortunately censored by the historian Jared Sparks, was customarily an early riser, and the next morning was no exception to his routine. He first repaired on October 31 across State Street to the residence of the Honorable Tristram Dalton, then United States Senator, who had invited the professional men of the town to meet him. While at breakfast the President became engaged in talk with the Reverend John Murray of Newburyport. (We must not confuse this divine with John Murray, the Universalist of Boston. They were popularly distinguished each from the other as Damnation and Salvation Murray.) In the midst of the conversation a servant of Mr. Dalton's entered and told the Senator that an old man was in the entry who wished to speak to President Washington. When Mr. Dalton said that the President was engaged, the

words caught the ear of General Washington, who may
have been having difficulty following the Reverend Mr.
Murray's discourse, because he sprang immediately to his
feet and went to the entry. The Reverend Mr. Murray
accompanied him, and they perceived an old soldier standing there who said, "God bless you, *Major Washington,*"
and the President immediately recognized him.

"Cotton, how do you do," he said. "I am glad to see
you," and taking a guinea from his pocket he gave it to the
elderly Cotton.

Returning to breakfast, the General told the Reverend
Mr. Murray that this man had been a faithful servant to
him in the old French and Indian War and he had not seen
him for thirty years.

Cotton, who was known in Newburyport as "Colonel"
Cotton because of his military exploits, earned a meager
living there running errands. He made a hole through the
guinea and hung it around his neck until poverty forced
him to part with it. It is reassuring to note that the house
of the Honorable Tristram Dalton still stands on State
Street, undefaced by any major alteration. It is possible to
enter its wide front hall today and to stand on the very
spot where His Excellency greeted Colonel Cotton.

The President left town by either High or Merrimack
Streets and proceeded down the Ferry Road in order to
cross the river to Amesbury. The Marine Society had a
specially prepared barge waiting for him, manned by
bargemen dressed in white. As he crossed the river Captain
Joseph A. de Murrietta, of Tenerife, whose ship was
anchored upstream, for the purpose of filling her casks
with fresh water, fired a twenty-one-gun salute.

"We cannot but admire," the *Essex Journal and New Hampshire Packet* tells us, "among the many amiable traits of the President's character, that of his politeness to foreigners, which was repeated on this occasion."

We are not told in what manner President Washington exhibited the politeness. History is often punctuated by such annoying gaps of detail. It may be fitting to conclude these notes on the visit of the greatest man, with the possible exception of Ralph Waldo Emerson, ever to tread the streets of Newburyport, with a curious word-of-mouth anecdote that has persisted into the present. In the late twenties a resident of Newburyport told me that he once knew a very old man whose grandfather, as a boy, had been present on the Salisbury Green when President Washington stood listening to another address of welcome. During the address the old man's grandfather saw the President reach into his waistcoat pocket, take out a digestive tablet and swallow it.

Timothy Dexter, if he was not ill, was certainly on State Street that afternoon when the President listened to the town's address of welcome before the Tracy mansion. Since the beneficent measures of Alexander Hamilton were yet to have their repercussion, Dexter would have been dressed plainly, but it may have been that he had marched with the town officers in his capacity as Informer of Deer. He was a stocky man in his forties. His shrewd, sparely modeled features were neither ugly nor handsome enough to attract anyone's attention. Judging from snatches of his writings, he gazed with envy at the scene before the Tracy mansion and at the local gentry. He was seldom enthusiastic re-

garding the upper classes, and to prove it we may quote a
few sentences he wrote some time later.

> All our broken merchants [he wrote] cant have beaths
> of proffett; goue and till the ground goue to work . . . all
> that has bin to Coleage, goue with slipers, and promis to
> pay, and Never pay only with A Lye; I gess 4 fifth is
> Coleage Lant, or devel Lant, or pretended to be onnest free
> masione, but are to the Contry; forgive me for gessing; I
> hope it is Not so.

He saw two broken merchants that afternoon. Mr. Jonathan Jackson, who was renting the Tracy house probably
as a favor to its owner, and Nathaniel Tracy were present,
dressed in the lace-and-cambric formality then the fashion,
and the house was a fine background for the costumes and
uniforms of the company.

Samuel Knapp refers to the Tracy mansion as a palace,
which could not "in justice be called by a lesser name." It
is difficult to share his enthusiasm when one examines what
remains of the Tracy house, now converted into the Newburyport Public Library. It was so completely altered, with
the very best intentions, in the Civil War period that not
much of its palatial quality is left. Its brick has a grim uncompromising color. The old panes and sashes are gone
from its windows and so are its shutters. Only two rooms
still have their old woodwork remaining — the directors'
room on the right of the great hall and the children's reading room on the left. The rest of the interior has been distorted into Johnson-U.S. Grant decor. The staircase and
the upper rooms are gone as completely as the great days
of the Tracys, their silver and their wine cellars lost behind
a façade of golden oak and the musty odor of books. The

size of the house is almost all that gives a hint of the proud days of its youth. But it still manages to stand aloof from later interpolations on State Street, including the startling façade of the Institution for Savings across the way and the Romanesque of the Young Men's Christian Association a few doors down.

The clouds of trouble had already gathered over the Tracy house when Dexter examined its exterior on that notable October afternoon. It had been built in 1771 by the elderly and wealthy merchant, Patrick Tracy, the first of the Tracy line to come from Ireland to America. His portrait, by an unknown artist, reproduced in the Currier history, has the fluency of the Gainsborough-Reynolds school. Patrick Tracy, stocky, square-jawed and composed, is dressed in pre-Revolutionary smallclothes. The thumb of his right hand is in the pocket of his capacious waistcoat, pushing back a coat, which a London tailor might have thought a shade too long. His left hand rests on a huge anchor, behind which stand barrels and bales, indicating that his occupation was involved with the oldest of the arts and the newest of the professions. He built the State Street house as a gift for his handsome son Nathaniel, a luxurious residence even for a very rich man's son, and it was further improved by Nathaniel during his privateering prosperity. The staircase, from the hall of the Nathaniel Tracy house, was purchased by Ben: Perley Poore, when the house was being remodeled for the public library, and installed in Mr. Poore's remarkable house on Indian Hill in West Newbury, where, before the house was burned in the summer of 1959, it was possible to admire the exquisite turnings of the balusters that appeared lighter and more

graceful than the surviving paneling. There are tales of
its gilded mirrors and rich carpets and of the generous
Tracy hospitality, but already, when Washington slept
there, the mansion was only a reminder of what the Tracys
had been some years back.

The man who had brought millions in prize money into
Newburyport, who had given $160,000 to the American
cause, had been obliged drastically to retrench. He could
no longer afford to live in his mansion, but he still held title
to it, hoping, seemingly, for better days; but he was to be
a man of moderate circumstances subsequently, although
moving in the best circles of Boston and New England society and universally respected. He finally was obliged to

deed the house to his friend, Thomas Russell of Boston, in
1791, and shortly thereafter Mr. Russell received a favorable offer for the dwelling and probably for the bulk of its
furnishings. Mr. Russell may not have known who the
prospective purchaser was, nor cared. Mr. Russell may have
been interested only in hard cash, since there was need, as
Samuel Knapp hints, due to a crisis in the Tracy affairs, for
a rapid turnover at a sacrifice.

But Newburyport was shocked (because Newburyport
has always been proud of its more magnificent figures)
when the rumor was confirmed that Timothy Dexter had
bought the house, and with that confirmation blind faith in
solid order was shaken. The effect upon Timothy Dexter,
Madam Dexter and their son Sam and daughter Nancy,
now a pretty though featherbrained grown-up girl, was
still more pronounced, since very abruptly they were
forced to change the sober routines of a lifetime and to
move from middle-class penury into a way of life with
which they were unfamiliar, except from superficial observation. The main difficulty with such an adjustment for
both Timothy and Madam Dexter was that they were a
middle-aged couple, lacking in resilience and with fixed
habits. Until this date they had lived with moderate con-
geniality, both hard-working, Mrs. Dexter tending the
leather store and her notion shop on the occasions when
Dexter was out bargaining for land and building the savings which he invested in Continentals. They were inured
to long hours and plain living. For every class it was a hard-
drinking period. The hideously cold winters and lack of
central heating rendered the ingestion of hot rum throughout the day almost obligatory, and a belief existed that cold

water was dangerous for the stomach, as it was, on account of ill-controlled surface drainage. Yet there were no rumors that Timothy Dexter was a drunkard. Semiliterate, his hands calloused by years of honest toil and stained by tannic acid, he was no longer fitted to be mobile upward.

When good fortune forced Timothy Dexter and his family to break the mold of a lifetime, the shock was so massive that it unhinged him. The one useful thing the wealth achieved was the picturesque change that it wrought upon the character of Dexter himself. It appeared that he enjoyed being rich very much indeed; his lapse into eccentric behavior began at once, and immediately he wanted everything that wealth might control.

The change in Dexter became apparent as soon as he moved into the Tracy mansion. We cannot fix the date of his metmorphosis exactly, except that he began his residence there between 1791 and the time he sold the old house and the Sign of the Glove on the corner of Green and Merrimack Streets in 1792. Gossip has preserved a story regarding one of Dexter's early suppers in the mansion. I was told some years ago by an old inhabitant that there used to be a dent in the handsome paneling above the mantelpiece in the Tracy dining room made by Timothy Dexter on an evening when Madam Dexter served him a pot of baked beans. It is said that he flew into a rage, seized the bean pot and hurled it at the wall, shouting that he was through with beans and the simple life forever. True or not, like all Dexter anecdotes it illuminates his character. He was not only through with beans but through with his past. He was moving into a strange new world, but so, too, was New-buryport. Like Dexter the town was burgeoning and ex-

hibiting enlargements in taste and extravagance that made
it a wholly different place from the settlement of Dexter's
young manhood. It was moving into the formalities and
follies of the Federalist era, and like the Federalists the
town felt that this brief span would last forever. It was
growing proud of its culture, proud of the tone of its society, which some connoisseurs said was superior to that of
Boston or Salem. Better to understand Dexter and his problem, it may be well to devote some thought to this Federalist
Newburyport — then a glorious sort of Never-Never Land
that cannot exist again.

Footnote to Nostalgia

WHEN I WAS SIXTEEN YEARS OLD I wrote a poem on Newburyport, a verse of which I quote, not out of pride but because it is so factually correct as to be obvious.

> It's an old town by the river,
> Aye, look at it once again,
> For its fame has gone forever,
> Lost to the minds of men.

If I had foreseen the immediate result of this effort, I would never have written it. Its ink was hardly dry when my mother, who was under the illusion that I was a prodigy, asked me if I would row her down the Merrimack to Deer Island, because she owed a call to Mrs. Harriet Prescott Spofford, who lived in a house that had been a tavern frequented by gay parties of young people in the Federalist era and visited also by Timothy Dexter, who, on at least one occasion, became intoxicated there. I should have suspected my mother's motive when she asked me to row her down-river, but instead I was delighted to pay a call on Mrs. Spofford, to see her house with its garden and its view of the river and to stand momentarily in the presence of greatness. Mrs. Spofford was at that time the dean of Newburyport letters, and a worthy one too, as you will discover if you look into her many books. She was an elderly lady then, tranquil, kind and hospitable. I was sitting balancing my teacup, lulled by a sense of security, when my mother produced my poem and laughed at my adolescent anguish.

"Don't be rude," my mother said. "Don't you see that Mrs. Spofford is anxious to read it?"

It was true that in 1910, just as we were leaving the horse-and-buggy age and the gaslight for upheavals that have constantly increased, that the fame of Newburyport, Mass., was already lost to the minds of men.

If it was so then, it is vastly truer now. I had been conscious in my youth of the grace and beauty of Newburyport's old houses. I am even more acutely aware of them now that their beauty has a tragic quality that increases as their functional purpose as dwellings is disappearing. High Street, the broad thoroughfare that traverses the length of Newburyport, was said thirty years ago to be the most beautiful residential street in America. Today it is much harder to accept such a superlative, because the last thirty years have dealt more roughly with it than the previous hundred did. Its elms, sadly smashed by the hurricanes of 1938, 1944 and 1954, are now awaiting seemingly inevitable extinction by Dutch elm disease. The rectangular houses that they shaded are not so neat as they were thirty years back. In spite of their exquisite cornices and the spare grace of their mantels and moldings executed by Newburyport shipwrights in off-season, each year finds them becoming a greater burden to their owners.

They were planned for large families, and are now too large for compact living, and the cost of heating them grows increasingly prohibitive. The choreman-gardener, once a keystone in polite Newburyport economy, is on the point of vanishing, and, with inflation, the wages asked by those still in existence are growing harder to meet. With such difficulties increasing, the desirability of Newburyport's finest residences proportionately diminishes. Some are divided into apartments. Some are funeral and nursing homes. For years the Wheelwright house on the High Street ridge has been a home for aged ladies. One must not criticize any present use to which these dwellings can be put, but obviously their purpose has changed. Fences that separate some of them from the street are falling into disrepair. Years ago the fence before the Dexter house was removed because of expense of maintenance, and the same may soon happen to several handsomer specimens. The magnificent pictorial paper in the Wheelwright house has been scraped away to create a more cheerful atmosphere.

It is, of course, an indication of age and conservatism to bemoan all species of change that mark the path of progress but we must continue for purposes of comparison. Along State Street, starting at Pleasant Street, a perpendicular intersection, and thence to Market Square, very few buildings in the business blocks date later than the first decade of 1800. William Perry, a restorer of Williamsburg, Virginia, once explored the possibility of altering the façades of the shops along the street so that they would possess an earlier character that would make State Street into a period piece. The cost, he estimated (pre-war), would amount to only $250,000, and the change might considerably increase business. The idea aroused a transient interest. Mr. Perry did redesign the front of the old Wolfe Tavern (now de-

molished), and farther down the street the First National
and the A & P stores (now removed to the town's outskirts
because of parking problems) also made Colonial efforts,
but the idea has now been forgotten with the advent of
plastic motifs that give the most authentic part of State
Street a jukebox air. But Newburyport has not lost all its
ancient charm. The grip of the Federalist era, which gave
it its unique splendor, is still aesthetically strong. The
church spires are still there, and one of them has been called
the finest wooden spire in existence. Their bells still ring,
but they emphasize less and less the silence of the night,
nor do they frame by their sound the unity of the place.
Newburyport is fluid. It grows constantly harder to believe
that it once had an independent ambition thought to be
imperishable. There were designs afoot to make Newburyport the hub of the universe when Timothy Dexter was
alive. His epoch resembled ours in its faith in progress, but
there was less dread in the older belief. The prospect of
hell's fire lay in the hereafter. Mankind had yet to produce
it upon earth.

One can still gain a faint impression of what Newburyport was like in its prime on a night in spring. The only
trouble is that there is no longer such a thing as a quiet
night, but I still can remember one, although to do so I
must again return to my adolescence. When I was seventeen I undertook to walk from Newburyport to Boston, a
project in which I was joined by my cousin, John Marquand
Walker, then engaged in learning the textile business at the
Warner Mill (now an abandoned shell of brick) and Gerald
Bradford, who at that time was attending high school with
me. I forget why we took the long way to Boston, which is

the approximate route that Timothy Dexter traveled, instead of saving mileage by using the Newburyport Turnpike.

We decided to begin the walk at night, since at that time the road would be nearly deserted. It would surely be highly dangerous to take such a stroll at present. Elminating the probability of being killed by a truck or motor car, there would remain the certainty of being stopped by the police. The hour we selected was midnight, and two of us made it in, I imagine, better time than Timothy Dexter. I recall sitting down in Salem to a breakfast of oatmeal, cream and coffee and blacking out momentarily when the heavy food filled my stomach. A mile or two beyond Salem, Gerald Bradford announced that he was through with it. My cousin twitted me about my Salem mishap until we reached a point near Lynn, where we stopped at a small store that sold candy and soft drinks. Here I took a malicious delight in seeing him, after he had drunk a glass of Moxie, turn ashen, stagger to the rear of the store and collapse on a trestle table, upon which the owner had been making candy. However, he too recovered, and we continued our walk until we reached the Hotel Lenox at twelve-thirty in the afternoon. (I cannot remember at all why we wanted to go to the Hotel Lenox.)

My point lies not in the walk itself but in the first few minutes of it. It was May, a clear night with stars but no moon. The trees were in new leaf. The street lights were dim, and there were only a few night lights in the stores, yet there was enough to show the outlines of the houses. The bells began to ring, unevenly, because the church clocks never could be exactly synchronized. Then New-

buryport was asleep again, cut off from the contemporary
world. The old buildings looked newer; their antiquity was
gone. Although asleep, the town was more alive than in
daylight.

Nostalgia is, in many respects, a horrid word. In one of
its aspects, at least, it signifies an immature desire on the
part of millions of American adults to crawl back into the
past in order to avoid contemporary exigencies. But no retreat from the present can resurrect the past. If I, too, have
been resorting to nostalgia, I have one excuse. There is
scant possibility of presenting to anyone living the Newburyport that made Lord Timothy Dexter. But there is
the chance that by casting backwards over hearsay and
reminiscence, some of its beauty as well as its cold, disease,
and hardships may be given some vitality.

Now that we have alluded to New England Federalism,
it may not be out of order to enlarge on the subject, since
Federalism left what many consider its finest legacy to
Newburyport; and its doctrines and attitudes, whether one
agrees with them or not, formed the dogma of the Dexter
period. New England Federalism was both a political belief
and a provincial state of mind. Although its devotees were
members of the national Federalist party, cleavages existed
between Boston and Philadelphia, and broadened as one
approached Baltimore, Alexandria and Charleston. Samuel Eliot Morison has defined it in his *Maritime History
of Massachusetts* as follows:

> Sired by Neptune out of Puritanism, the teacher of its
> youth was Edmund Burke. Washington, Hamilton, and
> Fisher Ames formed the trinity of its worship. Timothy

Pickering was the kept politician of New England Federalism, Harrison Gray Otis its spellbinder, Boston its political and Hartford its intellectual capital, Harvard and Yale the seminaries of its priesthood.

New England Federalism derived much of its originality from the have-not quality of the region in which it once flourished. New England was never a land of plenty. The best its enthusiasts can say for its gales, its tardy springs, and the freeze and thaw of its winters is that these build character and promote the doctrine of the survival of the fittest. Actually New England never had much to depend on except character. Its people, through three centuries, have acquired great wealth, usually by industry and ingenuity. But, although Massachusetts trustees still contrive to conserve portions of fortunes built up in another day, the income of these fortunes is siphoned off by the Federal government, and only a trickle of this expropriation is allowed to return to its source.

High Street Federalists had an uncanny premonition of what would happen if they lost their political power. They believed in the sanctity of private property and in their right to its indefinite accumulation. They would have shrieked at the possibility of such a levy as an income tax. They believed that the main purpose of government was to protect private property. They believed particularly in governmental protection of shipping and all its perquisites. They believed, to a lesser degree but still emphatically, in long hours, and in the right of the individual (if he could) to work his way from the bottom up. They believed violently in the creation of a small, educated, and enlightened governing class. They abhorred liberal philosophies. They

loved order, hated waste, and when their thoughts turned from practical affairs they were frequently tedious, prolix and sanctimonious.

The Yankee stock predominant in Dexter's day and the tenets of Federalism also have been drained to a sort of permanent dregs, but in spite of the cultures of later immigrant groups, the character of New England has not disappeared. Boston is still its capital. A reservoir of industrial skill is left. The electronic age is moving in, and in spite of debilitation New England still attempts to depend upon itself. Sometimes one even suspects that Federalism is not wholly dead.

X
Little Did They Reck

FEDERALIST NEWBURYPORT possessed a vigor that kept it in a condition of constant change. It would not be fair to its ebullient spirit to confine its manifestations to any one month or year of the town's history. For instance, many of the handsomest houses were built after the death of Dexter, but they are a part of the Dexter period. The Cushing house on High Street, built in 1808, is one of them. The Honorable Caleb Cushing, first United States Ambassador to China, lived there once, and until recently the house was filled with Chinese objects that he had carried back, and there was a rumor that several barrels containing some of his china were in the cellar still unopened. I had always discounted this piece of hearsay until I was bold enough to ask Mr. Cushing's granddaughter, Miss Margaret, whether this was true. She surprised me by saying that she believed it was, and I shall not forget her answer when I asked her if she was not curious to see what was inside the barrels.

"Why should I be?" she said. "We have more than enough china upstairs."

So many Newburyport dwellings were built in large quantities during the brief reign of Federalism that a walk along the streets today still gives some impression of a restless, prosperous town. Also there is a splendid book on Newburyport houses, with excellent descriptions by John Mead Howells. It is only necessary to run hastily through its pages to gain an impression of Newburyport's elegance and grace and luxury, compromising with austerity, as reflected in the Federalist doorways and exteriors.

If its houses are the best available illustrations of life as it was lived in this Newburyport, several attempts have been made by former inhabitants to describe it through the written word. But before turning to the badly foxed pages, it may pay to keep in mind the newness of everything in Dexter's Newburyport, and for some reason hardly anyone has mentioned this aspect of post-Revolutionary Massachusetts. Esther Forbes is an exception when she alludes in her novel *The Running of the Tide* to the brash modernity of the Salem houses being built by the architect McIntire. There was the same modernity in Newburyport. There was a smell of fresh paint — the houses, by the way, appear to have been painted chiefly white or yellow — and of new plaster and pine shavings. Another thing to remember, as we saw in the print of Newburyport, is that the town's great elms, now doomed to death, were hardly more than saplings. The streets were unpaved. The sidewalks were done in gravel more frequently than brick. In wet weather one's walking shoes were caked with mud, and the iron scrapers, some very handsome, on the doorsteps of the period houses once served a useful purpose. Newburyport was not quaint when it was flushed with its prosperity. Unfortunately these parts of the picture do not come clearly through the following descriptions of the town.

Let us begin with Samuel Knapp. The town he describes, writing in 1838, is dim in his memory, but some details must be authentic.

The town of Newburyport is situated on the right bank of the Merrimack. The whole territory belonging to the corporation is but little more than six hundred acres, and nearly one half of this is low pasture lands, but the thickly settled part is a lovely spot of ground. The southerly line is on an elevation about sixty or seventy feet from the surface of the river. The main street, called High street, running about a mile and a quarter from east to west on the town boundary, extends either way much further, making a delightful riding course of more than three miles in distance. The streets running at right angles with High street to the water are intersected by others, throwing a great portion of the whole site into squares convenient for building lots. The soil is light, gravelly and warm, well suited for gardens, for which the town is famous. Many of the buildings are still of wood: forty years ago they were chiefly so. The water here is good and the streets are wide and kept clean, and every thing about the "sweet village," bore marks of industry, thrift and comfort. Numerous churches and school-houses were placed at convenient distances. The shipping was extensive, for the size of the place. The town was thrifty for many years before the revolution, and when the war broke out several merchants left Boston to carry on their commerce in Newburyport. Their business flourished from the peace of 1783, until the embargo of 1807, when it received a grievous wound, but, thank heaven, not a vital stab as many thought it would have proved, for it is slowly rising from its difficulties. The education of this people was plain and wholesome. Reading, writing and arithmetic were taught to all, and their moral precepts were all drawn from one book. The Bible was read from lisping infancy to purblind decrepitude. There never was any canaille here: some few there are, as everywhere, the unfortunate and poor; but the mass of people were well to do; intelligent and active, they of course were happy. The wealthy and intellectual portion of the community formed a circle that had sufficient of the comforts and refinements of life to give society a charm which is seldom found in overgrown cities. The population was not so large as to hide any individual, however humble. Each stood out as it were from the canvas, and could be examined by every one who wished to observe.

Knapp's condescension is more impressive than his style. No one need be gracious toward Newburyport even now. One may like or dislike it, and there are substantial reasons for either view, but graciousness is not indicated. Newburyport was not a "sweet" village. According to Mr. Knapp himself, in those days bibulous young bucks, who doubtless were trying to imitate the London Corinthians of the Regency, amused themselves by eating one-hundred-dollar bills in sandwiches, neither a tasty nor sustaining form of nourishment, and certainly not "sweet."

He was more correct about the Bible. Newburyport in Dexter's era was a hotbed of Protestantism, in which leaders of its various sects debated upon original sin and infant damnation, taking out time occasionally to inveigh against the Pope of Rome. What would these divines, who could deliver a two- or three-hour sermon in an unheated church, remark could they see a Roman Catholic enclave dominating the town's center, with a parochial school, a nunnery,

and a church that draws more worshipers today than any
other? These comments are not designed as a criticism of
the foundation of all the Christian faith, but only as pointing to a change in time and thought and to a vast diminu-
tion of prejudice. Newburyport today is far removed from
the stern period when Governor Endicott cut the cross
from the Union Jack because it was a symbol of papacy.[1]
The fixation of Governor Endicott and the ingestion of
hundred-dollar bills in sandwiches, though poles apart,
were simultaneously accepted. It is fortunate that we have
another description of Newburyport that makes a dramatic
contrast to that of Mr. Knapp in the works of Mrs. Emery.
It is, we presume, her grandmother who was speaking in
the memories of Mrs. Emery, just as I have occassionally
quoted my great-aunt in accordance with my own inexact

---

[1] In this early Colonial period also Governor Thomas Dudley wrote the following
lines, found in his pocket at the time of his death:

> Dim Eyes, Deaf Ears, Cold Stomach, shew
> My dissolution is in View
> Eleven times Seven near liv'd have I,
> And now God calls, I willing Die.
> My Shuttle's shot, my Race is run,
> My Sun is set, my Day is done.
> My Span is measur'd, Tale is told,
> My flower is faded, and grown old.
> My Dream is vanish'd, Shadow's fled
> My Soul with Christ, my Body Dead.
> Farewel Dear Wife, Children and Friends,
> Hate Heresie, make Blessed Ends.
> Bear Poverty, live with good Men;
> So shall we live with Joy agen.
> Let Men of God in Courts and Churches watch
> O're such as do a Toleration hatch,
> Lest that Ill Egg, bring forth a Cockatrice,
> To poison all with Heresie and Vice.
> If Men be left, and otherwise Combine,
> My Epitaph's, I DY'D NO LIBERTINE.

(From *Magnalia Christi Americana*, by COTTON MATHER, Book II, p. 17.)

recollections. Mrs. Emery begins a chapter of her book with a description of Newburyport before its holocaust of 1811. The simple slate headstones marking the resting places of Mr. and Mrs. Dexter, with their careful epitaphs, reflected the glare of the Fire; but although the hero of this biography had gone to his reward, the setting which Mrs. Emery describes was his and depicts a wholly different climate from the one that Mr. Knapp has conjured. Mrs. Emery throws herself emotionally into her subject, and aptly quotes Shakespeare to introduce her tragedy.

There is a destiny that shapes our ends, rough hew them as we will.

(It should be "divinity" not "destiny," and "how we may"— but the sense is much the same. The time is at the end of May, one hundred and forty-nine years ago.)

The memorable Friday evening, the thirty-first of May, 1811, the sun set in unclouded splendor, gilding the church spires, and gleaming upon tree tops, window panes, and the masts of the little fleet anchored at the wharves up and down the river. For the last time its rays illumined the ancient town; when it sank behind the western heights it bade a final adieu to many an antique landmark and to many a goodly heritage. The last lingering gleam died away from the old "port," which henceforth would only be known in tradition and song. For the last time busy feet trod those long lines of lofty warehouses; carts and drays rattled up and down the wharves; the evening stage coaches dashed up to the Old Wolfe tavern; merchant and artisan turned the key, and wended their way homeward; the tea urn steamed on the luxurious board in stately mansions, and the more frugal supper was served in the dwellings of the mechanic and laborer. Little did they reck that ere another day should dawn, each would be reduced to a perfect equality, alike homeless and penniless. That the old town of the primeval settlers and of Revolutionary fame would have passed into oblivion, that one period had ended, that henceforth a new town was to arise, a new order of things to be instituted, new customs and business to be established, new men and measures to be represented; but the old town of Newburyport, with its commerce, its prestige and aristocratic splendor had gone forevermore.

A true estimate of the town must fall somewhere between these two accounts. The coaches would have been eclipsed by the farmers' vehicles in Market Square, and Bible-reading Newburyporters were developing a catholic literary taste. Besides these descriptions, the files of the Newburyport *Herald* contain a series of recollections written by a Mr. George Wood in his old age, about the town as it was in his childhood — approximately 1806.

"I shall let my pen slide on," he writes, "without effort or control." And he does. The result is a listing of a jumble of houses around State Street and Market Square, gambrel-roofed dwellings, ship chandlers' shops, clockmakers' shops, book-printers' places of business, concert halls, churches, breweries, distilleries. These are presented to us by Mr. Wood with the profusion of the unmatched pieces in a jigsaw puzzle; and with the places Mr. Wood gives us names and descriptions of departed inhabitants — James Prince, Esq., of State Street, with his cocked hat, ruffled shirt and wristbands, breeches and knee-buckles and large silver shoe buckles; the sternly orthodox Dr. Samuel Spring, with his hair curled into ringlets down his shoulders, and his long gold-headed cane; Mr. Enoch Toppan of Pleasant Street, a pump and block maker who could play a church organ, make up impromptu poems, and also pull teeth at twenty-five cents apiece. Yet a sort of order emerges out of Mr. Wood's confusion that conveys the idea that Newburyport, in spite of its smaller population, was a lively place. Market Square was the heart of the town, but the town was a crossroads then.

When the church belonging to the First Religious Society, which stood in the center of the Square, was demolished near the turn of the eighteenth century, a town pump was installed in its place. It had, Mr. Wood tells us, "on two sides handles like the brakes of a fire engine; and around this pump the oyster men had their stalls and the fish dealers loved to congregate; in the outer circle came the farm carts with poultry and yarn stockings. . . . The words 'restaurant' and 'hotel' were unknown in those days of plain Saxon English. There was the Wolfe Tavern on State Street. . . . And if a body was hungry there were rude benches on four legs near the town pump with a pile of oysters on one end and saucers, crackers and a pepper pot and a vinegar cruet on the other and a man with his oyster knife ready to shell out a dozen. . . . But men were so regular in those days that a few only found it best to eat between meals or after meals."

Mr. Wood also describes his days in church as a small child, perishing with the winter cold, watching the minister in the pulpit all in black, with the tip ends of his thumb and forefinger visible because his gloves had been cut off to enable him to turn the pages of the Bible.

Those were the days [he writes] of ignorance and barbarism in matters of comfort . . . I remember well the great turmoil it made in the church when Mr. Jacob Perkins offered to build at his own cost a furnace he had invented which would keep the temperature of the church at sixty degrees . . . and this was debated long and eagerly. Those who went for warmth were denied as having any vitality of piety, and so it was, the poor little girls and boys not being counted in or cared for, the offer was refused, and during all my childhood I was left to the martyrdom of cold feet, cold legs, cold bosom and cold hands, while Mrs. Polly Titcomb, Mr. Daniel Burnham, and such like saints who were muffled up to their ears in furs and had each their foot stove, and were quite comfortable, talked as though those who lacked in the fires of divine love deserved to shiver.

We learn in this grab bag of miscellany that the taking of snuff was popular, that by 1806 large wigs were going out of fashion, and only one inhabitant wore a powdered wig. The heavy Queen Anne furniture had already given way to Chippendale and Sheraton. Men's clothing, too, was undergoing considerable change. A hot weather style was developing of wearing long nankeen trousers called "tongs." Small boys sailed boats on the Frog Pond. The ropewalk was gone and Bartlett's Mall had been built around it. There was an advanced school run by a Mr. Walsh, who was a devoted believer in the educational advantages of flogging. Religion had more immediate influence, spiritually and socially, on Protestant Newburyport than it exerts at present. The church of the First Religious Society on Pleasant Street, with its box pews and balconies, was designed to accommodate at least eight hundred worshipers. It was well filled when it was new, whereas now it is a rare Sunday that sees more than a hundred in its graceful interior, Calvinistically lighted by plain glass windows. Back in Dexter's day they were having arguments in Newburyport over church organs. There were conservatives who did not realize that the organ was here to stay, including the orthodox Dr. Spring. He referred to church organs as "boxes of whistles," and in his own church, when the choirmaster once stood up before the singing seats and produced a pitch pipe, Dr. Spring shouted at him, "Put away that Babylonish pipe!"

Although they may not have known it, Dr. Spring and the rest of them were fighting a rear-guard battle against the influx of an elegant materialism, because Newburyport was drifting into channels of sophistication and luxury that it has not seen since. At the close of the Revolutionary War there were already ten jewelers and watchmakers in town. It had also become a publishing center that was pirating works of contemporary English authors and printing translations and originals of the classics. The first arithmetic book in America was published in Newburyport by its author, Mr. Nicholas Pike. Bowditch's work on navigation was first printed there, as was Blount's *Coast Pilot,* and many maps, charts, and other nautical works. Not so long ago a local dealer in old books made a haphazard and far-from-complete collection of volumes with the Newburyport imprint. Even though he had barely scratched the surface, the volumes on his shelves ran into well over two hundred items.

Artists and engravers were also attracted to the town,

and patrons appeared who had put down advance subscrip-
tions toward the publishing or proposed works that aroused
their interest. In one instance Timothy Dexter is listed
among the subscribers to a volume which one doubts
whether he ever read:

Letters
to a
Young Lady
on a variety of
Useful and Interesting Subjects
Calculated to
Improve the Heart, Form the Manners
and
Enlighten the Understanding
"That our Daughters may be Polished Corners of the
Temple"
By the
Rev. John Bennett
Author of Strictures on Female Education

This intellectual activity could only have flourished in
the specialized environment that existed then when a town
with a population of under eight thousand could assume
the dimensions of a metropolis.

There was a concentration of remarkable people. Mr.
Pike, the mathematician, and Theophilus Parsons are only
two. There was an excellent inventor, Mr. Jacob Perkins,
whose name has been mentioned in connection with his
church furnace. He advertised many of his inventions in
the press, including other heating devices, a method of
gold-plating beads, a method of engraving bank notes, and
a machine for making nails. But the most famous citizen

ever produced by Newburyport, whose genius rose above
Parsons's, Perkins's, and the rest, is the shipbuilder, Or-
lando B. Merrill. In 1794 he invented the lift or water-line
model, which Samuel Eliot Morison in his *Maritime History* called "probably the greatest invention in the tech-
nique of naval architecture between the days of Drake and
the days of Ericsson" —a long span. The model has also
been said to have marked the greatest improvement in shipbuilding since the days of Homer. Its concept, like the
basis of most great discoveries, was simple. The lifts of the
miniature hull, measured with a foot rule, determined
the dimensions of the vessel and enabled the timbering to be
fashioned at long distances from the shipyard. When the
ship was completed, the model was sawed amidships, one
half going to the owner, the other remaining in the builder's shop. At the turn of the century, these models were in
such profusion in Newburyport that they could be purchased for only a few dollars. Appreciation of their beauties
has only become wide quite recently, and with it a new respect for their inventor.

Publishing and most creative activity has now moved
from Newburyport to larger cities. It has been years since
a book beyond the size of a pamphlet has been printed there,
and the principal printing establishment left is that of the
Newburyport Daily News. This contemporary journal,
though larger than the *Impartial Herald*, is, I am afraid,
the inferior of its Federalist ancestor, both from the point
of view of literacy and taste.

"Wee," Timothy Dexter once wrote of Newburyport,
"are first in the North," and a large number of his fellow
townsmen have agreed with him. There was a wave of

commercial ingenuity now sought for but never discovered by our present Chamber of Commerce. Goods retailed in Newburyport have, with some brilliant exceptions, retrogressed in quality. The proprietor of one of the town haberdasheries told me recently that it was useless to stock the best grades of merchandise, because customers simply did not want them. This is only one sign of a change in buying habits, now that goods in great variety and quality can be obtained at shopping centers off the main highways. On the contrary, in the Federalist era you could buy almost anything in Newburyport, from a ship to a coach with a coat of arms, or a silver tea service, or a dining table.

We find that Timothy Dexter, incidentally, had purchased a ship, a barkentine, called for reasons now unknown *Mehitabel*, at about the time he purchased the Tracy house. This ownership placed him automatically in the merchant or shipowner class, and the cargoes carried by the *Mehitabel* no doubt formed a basis for subsequent legends of his business prowess. But the *Mehitabel* was only a unit of the fleet that now crowded about the wharves of Newburyport's narrow harbor. These ships with their complicated rigging and their variously painted hulls had a trimmer appearance than their Colonial predecessors. Although Newburyport's carrying trade was more limited than that of Boston and Salem — principally West Indies and the Baltic — ships might return with consignments from any spot in the world. Local lumber and fish, molasses and iron were traded for all sorts of luxury imports, including the finest laces, wines and jewelry.

One reads with astonishment of the wide range of goods offered by merchants and retailers in the advertisements of the *Impartial Herald*. In the retail or wholesale section of the town one might purchase silver service made to order, or select from "an elegant assortment of Lockets, gilt, pearl and glass Earrings, Broach Pins, Bracelets, Gold and Silver Cord, Spangles, Key Rings, India Rubber, Tooth Brushes and Powder." A step away a mercer displayed "Broadcloths, Casimeres of various colors. Striped Elastics, Superior fine color Shalloons, and Ratinettes, Baize of all colors, Yellow, Black and White Flannel, Wilton and Brussels carpets, Callimancoes, Black Ruffles, Prunella, Florentine Satin, Men's Plain Ribbed and Twilled Hose, Black, White, Blue and Pink Satin." The town supported a portrait and miniature painter, who also could work on "Real Hair Devices." There was a saddle and chaise maker, a wigmaker, and wine merchants with imported Malaga, Lisbon, Madeira and Sherry. Perfumery was on sale, and French pot and roll Pomatum, and a druggist at the Golden Mortar was ready to dispense Duffy's Elixir Salitis, Stoughton's Stomach Elixir, and Turlington's Balm of Life. In fact, there was nearly everything to meet the entire scale of material desire, from the staples of the country hawked from farmers' wagons to the latest adornments from across the water.

If one wished amusement, there was the diversion of conversation, and there were the taverns and the ship launchings. "Those persons who are fond of the amusement of horse racing," an advertisement then current reads, "are informed that some of the most capital horses in several neighboring towns are engaged to run on Stevens' Plains on Wednesday the 27th Inst., being election day." Occasionally, too, would come other greater attractions. There appeared, for instance, an educated pig, capable of entertaining ladies and gentlemen with feats of reading and addition. Incidentally, this pig's erudition was so great that he was finally burned at the stake by the Inquisition in Havana. We also read of an artist of the slack wire making his bow to the public. Among many other visiting marvels was one that may have been a preview of the automotive age. We are informed that

> M. Perette, Machinist of Paris and other large towns of Europe, a Pensioner to the French Republic, has the pleasure to inform the public that he has a self-moving carriage which has been much applauded by numerous spectators who have viewed it. An Eagle Automaton, suitably caparisoned, draws the carriage forward with as much rapidity as though it was drawn by horses. The driver seated in the carriage holds the reins and directs the course of this extraordinary carriage. M. Perette, intending to exhibit this wonderful piece of machinery a few times in the town, respectfully invites the Ladies and Gentlemen to attend, and flatters himself they will be highly gratified.

This announcement points to an important change in the cultural picture. The polished and sophisticated influence of France made itself increasingly felt in Newburyport as political disorders continued. *Émigrés* of exalted birth imported politeness to what, without them, would have been a much more awkward age. In contrast to a school of psalmody, which had just opened, we find Messrs. Renard and Dupatty were opening an academy of the dance; and, in language befitting an eminent artist, there appears the prospectus of M. Trille Labarre. This Gallic gentleman was a "Professor and Composer of Music and instructor to the Duchess of Orléans, Princess Liniski, Princess of Salmack, and general instructor of music to all Princes and Princesses who were lovers of music at the Courts of the principal cities where he has travelled in Europe." M. Labarre offered his services to teach a number of ladies and gentlemen the "Piano Fort, Spinet, Spanish and English Guitar, Flute and Violin."

These random examples may be enough to show that a tide of polite accomplishments was rising sufficient to shock the community's more sober sectors. Several schools flourished for genteel young ladies and gentlemen, besides which, in addition to these academies of dance and song, there also arrived an instructor of the sword, and teachers of drawing and painting. The Marquis de Chastellux, the Vicomte de Vaudreuil, M. de Talleyrand, and M. de Montesquieu were early witnesses of this finished era, and they found no cause to be shocked by any lack of worldliness in their entertainment. The town which had been new to Timothy Dexter now was growing newer still, and more of the world was at its doors than there will be again.

The sophistication of the new Federalist houses, with their handsome furnishings, a considerable portion of which was made by local artisans, made a suitable background for elegant social functions, such as weekly balls and routs to which the society was drawn in coaches manned by liveried footmen. The extent of Newburyport's high living may be gauged by the news that when personal property in Newburyport was assessed, several Newburyport merchants reported from one thousand to twelve hundred gallons of wine in their cellars.

With this growing affluence it is not surprising to learn that many persons believed that a noble order would be es-

tablished in the United States, with a peerage along English
lines. "The past," as Mr. Knapp has said, "seems a dream to
those who lived in it and almost a legend to those who take
it from history. From history, did I say? History was afraid
to record a tythe of the truth." In the light of such developments, conservatives can hardly be blamed for casting
back to the good old days that presented a simpler life.
"But how remote," Currier writes, "are we from duties
simple and enduring. A regular and uniform conduct
would seem to torment our gossips and gadders. They want
perpetual dissipation — all out of doors — full of vanity
and loaded with geegaws from London and Paris."

There is one record of the social amenities of the period
that deserves especial notice, both because of its vividness
and because it was written by a foreigner, who could evalu-
ate Newburyport society from his own sophisticated background. In November 1782 the Marquis de Chastellux, one
of the forty members of the French Academy, and a major
general of the French Army that served under the Comte
de Rochambeau, paid a visit to Newburyport while traveling through New England. He had with him, as traveling
companions, "Messieurs Lynch, de Montesquieu, the Baron
de Talleyrand and Mr. de Vaudreuil." This distinguished
group reached the town from Portsmouth along a road
which the Marquis tells us passed through a barren country. His narrative proceeds as follows in the second volume
of his travels:

> It was two o'clock when he reached Merimack ferry,
> and from the shore we saw the openings of the harbour,
> the channel of which passes near the northern extremity
> of Plumb Island, on which is a small fort, with a few can-

non and mortars. . . . After passing the ferry in little
flat boats, which held only five horses each, we went to Mr.
Davenport's inn, where we found a good dinner ready. I
had letters from Mr. Wentworth to Mr. John Tracy, the
most considerable merchant in the place; but, before I had
time to send them, he had heard of my arrival, and, as I
was arising from table, entered the room, and very politely
invited me to pass the evening with him. He was accompanied by a Colonel, whose name is too difficult for me to
write, having never been able to catch the manner of pro-
nouncing it; but it was something like Wigsteps.[2] This
Colonel remained with me till Mr. Tracy finished his business, when he came with two handsome carriages, well
equipped, and conducted me and my Aide de Campe to his
country house. This house stands a mile from the town in
a very beautiful situation; but of this I could myself form
no judgment, as it was already night. I went, however, by
moonlight, to see the garden, which is composed of different terraces. There is likewise a hot house and a number
of young trees. The house is very handsome and well
finished, and everything breathes that air of magnificence,
accompanied with simplicity, which is only to be found
amongst merchants. The evening passed rapidly by the aid
of agreeable conversation and a few glasses of punch. The
ladies we found assembled with Mrs. Tracy, her two sisters,
and their cousin, Miss Lee. Mrs. Tracy has an agreeable and
a sensible countenance, and her manners correspond with
her appearance. At ten o'clock an excellent supper was
served; we drank good wine. Miss Lee sung, and prevailed
on Messieurs de Vaudreuil and Talleyrand to sing also;
towards midnight the ladies withdrew, but we continued
drinking Madeira and Xery. Mr. Tracy, according to the

[2] Probably Colonel Edward Wigglesworth.

custom of the country, offered us pipes, which were accepted by Mr. de Talleyrand, and M. de Montesquieu, the consequence of which was that they became intoxicated and were led home, where they were happy to get to bed. As to myself, I remained perfectly cool, and continued to converse on trade and politics with Mr. Tracy, who interested me greatly with an account of all the vicissitudes of his fortune since the beginning of the war. . . . I left Newburyport the 13th at ten in the morning, and often stopped before I lost sight of this pretty little town, for I had great pleasure in enjoying the different aspects it presents. It is in general well built, and is daily increasing in new buildings. The ware houses of the merchants, which are near their own homes, serve by way of ornament, and in point of architecture resemble not a little our own large greenhouses.

The house in which the Marquis was entertained stands on High Street next to the residence of Jonathan Jackson, and it has undergone fewer alterations. The Baron de Talleyrand, incidentally, must not be mistaken for the great French foreign minister, who did not arrive in America until 1794 and who, unlike many other distinguished French refugees, may never have seen Newburyport.

Perhaps this ancient gossip has gone far enough to give an idea of the polite and calcified world that Timothy Dexter entered very suddenly, along with his abruptly acquired wealth. He bought the barkentine *Mehitabel* in 1790. He purchased the Tracy house on State Street in 1791, and another ship, the *Congress*, in 1792. He also owned a coach, with a pair of cream-colored horses. In fact, the Dexter family had everything they needed except man-

PHILIP KAPPEL

ners. It is saddening to discover that prosperity disrupted
their lives. Madam Dexter became a scold. Nancy Dexter
suffered eventually from an acute nervous collapse, and
Sam did not succeed in becoming an educated gentleman.
It would seem that Mr. Dexter was the only one who enjoyed his new environment. In spite of his years — forty-
four — and in spite of his lack of education, now that his
working capital had increased he became feverishly engaged
in the business of buying and selling. If he had lost his emotional balance and his sense of proportion in certain respects, he did not lose his commercial instinct for survival
when he came up into the world. He was apt to be drunk
nearly every evening, but he only transacted business when
he was sober. Gossip regarding his methods arose as sud-

denly as his fortune. Questions began to be asked in Newburyport that are still not answered. How did Timothy
Dexter make his money, and did he have as much as he appeared to possess? Is it true that he became so eccentric that
he sent mittens and warming pans to the West Indies? These
are subjects that deserve a chapter of their own, and we
shall have an opportunity to examine them in the light of
Dexter's personal testimony.

X I

How Did Dexter Make His Money?

WE HAVE SEEN already that it is extremely difficult to draw correct conclusions regarding the personality or the abilities of Timothy Dexter because of the rumors that surround him. An attempt to do so resembles the effort we must make to descry the real Dexter in the famous caricature that was made of him in 1805. It depicts an aging man carrying a tall cane, wearing an enormous hat with tassels, a coat with long tails, stock and waistcoat, and pantaloons tied by ribbons at the ankles. But behind this exaggeration, obviously designed to excite mirth, the pose and the features give the impression of reality. He is not so funny as his artist intended him, and this conclusion is confirmed from another source. In 1886 Mr. William Cleaves Todd in his essay deflating the Dexter myth makes the following statement:

> A lady in Newburyport has a portrait of Dexter taken by an artist in New Haven, where his daughter was married. He is represented dressed as a gentleman of that day, wearing a wig, a ruffled bosom and ruffled wrist bands, and his face certainly indicates no lack of intelligence.

I regret that I have never seen the portrait and I do not know where it may be, but I have talked with several Newburyporters who had seen it and who all agreed that Dexter looked handsome and intelligent. It may very well be that the portrait was a flattery, just as the Dexter engraving was a jest, and that the true Dexter fell between extremes. The same may be said of the Dexter character, which must lie somewhere between legal fact and popular inflation.

It is certain from his early days onward that he acquired money by skill and industry. The Registry of Deeds in Salem records that on January 2, 1770, Timothy Dexter purchased real estate for which he paid fifty-nine pounds and eight shillings. This transaction took place before his marriage, and only a short time after he arrived in Newburyport when by his own account he had less than ten dollars in cash. As one of Dexter's contemporaries wrote with heavy humor, "It must now be the wish of every scientific person to possess an accurate life of this great character, but where is the historian who can elucidate the man?" There is, of course, no one. Instead there are only a few facts that can be separated from myth. Among these are the deeds and conveyances of Dexter's registered in Salem in which, according to the custom of his time, his position in society was registered with the deed. In these papers Dexter was first termed "leather dresser," then "trader," then "merchant," then "gentleman," although, as Mr. Todd remarks, the last designation seems a strange misnomer. Nevertheless, this increase in legal respect reveals that Dexter rose by his own efforts in a competitive community until he became respected as a man of business.

Many of his contemporaries have hard words for him, but never once was he called foolish in merchandising, an art that was taken very seriously in this ambitious town.

What confuses the factual list of his achievements is the *nouveau riche* Dexter depicted in folklore. Here we discover a more dramatic image. Instead of a plodding Yankee trader we have a lucky fool listening seriously to the frivolous advice of town pranksters, who gathered around him to partake of his hospitality and to impose upon his ignorance. Carried away by their humor, they advised him to send coal to Newcastle and consignments of cats, mittens and warming pans to the West Indies. And somehow miraculously each of these primarily ridiculous ventures, which included heavy shipments of Bibles, reaped tremendous profits. These tales already flourished in Dexter's lifetime, especially the one of the warming pans, and they have not been overdrawn subsequently because Timothy Dexter himself exaggerated them in his own writings. He had evidently been asked by many inhabitants how he made his money, for he finally, a few years before his demise, wrote his own answer, ending with an admonition—"Now be still; let me A lone. Don't wonder Noe more houe I got my money, boaz."

The boys continue to wonder, but a great deal more may be learned from Timothy Dexter's extravagant, offhand and probably senile explanation than meets the eye.

How did Dexter make his money, ye says? Bying whale bone for staing for ships, in grosing three hundred & 40 tuns — bort all in boston salum, and all in Noue york, under Cover; Oppenly told them for my ships; thay all

laffed, so I had at my oan pris; I had four Counning men
for Rounners. Thay found the horne, as I told them to act
the fool. I was Full of Cash. I had nine tun of silver on
hand, at that time. all that time, the Creaters more or less
laffing, it spread very fast; here is the Rub — in fifty days
thay smelt a Rat — found whare it was gone, to Nouebry
Port — speklelaters swarmed like hell houns — to be short
with it, I made seventey five per sent — one tun and halfe
of silver on hand, and over.

one more spect — Drole a Nuf — I Dreamed of worm-
ing pans three nites, that they would doue in the west
inges; I got no more than fortey two thousand — put
them in nine vessels, for difrent ports, that tuk good hold.
I cleared siventy nine per sent. the pans thay made yous
of them for Coucking —

"very good, masser, for Coukey — blessed good in
Deade, missey; got nise handel; Now burn my fase, the
best thing I Ever see in borne days."

I found I was very luckky in spekkelation. I Dreamed
that the good book was Run Down in this countrey, nine
years gone, so low as halfe prise, and Dull at that — the
bibel, I means; I had the Ready Cash by holl sale: I bort
twelve per cent under halfe pris; thay Cost fortey one
sents Each bibbel — twenty one thousand — I put them
into twenty one vessels, for the west inges, and sent a text
that all of them must have one bibel in Every familey, or
if not thay would goue to hell — and if thay had Dun
wiked, flie to the bibel, and on thare Neas, and kiss the
bibel three times, and look up to heaven annest for for-
givnes. my Capttens all had Compleat orders — here Coms
the good luck: I made one hundred persent & littel over.
then I found I had made money anuf; I hant speck alated
sence old times by government secourities I made or cleared

forty seven thousands Dolors — that is the old afare. Now
I toald all the sekrett. Now be still; let me A lone; Dont
wonder Noe more houe I got my money, boaz.

It seems to me that this passage has been greeted with
undue hilarity and with an equal lack of serious attention.
Anyone with the patience to analyze it and to cope with
its tortured diction will find that there is more here than
the untutored effort of an old man to express himself.
There is a quality of individuality that one associates with
better writing, which shows that the man who wrote it,
a vulgarian with a crude sense of humor, was also endowed
with a keenness of perception that has been too readily
discounted. Although our hero did not tell the whole truth,
nor did he intend to, he has offered some pertinent facts
that have been overlooked. At least part of his confession
makes sense, and I am afraid that Mr. Todd, who has made
a most intelligent study of the Dexter money-making
legend, never weighed this aspect.

"The only satisfactory explanation," he tells us, "of these
stories, which Dexter tells to those inquiring minds so anxious to learn the secret of how he made his money, is that
they were the creation of his own brain, a great joke worthy
of Mark Twain, successfully imposed on the community,
— that instead of being the fool he is commonly regarded,
he fooled others."

This is the kindest thing that Mr. Todd has to say of
Mr. Dexter, and his generosity is canceled by his ultimate
conclusion. "As a man he was worthless, and only deserves
the space devoted to him as an example of erroneous biography and tradition."

There is one point that Mr. Todd has neglected, which is that no wealthy and successful man has ever been so wholly frank as to tell exactly how he made his money. There is invariably some gap in a true success story. Every speculator boasts only of his successes, and never confesses the full extent of his failures. This would seem to be exactly what Mr. Dexter did in his own informal way. Mr. Todd, I think, should have made allowances.

Samuel Eliot Morison in his *Maritime History of Massachusetts* has described the business day of a Federalist merchant. His merchant prince is a Bostonian, but Newburyport merchants, though they did not admit it, aped many of the habits of Boston. At eight or eight-thirty in the morning this fictitious example descended to the living quarters of his mansion dressed in a China-silk dressing gown and a cap, as Copley painted his father and as Nicholas Boylston is depicted in the Faculty Room of Harvard. (Dexter may have dressed in the same manner, a theory that can be substantiated by the opening lines of a satirical poem on Dexter as a writer: "My lord of royal silken robe," the poem begins.) There were short family prayers "and a hearty breakfast by a blazing hickory fire."

Then the mysteries of the toilet, performed by body servant or, preferably, by a neighborhood Figaro, a San Domingo refugee who discreetly gossips while he performs the rite of shaving. Hair is dressed, tied in a queue, and powdered; unless there is a white wig to be nicely adjusted. A fresh white cravat with long lapels, is folded and skillfully tied. Then for the nether limbs. Linen drawers are tied down, silk stockings pulled up smooth, and gartered against all chance of ungentlemanly wrinkling; buff nankeen breeches arranged neatly over them and silver buckle drawn tight. Low-hung waistcoat and broad-skirted coat of light-colored broadcloth come next. After a few parting suggestions to his lady, Master takes a stout gold-headed Malacca-joint cane, three-cornered hat, scarlet cloak if chilly, and sallies forth on foot, followed by Cicero, the colored butler, with huge market-basket.

He then proceeds, through Dock Square, jammed with farm wagons and hucksters, to his countinghouse, where he discusses, over a hot rum punch if it is winter, various opportunities of trade, but we need go no further.

Timothy Dexter, after a hearty breakfast, walked to Market Square, where he entered the countinghouses and chatted with the clerks, who may have quizzed him but were glad of his acquaintance. He inquired about the latest imports and the newest assortment of goods for sale — "assortment," by the way, was one of his favorite words. He walked about the wharves and watched the unloading of the cargoes. We do not know whether as the owner of two ships he had a countinghouse of his own, but one assumes he had office space somewhere, and a clerk. Judging also by his real estate ventures at the Registry of Deeds, he was an in-and-out trader, dealing in odd lots of goods and often shipping them in small consignments on other people's vessels. If one thinks of Timothy Dexter's trading in this manner, his explanation of his money-making moves close to sense.

After purchasing the Tracy house, Timothy Dexter was on the way to becoming a prominent figure in Newburyport, surrounded by flatterers and hangers-on who exaggerated his speculative achievements and made them unusually bizarre, and Mr. Todd points out this distortion of fact in his critique. He starts with Dexter's speculation in whalebone. Mr. Dexter, as you have read, was told by one of his ship's riggers that there was need for stay stuff, referring, of course, to the standing rigging of a sailing ship. Mr. Dexter gave a convincing pretense of believing that the rigger meant whalebone, then used in ladies' corsets. Mr. Todd points out that the amount of whalebone that Dexter alleged he purchased was fantastic and not even in existence, and he scoffs at Dexter's nine tons of silver, but he adds one interesting detail to the legend. "The tradition," he tells us, "is that as soon as he had purchased it the fashion for broad skirts was introduced, and it [whalebone] was all in demand. How far a ton of whalebone would go in satisfying the expansive desires of the ladies of that time, no data exists for calculation. Most were practical, hard-working and economical from necessity; merely fashionable ladies were rare and visits to Newport and Saratoga unknown. As to the foolish reason for the purchase, it was characteristic of him to give it, if he wished to buy."

From this it would seem that Mr. Todd advances the theory that most women in the early United States did not wear corsets, in spite of the certainty that Puritan women usually were spoken of as being strait-laced. There is no good reason to believe Dexter's story of sending runners to New York and of cornering the national whalebone market, but there is also no reason not to give him the credit for buying some lots of whalebone and selling when it was in demand or making a joke of it and calling it "stay stuff."

Mr. Todd next moves to a point at which I believe he is grievously at fault. He takes literally the Dexter statement of having nine tons of silver on hand, which he says, in round numbers, would be three hundred thousand dollars. Yet if one examines the Dexter statement, remembering that Dexter was an unlettered man, it is sensible. Dexter was frequently obliged to compute in the pound sterling, and there is no reason why he should not have considered a British pound as representing an actual pound of silver. Thus if he computed in this manner, a ton of silver represented two thousand British pounds. Nine tons of silver would represent eighteen thousand pounds, a far from fantastic sum, since the pound was then valued at about three-and-a-third dollars. It is very possible that Dexter had sixty thousand dollars in cash on hand at this moment. I have never been able to see why no one seems to have thought previously of this simple explanation of the fabulous Dexter fortune. Yet even his poet laureate, Jonathan Plummer, who must have come into Dexter's life about this time, in his ode to Lord Dexter writes the following couplet:

> Lord Dexter, like King Solomon
> Has gold and silver by the ton.

We can go further in analyzing the Dexter fortune. He tells us that he cleared forty-seven thousand dollars in Government securities, and this, judging from his final estate, could have been correct. We also find him complaining that his rascally son-in-law, of whom we shall hear more later, cost him more than a ton of silver. Other fathers-in-law, when dowries and settlements were more the fashion than now, must also have paid out sums of between six and seven thousand dollars so that their daughters might be happily established.

Mrs. E. Vale Smith has promoted the legend of Dexter and the mittens, and there is a flaw, too, in this tale. No commercial knitting worthy of the name was practiced in the early Republic. The making of mittens was a housewife's duty, and her product was confined to the family circle. It would have taken considerable labor to gather a consignment of mittens in Newburyport, whereas mittens were knit in quantity by European peasantry. Still one must remember that Newburyport was a market center where the consignments of many cargoes were unloaded, resold and reshipped. It is conceivable, since Newburyport traded with the Baltic, that some ship's captain brought home a small lot of Baltic mittens, which was finally sold at a loss and consigned to the West Indies, from whence they were truly sent back to North Europe and sold at a profit.

The legend of the warming pans, by far the most striking, is a hotter subject, and obviously the number that Mr. Dexter mentions is fantastic. It would have been virtually impossible to have collected forty-two thousand warming pans in Newburyport and to have put them in nine different vessels, as Mr. Todd has indicated.

No hardware [he writes] was made in this country until a little more than half a century ago [Mr. Todd's critique was written in 1886] and all the warming pans in use came from Great Britain. The amount named would have cost $150,000, to be paid for in hard money, as bills of exchange were then but little used. Such an importation and exportation would have required months of time, and would have made a sensation indeed, for, though common, a large part of the families had none, and they are now rare old curiosities. Is it possible, rating his intelligence very low, that, if he had attempted such a speculation, he would not have been persuaded of its folly long before he could have executed it? Except for the purpose for which they were made they are of no value. Dexter says they were sold in the West Indies as cooking utensils, but a glance shows how inconvenient they would be for such use. The tradition is that they were sold to dip and strain molasses, but they are poorly adapted to this, and nearly a century ago, when sugar plantations were few in the West Indies, but a small part of 42,000 would have satisfied any such demand. Did any visitor to the West Indies ever see or hear of one of those 42,000 warming pans?

It is easy enough to answer Mr. Todd's last question first. Certainly forty-two thousand warming pans would have been more than enough for the sugar plantations in the West Indies, and no visitor in 1886 could possibly have seen a vestige of them. With the end of slavery the plantations on the so-called "sugar islands" like St. Thomas, where the warming pans would most likely have been purchased, had long ago been abandoned, and change and revolution had shaken Guadeloupe and Haiti, even if a Yankee ship had been welcomed at any of these places, and Spanish lands were closed to Yankee commerce.[1]

It is Mr. Knapp, inaccurate as he has often proved to be, who gives this legend substance:

Some of the merchant's clerks were fond of quizzing him; at one time they put him up to sending a large lot of warming pans to the West Indies, as a part of an assorted cargo. The captain, a young and ingenious man, finding

[1] Philip Kappel, the illustrator of this book, says that he has recently seen a considerable number of warming pans in Jamaica.

this article on the invoice, set his Yankee talents to work to find a sale for them. He took off the covers, and had handsome handles put to them, and called them skimmers, and the large part ladles. He then had them introduced into a large sugar-making establishment, and they were much approved of as the best machines of their kind invented.

This boils Mr. Dexter's own exaggeration down to a manageable proportion, and it is possible to assume that Mr. Knapp was right and that Dexter did send a small lot of warming pans to the West Indies. Although Knapp wrote his book in 1838, he had lived in Newburyport in Dexter's time and had often observed him. The Life itself was actually written from notes made near this period. "Sibylline leaves," Knapp calls them, "dragged up from the cells of the cavern." But, we can produce a further substantiation. The warming pan transaction, like all of Dexter's speculations, occurred roughly between 1790, when he made his money, and the year 1796, when he shook the dust of Newburyport off his feet and moved to Chester, New Hampshire. This country seat was too far from Newburyport to make speculation easy and his residing there must have put a period to any large-scale trading. "I found," he tells us, "I had made money enuf I hant spekalated sence old time." Dexter himself died in the year 1806, so that there was not much of an interval before his death for the warming pan legend to be invented, if it had not been founded on some sort of fact; and actually the transaction is mentioned in the grudging obituary accorded Dexter by the Newburyport *Herald*.

The fortunate and singular manner of his speculations [we read] by which he became possessed of a handsome property, are well known, and his sending a cargo of warming pans to the W. Indies, where they were converted into molasses ladles, and sold to a good profit, is but one of the most peculiar.

There is no profit in continuing further with this phase of the Dexter myth. No figures have survived but those of Dexter.[2] The safest conclusion is that Dexter was one of an army of small-time Yankee traders whose aggressiveness earned them a world-wide reputation. In a small way, at least, Dexter was unusually clever, and doubtless enjoyed giving the impression of being more ignorant and stupid than he was, a ruse still used by businessmen today. In fact, years after his death there was a rumor that Newburyport children chanted a little rhyme:

> Dexter is a smart old man;
> Try and catch him if you can.

The most remarkable aspect of these and other tales of the Dexter business triumphs is the enormity of the fantasy. If it spread from small beginnings, it is a monument of imagination. The Dexter legend as well as the Dexter character is a purely local product. It happens that Lord Dexter has explained himself more eloquently and more accurately in a remark regarding his own life than have his biographers and critics.

> Trouth, I afirme [he has written], I am so much of A fule the Rougs want to git my Jouels & Loaves & littel fishes, without my leave thay all Caled me a foull, forty

---

[2] The business transactions of Timothy Dexter and of Newburyport's other Federalist merchants can never be checked. The customhouse of the port, together with its records, was destroyed in the Fire of 1811. Thus the truth about warming pans, Bibles and whalebone went up in smoke more than a century ago.

years; Now I will Call all foulls but onnes men; Now to prove me a foull, I never Could sing, Nor play Cards, Nor Dance, Nor tell a Long story, Nor play on any mouskel, Nor pray, Nor make a pen; when I was young, I could play on a Jous harp — it would make my mouth warter. A good laff is beter than Crying; a Clam will Cry and warter wen they are out of there Ellement — so wee the same.

Here was excellent material to work on, and Newburyport did its best. The mute inglorious artists who made him are now nearly all forgotten, except for his laureate, Jonathan Plummer, who wrote the Dexter Odes, but the net result is still a magnificent tribute to their genius.

X I I

The Bridge Builder

With the possible exception of Dexter's early leather-dressing days, the years that he dwelt in the Tracy mansion appear to have been the busiest and most disturbed in his life. Some contemporary observers have said that Dexter did not become markedly eccentric until his return from his sojourn in Chester, New Hampshire, a short time later, but he was already attracting more than average attention and not alone because of his eccentric speculations. His character was already being embellished by gossips and admirers who might be termed, in the parlance of today, his public relations echelon. Although this great art of personal salesmanship and character building was not recognized in Dexter's time, Dexter himself subconsciously grasped its potentialities. He was beginning to send his own ideas to the *Impartial Herald* in the form of advertisements and communications; and he was aided by another disturbed genius.

By coincidence, when Timothy Dexter moved to State Street, there was already in Market Square a singular young man gifted with a rhetorical ability that might have carried him far today. His name was Jonathan Plummer, a name

PHILIP KAPPEL

that indicates he came from solid old Newbury stock, and, as his writings show, he had received a good primary education that was backed by considerable reading. Although he was on the unemployable literary fringe, handicapped by pride, a high temper and a malicious tongue, he contrived to earn a living that may have been above the average. As a boy he attended a revivalist meeting and, moved by the mass hysteria, delivered a sermon of astounding eloquence that was superior to that of the preacher who conducted the ceremony. This *démarche* gave him a local reputation, but he never took holy orders. He became sometimes a teacher, sometimes a writer of broadsides, and sometimes a ranter and reciter in Market Square, and again a salesman of fresh fish, and also, one hears, of pornographic literature. Jonathan Plummer in his autobiography gives a good description of his varied activities. "I had," he says, "some practice as a physician, and earned something with my pen, but for several years was obliged chiefly to follow various kinds of business accounted less honorable, viz: Farming, repeating selected passages from authors, selling halibut, sawing wood, selling books and ballads in the streets, serving as post boy, filling beds with straw and wheeling them to the owners thereof, collecting rags, &c."

We are fortunate enough to have a drawing of him, done from life, a dumpy man in knee breeches with stout legs, carrying his famous basket that contained fish, broadsides of his own compositions, and pornography, in various layers. Happily some of the Plummer broadsides are still in existence, treasured by museums and historical societies. These contain gruesome stories of murder and of the assorted epidemics that beset the community, interspersed with the author's random thoughts and sermons. It is noticeable, in spite of the startling subjects that Jonathan Plummer selected, that most of these works afford dull reading. There are, however, brilliant exceptions, which include the Plummer last will and testament, and also his verses praising Timothy Dexter, who inspired his finest work.

There is still in existence a Plummer opus that probably contains his first reference to Timothy Dexter. It is entitled:

Plummer's Declaration of War with
The Fair Ladies of the Five Northern States
and
The Author's Congratulatory Address
to Citizen Timothy Dexter on his
Attaining an Independent Fortune.

The eighteenth-century periodic balance in the Plummer
praise of Dexter, in this broadside, exhibits Plummer's
powers of imitation and also shows how readily he could
move from nasal Calvinism to the world of polite letters:

To Citizen Dexter [he writes], the favorite of the Goddess who presides over riches. Wise and wealthy citizen:

Julius Caesar, a renowned and ever victorious Roman
Emperor, being once at sea, in a tremendous storm, banished
the fears of his pilot, who expressed great concern, by informing them that he bore Caesar and his fortune. Now,
sir, I beg leave to inform you that I have been very fearful
that I should draw nothing in the present Connecticut
Manufactury Lottery, and my diffidence is so great that I
have not yet ventured to lay out in it a single cent, nor can
I yet resolve, so far, to trust my ragged fortune.

In this disagreeable situation to whom but you, my
generous patron, can I look for the favor which Caesar
granted his despairing pilot? In the name then of Apollo,
my immortal master, let your drooping Poet receive one
or two of these tickets from your bounteous hand. This
favor granted,

My joy shall then, from shore to shore,
Resound till time shall be no more.

I shall then have substantial reason to hope that a part
of the fortune, not of the conquering Caesar, but of the
lucky, the successful Dexter, will attend me. My muse

whispers that tickets bought by so fortunate a gentleman
benevolently given by you, and gratefully received by me,
will be very likely to draw some capital prize. I am, sir,
your very humble servant and affectionate bard,

JONATHAN PLUMMER, JUN.

The search today through Newburyport's Market
Square reveals a few Plummer successors but none endowed
with his willingness to attempt any given literary height.
Our respect for his abilities will grow, the more we become
acquainted with them. There is one point that should not
be missed in this early quotation. The Plummer reference
to Dexter as his generous patron indicates that the two had
already arrived at an understanding, and the relationship
must already have been mutually rewarding. In fact, it
would not be biographically rash to surmise that much of
Dexter's writings are the result of the Market Square
huckster's advice and inspiration.

It would be pleasant to be able to state categorically that
Mr. Dexter, in his capacity as patron, rewarded Mr.
Plummer with the Connecticut lottery tickets for which
he asked, but here the veil falls, as it does so often over
Mr. Dexter's most active years. We do know, however,
from Plummer's own words, that Mr. Dexter, during his
stay in the Tracy house, rewarded his poet with a handsome
suit of black broadcloth. (It is doubtful whether Mr.
Plummer went so far at this period as to term himself Dexter's laureate, but he did call himself Mr. Dexter's poet.)
The Dexter patronage began early in their acquaintance;
and in the eighteenth century this sort of subsidy was less
peculiar than now, since Guggenheim Fellowships or Ford
Foundations were part of the future. It surely is more than

coincidence that from the start of this burgeoning friendship, Dexter began to turn his mind to the written word.
Imagination alone can supply a picture of literary evenings
at the Dexter house, during which Jonathan Plummer and
others listened to readings from Dexter's works. As for the
writings themselves, imagination is unnecessary, since
many of them still survive in the columns of the *Impartial
Herald* as well as in Mr. Dexter's own book, *A Pickle for
the Knowing Ones; or, Plain Truths in a Homespun Dress.*

The earliest contribution that he made to the *Impartial
Herald*, while bearing the stamp of his personality, is dull
compared with his later works and shows signs of literary
tampering. In view of the later sardonic attitude he assumed toward the clergy, to whom he usually referred as
"preasts," it is worthy of notice that the first Dexter effort
dealt with a broad religious theme. (During Dexter's greatest years, when a minister called upon him and his son Sam,
it is only fair to state that Mr. Dexter asked his guest to
pray, and after the minister complied, Dexter is quoted as
saying, "Sam, wasn't that a damn good prayer?") The title
of Dexter's contribution, more promising than the contents, is "Dexter's Chatchize, For *Men* and not for Children." It occupied nearly a column which any child may
still read without risk of moral contagion. Throughout we
find its author on his best behavior, facing up to the facts
of life as well as to the world hereafter. Someone must have
helped give form to the homily, since the general style of
the "Chatchize" is not at all like the later Dexter.

> Now as I write, I flatter myself I write by inspiration —
> my pen seems guided by the higher power. I write for the
> good of bodies and souls. If we do well in this life surely we

stand a better chance if there be anything after death. . . .
If you have a weak brother or sister take them along and
give light to those in the dark, and bring them into the
right path — that is love. Love aims to truth and true
justice — and with tender feeling it is how men have a
desire to make happy men, women and children and even
the dumb beasts.

The significant part of the "Chatchize" is at the end:

> Mr. Printers, I hope my weak brothers won't be dis-
> turbed about my scratching a little in the newspaper. I do
> it to learn myself to write and spell which I never knew
> how; I am now at leisure and a man of pleasure. I mean
> no hurt — I let you know what I know without reading
> — what I know only by experience — Clear Nature has
> been my school master — nothing borrowed by reading,
> or very little — Nature is my great study.

This apologia serves perfectly as a preface to his collected
works. He was a self-made man who, like many in his category, loved and admired the written word.

His second contribution to the *Impartial Herald* shows
fewer signs of editorial tampering. Its title, probably the
product of the *Herald*'s editor, is "Wonder of Wonders!"
Although this piece bears no signature and may be frag-
mentary, its style so resembles later efforts that it is customarily attributed to Timothy Dexter, even by as careful
an essayist as Dr. Oliver Wendell Holmes.

> How great the soul is! Do you not all admire and wonder
> to see and behold and hear? Can you all believe half the
> truth and admire to hear the wonders how great the soul
> is! — that of a man [who] is drownded in the sea, what
> a great bubble comes up at the top of the water — the last

of the man dying under water! This is wind — is the soul that is the last to ascent out of the deep to glory. The bubble is the soul. A young fellow is for gunning for the good of bodies and souls.

This product must be the result of encouragement by his growing circle of friends, "youthful admirers," as they have been termed by one historian. It was supplemented at about this period by an incident that was sentimental rather than literary.

Dexter, like other New England merchants, was shocked by the excesses of the French Revolution and deeply disturbed by the tragic situation of King Louis XVI and his family. Without going so far as some of his contemporaries in making plans to rescue the royal family, Mr. Dexter was heard to say on several occasions that he would welcome and give financial support to the King of France if he landed on these shores, and the opportunity finally came for him to give public expression to this loyalty. The date was in the winter of 1793, at a time when news still traveled slowly. It is said that Mr. Dexter was in Boston on business, for this was one of his more active years of speculation, when news was received of the French King's execution. He hurried back to Newburyport in his own coach before word of the tragedy could reach there. On that same evening, with the help of admirers, he bribed the sextons of Newburyport's churches to toll the bells in the early evening. The simultaneous sound of the bells caused immediate excitement. A crowd began to gather on State Street, expressing group bewilderment until the door of the Tracy mansion opened and Mr. Dexter appeared and made what may have been his first speech, announcing that the bells were tolling to mourn the death of the King of France. The crowd enjoyed the whole proceeding to such an extent that groups of young boys began to shout "Huzza for Mr. Dexter!" Our informant adds that never was Mr. Dexter more moved or more pleased than he was by this acclaim and by the general good will that surrounded him.

This incident, not mentioned in the *Impartial Herald*, may have marked a turning point in Mr. Dexter's career in that it was the first time that he had personally experienced public adulation on a large scale, and, as with many others, it was a heady wine. He became increasingly particular about his coach and his horses, buying a succession of splendidly matched pairs. Finally when his equipage appeared the boys of Newburyport, stimulated by the possibility that some gratuity might be tossed from the coach windows, began to run after it shouting "Huzza for Mr. Dexter's horses!" All this while the base of his hospitality appears to have been broadening. He reacted immediately to appreciation and praise.

These last statements must be founded on hearsay, because after his thoughts on the soul the name of Timothy Dexter does not appear in the public prints until July 1793, when he made another speech upon a very happy occasion.

The problems of traffic in Newburyport have never been wholly solved. Now that the Merrimack River has been abandoned as a commercial waterway (not for years has a single coal barge been towed up that stream to Haverhill), and since the traffic on the railroad has dwindled to a ludicrous trickle, the town depends for survival upon an intricate highway system that supports streams of trucks, trailers, motor boats and even the United States mail. But now that the population of Massachusetts has become more individually mobile than its citizens could have anticipated in their wildest dreams of wish fulfillment, even the most modern highways cannot accommodate the commercial and pleasure vehicles that crowd them.

It is consoling to find that Newburyport faced much the same sort of crisis in the last decade of the eighteenth century. The north-south traffic was increasing then, as it is today. The several ferries that plied across the lower Merrimack were inadequate to serve a growing congestion. The Parker River had been bridged in two places, but the bridging of the lower Merrimack, which was becoming a vital necessity, was a greater engineering problem and also demanded a much larger outlay of private capital, since government aid was then almost negligible.

Fortunately for the group of investors who were willing to gamble their private resources on the construction of a toll bridge across this swift tidal stream, the Merrimack, some miles from its mouth, runs between narrow banks with an island of about six acres, Deer Island, nearly in its center. The island, acting as a pier with its northern end high above the highest tides, afforded an excellent location for spanning the river with two wooden bridges, one from the Newburyport bank to Deer Island and the other from Deer Island to the opposite shore. There was also a Newburyport builder, Timothy Palmer, possessing all the skills and ingenuity needed for the undertaking. A company was formed known as the Essex-Merrimack Bridge Company, in which Timothy Dexter was a substantial investor, with his name on the books for over a hundred shares. Timothy Palmer, when capital was available, used methods of con-

struction which he later patented. The portion of the
bridge connecting the island with the Salisbury shore was
provided with a draw so that vessels might pass upstream.
A house was built on the island for the toll collector and
the bridge tender. The construction was finished in 1792
and the enterprise was so successful that Dexter was an enthusiastic believer in bridges for the rest of his life.

"Nater," he has written, "has formed N Port and part of
Noubry as well for pease and war altogether as well as the
Lord would wish to have it."

If this statement is too sweeping, he was right regarding
the bridge location. One may see the span still, a different
bridge, but the same island, with the same house upon it —
a house that was to become a tavern and the house in which
Mrs. Spofford lived on that occasion when I rowed my
mother to the island. But the main purpose of the Essex-
Merrimack Bridge has now almost vanished. A new bridge
has now been built a hundred yards or so upstream, over
which Maine and New Hampshire traffic pours like water
breaking through a dike. The old bridge, once a bottleneck,
is almost deserted now, merely a rustic connection between
Newburyport and Amesbury. There has even been talk of
abandoning it altogether, and its fate rests in the hands of
our highway authorities. Yet there are hopes that the bridge
may remain, since Massachusetts roads now cost more per
mile to build than many others in the nation and since an
economy like giving up an old bridge may matter little one
way or the other.

A very early photograph of the Timothy Palmer construction shows a rambling and unprepossessing mass of
heavy timbers, with small indication of the builder's new

inventions. On examining the picture, it is useful to remember again that once all things were new. Thus in July of
1793 the Essex-Merrimack Bridge was modern and original.
There was every reason for some citizens of Newburyport,
including Mr. Dexter, to cross over, on the Fourth of July,
1793, to Deer Island and to celebrate the whole accomplish-
ment by a suitable wine and food collation. A clear, clean
river flowed beneath the span. There were pastures and
cornfields on either side of the water and traces of tall
forest. Looking downstream one saw the masts and spars
of shipping. There was no Dutch elm disease to ruin the
trees recently planted along its newly developed streets, no
gypsy and browntail moth, no Japanese beetle, no chestnut

blight, no factory towns farther up the stream where, Upton Sinclair tells us, girls bartered their virtue for a sandwich. We can only bring back the objective thought that these Newburyporters on the Fourth of July, after a few cool drinks of rum punch, could easily believe that now the bridge was built Newburyport was on its way to becoming the metropolis of tomorrow. The weather was pleasant, the foliage was green. It was an occasion for mutual congratulation.

Toward the end of the collation Mr. Dexter was moved to get upon the table and deliver a speech, and his action was reported in the *Impartial Herald*. Some observers said the speech was incomprehensible. Others said it was truly Ciceronian, and still others believed it was delivered in French. At least, Mr. Dexter held the attention of his audience, if only because he was a heavy shareholder in the Essex-Merrimack Bridge project.

"People has offen asked me," he tells us, "why I did not bye the holl—I have offen told them mankind was mankind it would not doue—nor would it doue for a foue people to hold all the publick seccoureteys for mankind has so much of what wee call the Devel or Rouring Lions or wouls."

Perhaps his remarks on that happy Fourth of July ran in a similar channel. At any rate, the event had repercussions, for we find that Mr. Dexter subsequently sent a letter together with his Deer Island speech to the editor of the *Essex Journal and New Hampshire Packet*. (When I last saw this newspaper, it was stored in the cellar of the Tracy mansion, and the cellar, being unbeautified, gave many hints of the former pretensions of the old building. It could be that the newspaper files of the Newburyport Public

Library were lodged in the old Dexter wine cellar. I have
always liked to believe so.)

> Mr. MyCall [the letter reads], Messrs. Blunt and Robin-
> son took notice in their last *Herald* that I delivered on the
> fourth instant on Deer Island a speech in French. This
> speech I now send you in English, and, should you think
> it worthy of a place in your useful paper, you may insert.
> I did not deliver all that I intended on account of the ill-
> breeding of a blue puppy, who impertinently endeavored to
> upset my pulpit, or rather the table on which I stood. The
> public, considering the small chance I have had to learn
> French, are a little surprised to hear of my having endeav-
> ored to speak it; but, if Gentlemen and Ladies will give
> themselves the liberty to reflect that Frenchmen express
> themselves very much by gestures, and that Englishmen
> have made such a proficiency in this art that a whole play
> can now be acted without speaking a word, they will cease
> to wonder.
>
> TIMOTHY DEXTER

If Mr. Dexter never wrote a word of this, the passage is
still significant as showing the hand or hands of the *deus ex
machina* that made our New England leather dresser into
what he eventually became. One wonders whether the blue
puppy mentioned here was a biped or a quadruped. He
could hardly have been the improbable dog shown in the
Akin [1] engraving of Mr. Dexter done in 1805, a year be-

---

[1] Mr. Akin, who did this engraving, conceived a violent dislike for Mr. Edmund
M. Blount (Blunt), publisher of the *Coast Pilot*. It is said that Mr. Akin's vindictive-
ness carried him so far as to have a cartoon he drew of Mr. Blount transferred to
the bottom of several Liverpoolware chamberpots, which he distributed about Newburyport. It is impossible to vouch for the accuracy of this rumor, but I did know
an old inhabitant who said that he believed he had seen a piece of this crockery in
his childhood.

fore his death. This dog was a piglike quadruped that was
said to be his constant companion, without a hair, but with
a skin black and wrinkled, like that of an elephant. The dog
was, one historian tells us, "as remarkable among his species
as his master among men. . . . From his *structure,* which
should have partially indicated his family, it was impossible
to approximate, even to a suspicion, his pedigree."

It was said, Mr. Knapp tells us, "that Dexter's dog would
never leave his master's feet when he was at all intoxicated.
What a satire on the presumption of man, who arrogates to
himself to be lord of creation." The faithful dog of the
Akin engraving was, I should guess, a Mexican hairless, a
rarity even now in this part of the country.

The speech itself, which follows the communication, was written by the guiding spirits that now had Timothy Dexter's future well in hand. Was it Jonathan Plummer who wrote it, or was it one of the young bucks of Newburyport mentioned by Samuel Knapp, who ate hundred-dollar bills in sandwiches?

Ladies and Gentlemen, this day, the eighteenth year of our glorious independence commences — Justice, order, commerce, agriculture, the sciences and tranquillity reign triumphant in these United and happy States — America is the asylum for the afflicted, persecuted, tormented sons & daughters of Europe. Our progress towards the glorious point of perfection is unparalleled in the annals of mankind.

Permit me, then, my wife and jolly souls, to congratulate

you on this joyful occasion — Let our deportment be suitable for the joyful purpose for which we are assembled — Let good nature, breeding, concord, benevolence, piety, understanding, wit, humor, Punch and wine grace bless adorn and crown us henceforth and forever. Amen.

We may pause here, confident that we have said enough and more than enough to show how willingly Dexter cooperated to form his legend. Even at this time, in spite of our being told that people noticed no great peculiarity in Timothy Dexter during his ownership of the Tracy mansion, his general condition must have been disturbed. But what of his home life during this active epoch of composition, speculation and investment? What were Madam Dexter, Samuel and Nancy doing during their stay in the Tracy house? We can give a factual answer, seasoned with only a little logical surmise.

X I I I

Some Penalties of Affluence

THE INHABITANTS of Newburyport, tolerant though they have always been of eccentricities in their fellow citizens, are also blessed with a tendency toward moral stricture. Thus on one side of the medal there was a communal delight in the Dexter coaches and horses, his leap to fortune and the Deer Island speech, while on the other side many citizens, less fortunately situated financially, were glad to have it proved to them that wealth and domestic happiness do not necessarily go hand in hand.

This was now being demonstrated by upsets in the Dexter ménage. The relations of the whole family group were undergoing disastrous erosion as its members began adjusting themselves to the challenges of affluence. Sam and Nancy, who might have coped with the simpler manners of tanners' row, were helpless when in contact with High Street. In fact, after perusing the antiseptic description of them given by Samuel Knapp, it would be kinder to omit them entirely, but this act would be moral cowardice.

The kindest thing that one can say is that their faults were beyond their control. Without domestic counselors to help them, both children turned out miserable failures, unable to meet the demands of their age, which would ap-

pear to have been, in spite of a well-trimmed moral bordering, more tolerant than ours. Sam Dexter, not popular anywhere in town, is the especial anathema of Mr. Knapp.
Samuel "Lord" Dexter, he was to be called in later days by
his more humorous contemporaries. He grew in size more
rapidly than most boys, but in spite of an expensive education, the boy was naturally imbecile and his mind was
stored with nothing useful or ornamental. He was "capricious in his appetites," extremely cowardly, and, in toto,
rotten to the core. He had only one redeeming feature
among his contemporaries, and this was his profusion. He
bribed boys with cake, fruit and confectionery, for protection from insult and for assistance with lessons. The
only ingenuity and talent he ever exhibited, according to
the Knapp observation, was his skill in inventing lies. The
boys despised him, his teachers pitied him. This should be
enough to demonstrate that money is not always a help in
building character. But Mr. Knapp conducts us still further down Sam Dexter's primrose path, which, if only for
moral reasons, we must follow.

School became irksome to young Samuel, as it still does
in spite of modern efforts to sugar-coat the difficultly in-
gested pill of learning. The tradition of the sea and of the
thriving port being a part of his youthful atmosphere, he
asked his father to allow him to sail on one of the Dexter
ships on a European voyage in the capacity of factor or
supercargo, a position often given promising scions of New
England mercantile houses. Once across the Atlantic he
squandered the entire value of his father's ship's cargo at
the gaming table, and thereafter quarreled incessantly with
his disappointed parent, whenever he was not plunging into

what Mr. Knapp refers to as "every species of dissipation."
In fact, he was a goose "from whom every knave plucked
a feather, to whom every Cyprian had a chain to hold him
as a cub."

There is only one excuse made for this unhappy profligate. There were, according to Mr. Knapp, lots of others
like him in Federalist Newburyport, who modeled themselves on the dissipations of Charles Fox and admired the
witty if off-color dramas of the playwright Sheridan. To
show their "nobility" they often skipped dollars on the
surface of ponds, not knowing that eighteenth-century life
and thought was waning, to give place to Jeffersonian
ideals. The echo of their behavior, as I have said, was vivid
in my childhood. My own great-grandfather was damaged
by this Corinthian spirit; and I have been told that my
grandfather, who was made of sterner stuff, once, when
alone in his New York house, poured a whole bottle of
spirits down the sink rather than face the temptation of
imbibing a portion. Once, also, I am told, when Mr. Edward Moseley of Newburyport, a gentleman some years my
grandfather's senior, said "What would you say if I were
to tell you I have not drunk a drop of liquor in twenty
years?" my grandfather replied, "I would say you were
a d——d liar." This persiflage, though doubtless apochry-
phal, shows that the antics of Samuel Dexter and other
young bloods had left their imprint. Samuel, we finally
learn, died at an untimely age, without having done the
slightest good to his generation and without a particle of
regret from anyone. "No drunken companion who had
partaken of his wine even said, 'He was a clever fellow; it
is a pity he went off so soon.' "

As for Nancy Dexter, the excoriation she received from Knapp is mitigated by her father's partiality for her, greater perhaps than the poor girl deserved, and in spite of all her difficulties he remembered her with care and affection in his will.

> We may as well speak of the daughter of Timothy Dexter now as at any other time [Knapp writes]. She bloomed for a while, a giggling belle of more than ordinary personal beauty; but her education was superficial as her brother's. The fame of her father's wealth brought about her a host of swindling, greedy gallants; but most of them retired after a visit or two, finding it impossible, with all their love of money, to bring their minds to make serious proposals to one so entirely unfitted for society.

It could also be that the whole Dexter background was calculated to frighten away young men, what with Madam Dexter's scolding, which was growing more pronounced, and what with Dexter and Samuel drunk at table, and poets and other entertainers making too frequent use of the house. Despite these obstacles to matrimony Nancy was married, in March 1792, to a peculiar young man of scholarly proclivities named Abraham Bishop, who took her to live in New Haven. Knapp refers to him as a grave, philosophical scholar who had traveled in Europe and the East. His learning and cosmopolitan politeness made a deep impression on Nancy and Madam Dexter. Dexter maintains that he was not impressed, but this is difficult to believe, since he made a cash settlement on Nancy and since he went to visit his daughter and son-in-law in New Haven, and stayed long enough to have his portrait done in that town and to attend Yale commencement, where, he tells us, "the man in the hat" gave an exhortation to the graduates. Still Dexter must have been jealous. From the very first, he says later, he suspected Abraham Bishop. It was Madam Dexter, he explains, who was responsible for the fatal step.

"Madam Dexter," he has written, "have my Dafter marey to A bishop — Cosed the agrement — the sole Cose." Mr. Bishop may have seemed handsome to Madam Dexter and Nancy, but to Dexter he appeared like a two-legged Connecticut bull, "short Neck boull head, thik hare, big sholders, black Corlley hare." He also was not in funds; in fact he was, Dexter tells us, "then nothing as for Cash; he being A fox and A old fox, he was After the graps . . . o, o, pity me, All good felow mortels; sade Creater A b, mad with Larning, & as pour as A snake, and as proud as Lousefer — he sade his father was worth twenty-thousand Dolors, & he was Not more than five thousand Dolors."

The unpleasant impression that Nancy's husband made on Dexter, both physical and financial, is projected further. Mr. Bishop was seldom gone from Dexter's later thoughts. "My gesing of the Creater is turned out," Dexter writes, "A cording to my gessing." Other sources reveal that Mr. Bishop was rude before the ceremony, requesting that the marriage be performed before the banns were published, and when Dexter objected, Mr. Bishop said that "Dexter might cry them — down in the Lower Region."

My frinds & Felow mortels [Dexter writes again], there is A first Cose of all things, most commonly: so it Came to pass that one Abraham bishup got A quainted with my Dafter — shee A babey, he Old in Eage and larning, and Coleage lant & lawyer lant and preast lant and masonik lant and Divel lant.

This experience explains Dexter's growing suspicion of scholars, clergymen and the Masonic order, of which Bishop was a member. "He hurt me and my family," Dexter adds, "one tun of silver." It would be pleasant if we could end the tale by saying that eventually the couple became reconciled to each other, but this did not happen. In spite of Abraham Bishop's scholarly example, Nancy became increasingly silly and simpering. They had a single daughter who was well brought up by Bishop but who died without issue. Mr. Bishop began beating and abusing Nancy, who, like her father and brother, turned to the bottle. Her mind, never strong, grew more and more flighty. Finally a divorce ensued, and she lived on for many years, kept out of public sight and supported by the provident care of her father, "one good deed," the moralist Knapp concludes, "which should be named in the waste of his life, where few green spots are to be found."

Dexter's business combinations, his extrovert proclivities, some of which we have described, as well as his increasing addiction to strong alcoholic beverages, taken in combination with the frustrations, furies and worries caused by his feckless children, created an atmosphere far from conducive to connubial felicity. The house was filled with good servants, like all prosperous Newburyport houses in those days, since domestic service was a very reasonable commodity, demanding an outlay in cash only a little beyond the cost of board and lodging.

All Newburyport families who amounted to anything at that time, Mrs. E. Vale Smith tells us, had a coachman and a footman, and Dexter had an excellent coachman for his coach, who hardly ever took time off and then only with

Mr. Dexter's express permission. In the light of the present, the domestic advertisements then in the press fill the reader with astonishment and nostalgia. Gardeners who understood hothouses were in demand, men to wait on table. The advertisements for women were fewer, because of the over-abundance of those seeking work.

However, despite the plethora of people ready to do things in the Tracy mansion, the relationship between Mr. and Mrs. Dexter was rapidly failing. We have quoted Dexter, in one of his many public confidences, as saying that he was knocked upon the head seven times and that several of these blows were given him by Mrs. Dexter. Normally the house must have been in an uproar, what with Mrs. Dexter's high temper and Dexter's mercurial moods, and there was always a turnover of servants plus a great deal of breakage, during convivial evenings. There were quarrels over Nancy and Mr. Bishop as well as more immediate causes for friction. There is no doubt also that Mr. Dexter was afflicted with what is politely known as a roving eye.

In the days of his wealth he was always susceptible to a pretty face, a well-turned ankle; and he may have had some excuse for small efforts at solace (a weakness never uncommon in Dexter's age group), since Mrs. Dexter was some years his senior, a scold who had lost her good looks long ago. But she was justified in her scolding, probably for many more years than one might expect. There is evidence that in the early days of their marriage Mr. Dexter became interested, at least in a religious way, in a house-keeper. This word for a general helper has often been used in New England as a conventional cloak that gives an air

of correctness to many living problems between men and
women which might otherwise have been debatable. In any
event, Mr. Dexter in 1805 wrote to the *Impartial Herald*
as follows: "Furthermore, if I am not converted, there is
not anyone converted as I think. I have been more than
twenty years converted (I am not joking about it) ever
since I got me a housekeeper."

Simple arithmetic will place the advent of this unknown
lady into the Dexter household back in the year 1775, only
five years after his marriage. We do not know what Mrs.
Dexter may have thought of the friendship, but the memory of this religious influence remained with Mr. Dexter
until the year 1802, for we then find him writing "one
thing fourder, I have bin converted upwards 30 years,
quite Ressned for the day, the grat day; I wish the preasts
Node as much as I think I do." The excuse for digging so
far into the ashes of his past lies in a frank advertisement

that he inserted in the *Impartial Herald* in the early days
of his prosperity.

> Wanted Direct, A very good Housekeeper — the age
> not less than 25, nor more than 35, with a good mind. I
> take myself to be a converted man and full of love. I want
> a good housekeeper, fully converted — a cook fit for my
> house, of a good constitution, so as to grace the house well
> and a very sensible person — not handsome but comely,
> willing to oblige by night or day. As I am very nervous,
> if she please me well, she will be handsomely paid as much
> as she can be asked in reason. She must take good care of
> the house at *one dollar* a week — must not go out nights
> — she must go to meeting and delight in doing good at
> home where she has her pay and good living. She must
> look well to my interest — and if she does well, at my
> decease, she will have a *noble sum of money to buy her a
> husband.*

This sort of *démarche* could only have increased the
scolding capacities of Madam Dexter, who may have
prided herself on her own housekeeping, but other events
tried her patience still further. At the period of the house-
keeper notice another advertisement appears in the *Impartial Herald* that may have been still more upsetting.

> To the Curious
> A beautiful African
> Lion
> To be seen every day in the week, Sunday excepted,
> during his continuance in town at one of the outbuildings
> in Mr. Dexter's yard.
> This Noble Animal is upwards of three feet high; meas-
> ures 7 feet from nostrils to tail; is of a beautiful dun

color, five years old, and uncommonly strong built. His legs and tail are as thick as those of a common sized ox; he was caught in the woods of Goree, in Africa, when a Whelp, and brought thence to New York. He is as tame as any domestic animal whatever, and is really worth the contemplation of the curious — Price of admittance, Nine pence, each person.

Entertainment was lavish then. At about this time an acrobat crossed State Street on a tight wire, something which I think no one has done since, but I believe Dexter is the only citizen ever to have kept a lion in his yard. It was an achievement, but not one of a sort to give tranquillity to his family.

As an example of how the Dexter legend proliferates after more than a hundred and fifty years, we may quote from a sprightly article on Timothy Dexter that appeared in *Argosy* magazine, May 1958. It is entitled "The Madness of Timothy Dexter." Its author is Mort Winthrop. Here you can read of the Dexter speculations, with many angles that have not been mentioned in this book. The mittens, Mr. Winthrop says, were shipped to the West Indies in July. Dexter, according to the Winthrop article, was planning to free Marie Antoinette, and, to arrange for her reception, cornered most of the food supply of Newburyport. During the noisy drinking bouts in the Tracy mansion, empty bottles were strewn over its spacious yard. The lion story has further elaborations.

One day he decided that if Newburyport wouldn't come to him willingly, he would beguile them into it. He offered — for a fee to cover board — to mind a lion while its owner took a vacation. He brought it from New York to Newburyport by carriage and set up its cage in his grounds. He then advertised in the local newspaper that for ninepence, he would treat all to a spectacular view of a seven-foot lion imported from Goree, Africa (wherever that is). For a week crowds filled his lawn, dropped their ninepences into his coffers, then all was quiet again.

I do not know from what sources Mr. Winthrop obtained these and other intriguing facts, but I like to think that he picked them up from conversing with residents of Newburyport. Lord Dexter is still being talked about.

Probably without his being aware of it, this combination of events was forcing Dexter, after about four years in the Tracy mansion, to the conclusion that it was not a happy home, and that Newburyport, after all his years in it, was no longer a peaceful domestic environment. We can follow these growing tensions because of his increasing habit of pouring out his troubles in print. "I have bin in hell," he writes, " all the time." He very well may have been, for a good part of it. He was plagued by reproofs, by Samuel's losses, and by his son-in-law's demands for money. The situation between Mrs. Dexter and himself finally reached a point where he attempted while living in the house with her to ignore her presence by referring to her only as a shadow, and now we find him referring to her as a "ghost" or "Mrs. Dexter that was," or "the ghost that was my wife." He has even left us evidence, confused because of his sentence structure, that he endeavored to compound some sort of separation agreement with Mrs. Dexter. A deed of trust was drawn by lawyer Theophilus Parsons. The explanation of the trust that Dexter has left us cannot be literally understood, but whatever it may have been, Mrs.

Dexter ignored it more successfully than he attempted to ignore her presence. In fact, Mrs. Dexter may have won the marital battle of the Tracy mansion, if she did not win the war.

It is hard to escape the conclusion, after an examination of Dexter's estate at the time of his death, that he may at this time have suffered a financial reverse. As we know, he announced that he gave up speculation because he had made enough, and at this point in the chronicle Dexter the merchant begins to disappear from the record, turning into Dexter the man of leisure. One thing at least is certain — the *Mehitabel* and the *Congress* disappeared, and either from lack of zeal on my part or dearth of recorded fact, I do not know what happened to them. The safest guess is that they were sold at a time when Timothy Dexter retired from trade.

Added to these major conjectures, further recorded events give more reasons for Mr. Dexter's great malaise. One concerns a generous offer that he made to the citizens of Newburyport. It is difficult to describe the conditions existing in Market Square, the town's commercial center, because of the chaotic state of the square itself. Pandemonium existed there, and leading citizens, now that the town grew wealthy, were increasingly discontented with the Square's general condition. It was not a showcase, as one would say today, for a community on the way to becoming a metropolis. Plans were being discussed to build a roofed-over market on the site of what is now occupied by the town fire station, when Dexter volunteered to build a brick structure at his own expense, provided it was given the name of Dexter Hall. The offer was rejected by the selectmen with thanks. This seems a short-sighted decision but one that hints at a growing local uneasiness regarding the Dexter personality, not dislike as much as suspicion, now that he had changed from leather to satin. This rejection unfortunately came at a time when the youth of Newburyport started playing a series of pranks on him which finally ended on December 10, 1795, with what, in Dexter's opinion, was a theft from the mansion, and he immediately rushed to his favorite sounding board, the *Impartial Herald*.

> Repent and Live [he wrote]. Whereas the Subscriber's House was broken into the night of the 10th Ins, and several bank bills taken therefrom, this is to inform those well known blackguards and pests to mankind, that I have full proof against them, but from a regard to their relations I do not wish to expose them; and if they will send me the bills in a letter it shall be kept a secret and no questions asked — if they do not, the Lord have mercy on their souls, for the day of Darkness is near upon them. T. DEXTER.

We cannot tell whether he mislaid the bills or whether they were stolen, or whether the miscreants brought them back, but it is clear that disturbances in the Tracy mansion continued, as is attested by a second announcement, couched like the first in terms that are not Dexter's own. This must have been composed by some friend in Dexter's hour of need.

> Mssrs. Blunt and March [he writes to the editors of the *Impartial Herald*]: I say to whom it may concern — to the majesty of the people of Newburyport, greeting —
> It costs Eight Hundred Dollars a year to support a watch

in this town, and yet gentlemen's windows are broken, fences pulled down, and cellars broken open and much other misdeameanors done at night. Are the watch asleep, or are they afraid to detect those who are guilty of such practices? Boast not of it, if you call this Liberty and Equality. Newburyport has had the name of being a very civil and worthy place; it is a great pity some bad boys or young men should disgrace it. I hope our worthy and honorable rulers will bring these lads to see themselves and lick the dust like serpents, and ask forgiveness of their betters, and do so no more, but repent and live.

Now fellow citizens, is it wisdom, is it policy, to use a man or men so shocking bad as to oblige them to leave the town where they paid one Dollar a day to support government?

A friend to good order, honor to whom it belongs, to great men a friend, to all citizens and honest men goodbye —

This indicates that Newburyport has long been a haven for juvenile delinquents, but the misdemeanors catalogued by Dexter make one wonder why he complained so loudly. Through the generations into a changing world, petty thefts, pilferings, trespassings and other torts by Newburyport's youth have continued to flourish under the tolerant eyes of those of us who used to be boys ourselves, including parents, teachers and law enforcement officers. Further, boys of Newburyport have moved to more glowing fields. Lately a group of teen-agers robbed a tomb and paraded dressed in funerary garments. Another enterprising Newburyport juvenile, hired by an old lady to do odd jobs around her yard, murdered her because he was short of pocket money. Two other youths, both in their teens, shot and killed the proprietor of a small local grocery, and more recently some playful boys beat up a local storekeeper on Plum Island, but here, I am told, the irate storekeeper may have picked the quarrel, not the boys. Boys are still boys in Newburyport. They can do far better now than in the tamer Federalist era.

The final recorded complaint of Dexter is one that would now be inserted in the Lost-and-Found columns of the *Impartial Herald*'s successor, the *Newburyport Daily News*. In the April after the excitements around the Tracy mansion Mr. Dexter lost a pinchbeck watch on State Street with a small black turtle-shell case. "As it is a remarkable looking watch," he writes, "the thief must soon be detected."

In this case the watch was returned, and may very well have fallen from Dexter's pocket, as may the bills he lost in the previous December, but by this time things had gone too far.

Shortly after these events Dexter left Newburyport, abandoning business and friends and moving into Mrs. Dexter's home state to the rural seclusion of the crossroads town of Chester, New Hampshire. Mrs. Dexter's hand may have been in this, since she was one of the Gilman family, but it is said in Chester's local history that he moved there because his niece was married to the Reverend Nathan Bradstreet of that town. Chester was a quiet place, ideal as a locale in which Timothy Dexter might pull himself together. As he announced himself, he was very nervous, and he may have been in more need than we know of rural rest. He must have given up trading activity, because Chester, even with fast horses and the Essex-Merrimack Bridge, was

not within commuting distance of Newburyport countinghouses. Something drastic had happened, and any guess as
to what is as good as another. We shall endeavor to follow
him as best we can to his exile, which was somewhere inside
of two years. His eventual return to Newburyport, in-
vigorated and more active than ever, may still be a recommendation for Chester's salubrious climate.

It is an excellent diversion for a fine spring morning to
motor from Newburyport by back roads in an attempt to
follow the route of Dexter's coach and of the wagons carrying his personal property on his way to Chester, New
Hampshire. He passed for sure over the Essex-Merrimack
Bridge to the town of Amesbury, whence he may have gone
to Haverhill or he may have taken the venerable road to
Kingston and through the hamlet of North Danville to his
newly chosen home. I hope that he took this, because the
road is still off the beaten path, with some farmhouses
bordering it that Dexter might easily have admired. Scrub
forest has grown over the pastures since Dexter's day. The
great stands of white pine, much of which still stood in
1796, when Dexter made his journey, have vanished, making parts of the country reminiscent of scenes in a recent
best-seller, *Peyton Place*. The distance from Newburyport
to Chester is roughly twenty-five miles, a forty-minute
motor ride under present road conditions, but it would have
required a good day's journey to cover the route by coach.
As one moves further into this New Hampshire hinterland, past the wood lots and the houses and barns of another era, one is seized by an increasing feeling of curiosity.
Why did Dexter go so far from the seacoast? Why did he

select Chester instead of Exeter or Hampton? He remembered two brothers in his will, and his fondness for a brother's daughter may have drawn him thither, but in view of his attitude toward the clergy one doubts it. Without knowing anything about the excellences or social proclivities of the Reverend Mr. Bradstreet, it could hardly have been his persuasiveness that induced Mr. Dexter to move to Chester.

A safer conjecture is that Dexter, always interested in real estate, had invested in Chester properties for the long term. Chester, one can see as one approaches it, was then more than the quiet place it is today. Its long street with its substantial houses was then a part of an almost forgotten route of travel, altered by the coming of the railroad and the appearance of the textile mills on the Merrimack. It was once a stopping place for drovers and a center for the exchange of farm products that reminds one of the forgotten Sandisfield in the Berkshire Hills, the scene of Edith Wharton's *Ethan Frome*. One can easily imagine that its church and its stores, though more recent, stood in the same part of the town when Dexter's coach rolled down its main street. The rural peace of the community may have been as pleasant to Dexter as it is now to a traveler from the city. There was a tavern and there were some gay young blades. There was a market day, but at its best it could not have had the modernity of Newburyport.

In 1876 Henry Flagg French, an Assistant Secretary of the United States Treasury, and the father of the sculptor, Daniel Chester French, published some reminiscences entitled *Chester Fifty Years Ago*. His description of the town still suits it:

On the swell of land which divides the waters that flow directly into the Atlantic Ocean from those that flow into the Merrimack River stands the quiet village of Chester in New Hampshire. The soil is fertile though hard and stony; the air is pure and bracing like that of a mountain region, and the place, though but twenty-five miles, as the crow flies, from the ocean beach, is just beyond the chilling east winds of spring. It has always been said that the sea is visible and even that sails of vessels upon the sea may be seen from the housetops there on a clear morning.

Mr. French, though loyal to his native town, is then obliged to confess that he never saw the sea himself from Chester. The closest approximation was mist over the rolling countryside. The greatest relic of the town's dreams of a glorious future is its mile-long Chester Street, much wider, as Mr. French says, than the street of an ordinary town, but not so wide as that of Keene, New Hampshire. In Mr. French's boyhood local fires afforded great excitement. The town's hand pump would seldom function properly, but in spite of these ravages, the house once the property of Timothy Dexter is still standing on Chester Street, and is now owned by the French family. It is a substantial square dwelling, but not to be compared in point of size or elegance with the Tracy mansion. It has undergone many changes since Dexter last crossed its threshhold and since Henry Flagg French described the place. Mr. French speaks of a large barn and a stone-paved courtyard, the latter believed to have been constructed by Dexter. These adjuncts, together with large pigeoncots constructed by Mr. Dexter, have now disappeared. The stables once afforded accommodation for the Dexter coach and horses,

thus allowing the mobility that Dexter's increasing restiveness craved. The coach with armorial bearings, the coachman still in his livery, and an imported servant or two,
made the Dexter establishment conspicuous on Chester
Street, and Dexter, with his gold-headed cane, rounded out
a vignette which of necessity is mostly surmise but still an
educated guess.

What is difficult in a biographical reconstruction is to see
Chester from the Dexter point of view. Its rural peace, delightful today, must have been more dramatic then. Even
now Newburyport, though a less active place in commercial rating than it was in its prosperity, is a noisy contrast
to Chester's tranquillity. The eighteenth-century contrast
would have been far greater — no ships, no shipwrights, no
countinghouses, a smaller society with more limited social
ambitions. What was it, one wonders, facing Chester's
beautiful street today, that Dexter found to do in Chester
that might occupy his time? His quieter life must have
been a let-down after the excitements of the seaport, but
he had lived on a farm and understood farming, and so was
in a position to talk intelligently with local tradespeople
and agriculturalists. If the house was more cramped than
the Tracy mansion, the presence of fewer juvenile delinquents may have been soothing to his nerves, although one
doubts it, because his restlessness did not decrease during his
short sojourn in Chester. His home life was more simple
than it had been in Newburyport, and, on a long winter
evening, there was greater chance for domestic quiet, since
Dexter was now a man of leisure with pretenses to gentility
that would have prevented him from taking up his old
trade again, even had he desired to do so. It has been re-

marked by some who knew him that in his quieter moments
he was reasonable, generous and appreciative of family ties,
but it is hard to think of him spending an evening at the
Bradstreet parsonage. The tavern was no doubt his favorite
haunt and his personality, growing more buoyant, soon left
a greater imprint on Chester than it had on Newburyport.

One can imagine what he was like from the examples of
his writings that we have examined. When sober he had a
trader's wit plus a touch of the cracker barrel. He was
garrulous when drunk. He was vain and impatient. Like
Fielding's Parson Adams he enjoyed smoking his pipe, but
he disliked the long-stem clay pipes of the period. There is
a tradition that he broke the stems off short, and it is a fact
that the short clay pipe, once popular at the turn of the
century, was, and perhaps still is, called the T.D. pipe,
initials which are said to stand for Mr. Dexter, its inventor.
An evening in his company, even alleviated by good wine
and food — and there is no reason to believe that Dexter
had a cultivated palate — would have been a difficult ordeal
for any intelligent or well-bred person. If the Dexter droll-
eries were amusing for a while, in the end the old man,
I am afraid, was a crashing bore. His personality could not
have worn well, and it is not surprising to learn that he was
not universally popular in Chester. The impression that he
made was on the whole unfavorable, but he also created a
ripple of amusement, which resulted in another important
addition to the Dexter myth.

After the first months of his stay in the town he began to
be referred to by its common people as "Lord" Dexter.
Though this appellation may seem unique today, it was
once a common enough New England term, used in many

localities to describe pretentious neighbors. At this same period one of the Hoopers of Marblehead was called "King"
Hooper, because of his wealth and luxurious style of living,
and at least one other citizen of Newburyport has been
christened "Lord." Yet this term, when connected with
Dexter, had a catching quality, because it described accurately an aspect of his character that was causing general amusement. The town finally went so far as to exaggerate the honorific by calling him "Lord Timothy Dexter,
King of Chester." Instead of being mortified, Lord Dexter
was delighted with his title, a more significant one in those
days than now, since there were still rumors of an American nobility. His pride and pleasure in the Chester honorific
is embalmed in the opening dissertation in his *Pickle for the
Knowing Ones.*

> Ime the first Lord in the younited States of Amercay,
> Now of Newburyport. It is the voice of the peopel and I
> cant help it and so let it goe. Now as I must be Lord, there
> will foler many Lords pretty soune, for it don't hurt a Cat
> Nor the mouse, Nor the son, Nor the water Nor the Ears
> — then goe on — all is Easy; noe bons broken; all is well;
> all in love.

Being called "Lord" was a genuine salve to his ego, and
his memory often returns to the time when he was exalted,
"The first Lord Dexter made by the voice of hamsher state
— my brave fellows affirmed it — they gave me the title &
so Let it goue for as much as it will fetch — it wonte give
me any breade but take from me the Contrary." This last
passage points to the growth of an admiring claque and
hints at some forgotten jollification on some market day or

holiday. The brave fellows who affirmed it in the tavern are now safe in the Chester cemetery. The free beverages that Dexter accorded them are no longer on the record but, without knowing what they were doing, they had contributed to making Dexter a figure more universally remembered than the greatest local characters of Chester, who were as annoyed as you or I would have been by his presence. There was something else in him that made men remember him long after he was gone. He was becoming, in his own bizarre way, a part of the success motif still so slavishly respected in the United States, a dazzling and erratic fragment of the rags-to-riches story. In Chester itself there was a warm spot in some hearts for Lord Timothy Dexter. The name, in the unlettered countryside, had started to possess its own value in dreams of wish-fulfillment. If he had been asked, he might not have wanted to become a part of legend, but it was already beyond his power to change his destiny. His Chester sojourn had raised him to a unique position from which he had to move forward and from which he never could retreat.

> It is hard work to be a king [he writes], I say it is harder than tilling the ground — I know it is, for I find it is hard work to be A Lord — I don't desier the sound but to pleas the peopel at Large — Let it gou to brak the way — it dus for A sortment to help a good Lafe, to Cour the sick, spleany, gouty dul frames Lik my selfe with the goute and so on.

This is a significant paragraph for anyone who aspires to solve the Dexter riddle — if there ever was one. It proves, if Lord Dexter wrote it himself, *that he could spell with reasonable correctness when he so desired.* The first part of the passage is lucid and correct. Then suddenly he lapses into the Dexter lingua franca. Was it he or the printer who wished to put him back in character? Obviously we shall never know, but we do learn at least that he was able to see himself in perspective to the extent of realizing that he was partially a figure of fun. He knew that a good deal of his life was good for a "laff," and the suspicion again arises that he may often have been laughing at those who laughed at him, that he deliberately played the fool without being entirely the moron his contemporaries thought him. His character may have been more complex than it appears, but suddenly one doubts it. Suddenly the shrewdness and the humor go, leaving him the alcoholic and lecherous old man, who, in certain areas of living, did not behave at all well in Chester, or anywhere else.

X I V

The Unkind Nymph of Chester

As in the great Buddhist caves in Shansi Province, where some of the sandstone sculpture has been so worn as to leave only a hint to the imagination of what once existed there, so too are the fragments of gossip regarding Lord Dexter's weaknesses for the fair sex. The substance has gone long ago, and only a few typographical shadows have been left by Samuel Knapp and Jonathan Plummer. Enough of fact remains, however, to make it apparent that Lord Dexter's weakness for young and buxom femininity grew as his years increased and his gout along with them. There is no escaping the suspicion that his search for emotional release led him to attempt, in some way, to exercise the seignorial rights of his new nobility at either Chester or Hampton Beach, or perhaps at both places. Both is a better guess than one, judging by his behavior on his return to Newburyport.

Here then is another Dexter riddle. According to his own testimony he was severely chastised in Chester by a lawyer. This beating was given to him, as Jonathan Plummer will inform us in verse, because of his involvement with a nymph in Chester. On the other hand, the not-always-accurate Knapp announces that at about this time Lord

Dexter was also beaten at Hampton Beach by an enraged
lawyer because of advances not welcomed by a nymph —
until Dexter's blood ran into his boots.[1] Thus there may
have been two lawyers, on two different occasions, but the
one beating that seems to have most definitely altered Dexter's life occurred in Chester and not Hampton.

PHILIP KAPPEL

A Chester town history states, without a fixed date, that
Dexter, when standing before his house, shouted an un-
specified insult at an esteemed local jurist, Judge Liver-
more, as the Judge was riding down the street. The Judge
immediately dismounted and proceeded to thrash our hero
without mercy. We must rely on Knapp and Plummer for
assuming that sex was at the botom of the collision and on
Plummer alone for his versified hint that the Judge was
aroused to fury because of a local nymph's partiality to
Dexter. The cause is now debatable, but the beating was

---

[1] Mr. Winthrop, in his "Madness of Timothy Dexter," gives still another version.
"He was caught in the bushes with a teen-aged girl at nearby Hampton Beach, and
. . . the girl's champion-lawyer pounded him into insensibility during a dispute in
front of the town apothecary shop." Hampton was not nearby to Chester in the horse-
and-buggy days, and the bushes along the beach were very low, and I wish Mr. Winthrop had told us whether the apothecary shop was in Hampton or Chester.

real enough. Although Dexter has stated that his Chester
retreat was as fine as any from Canada to "solt" water, the
beating caused him to issue a warning to Chester somewhat
similar to the one he had previously given Newburyport.
His own explanation for the trouble seems specious. The
lawyer was mad because the people at large "declared me
Lord Dexter, King of Chester," and this same individual
had borrowed a hundred dollars of him, and while still
owing it, beat his "bene factter."

This contretemps on Chester Street could not have increased Dexter's local popularity. To make things worse, it
was either preceded or followed by another less sanguinary
but equally crucial quarrel, this time with a Baptist minister, to whose hypocrisy the King of Chester objected. But
Dexter can, and will, describe his own difficulties.

> For A Minster to git the tone is a grat pint, when I lived
> in hamsher, one Nue Lite babtis babler sobed A way just
> fineshing his sermon, he says, o good lord, I hop you will
> consider what fue hints I have given, and I will cleare it
> up sum time hence; I am much wore down Now, the wether
> being very warme to day. Less pray, & so went on, fire, fire
> & brimstone & grunting & sithing, and tried to cry & snifel
> & blow the sconks horn, & sum the old fules & yong fules
> sot to crying. I tuck my hat and went out. hou mankind &
> women kind is in posed upon all over the world more or
> less, by preast craft; o for shame! o for shame! I pittey
> them; be onnest; doue as you would wish others to doue
> unto you in all things; Noe fear of Death. Amen.

This sort of thing could only have one ending. Dexter's
proclamation threatening to leave Newburyport appeared
in January 1796. He served notice on Chester in September

of this same year, again in the *Impartial Herald*. It must have been a torrid summer in New Hampshire, and the emotion felt by Dexter has not lost its warmth in his Chester proclamation.

> My wish is all Liers may have there part of fier and brimstone in this world, or at least sum part of it; or Else the govement is Not good; it will want a pourging soone, if A lawyer is to way lay a man, and bruse him un massely All most to Death — A sittesen that pays twentey fore Dolers for Carages [there was then a tax on vehicles] and more than one Dolor A week to ment the hiways; and my being libberal is in part of this bloddy A fare. No savage would beat a man as I was beaten, almost to Death. I Did not know houe these men Came to keep sade lawyer from quite killing of me till sum time After; three men saw the Axion of the blodey scene with out massey, and carried sade Dexter in to the house, sun fanting, or Neare to; se and behold the orful site: bleading, and blind of one Eye, two brousings in two hours, at least. Noe Laws in this part of the world for a man of money to liv; thos I lend money to, and A lawyer, and others, thay youse me the wost; it maks Inemye; then thos Rogs, if there is Any, that call me A foull and pick A quarel with me About my Nous papers, so as to pay the lawyer Craft to make up the molton Calf — A molton Calfe, Not an Ox. Now the town of Chester has lost two *Hundred wate of Silver*, at least — I beleave more money. Now thay may have me in the town or A lawyer. Chouse for yourselves, my frinds and felow mortals. pease be with you All; Amen. — selagh.

The date of this warning makes it difficult to ascertain exactly how long Timothy Dexter did remain in Chester — perhaps for less than a year, certainly for less than two.

The chronology in a Chester history announces that in the year 1798, a long while after the beating, Lord Dexter offered to pave the whole of Chester Street in Chester at his own expense, if it were renamed Dexter Street. The offer was voted on at town meeting and rejected "almost unanimously" because of his eccentricities. This may have been a Parthian shot or an attempt to heap coals of fire upon ungrateful heads, because it is probable that Lord Dexter was gone from Chester by then. At best he would only have been perched there uncertainly, since in the early part of the year 1797 Newburyport was electrified by the news that Lord Dexter was moving into the great house formerly owned by Jonathan Jackson on High Street. Also in March of that same year Jonathan Plummer composed an ode welcoming his lordship back to town, which, because of its informative significance, will shortly be printed in full.

Dexter had left Newburyport in search of peace and quiet. After his exile, more full of vim than ever and in a higher state of autointoxication, he had not only received a beating in New Hampshire but an accolade of nobility. The beating may have seared his soul, but this was secondary. The honorific he had received meant everything to his future. It fitted perfectly with his acquisition of the Jackson place.

We have gone to some length already to describe this house and grounds, among the finest in Newburyport, but it may do no harm to recapitulate by quoting Lord Dexter's own description of them.

> Nater has formed the grounds Eaquel to what you would wish for, And by a man Eaquel to a Solomon, the onerable Jonathan Jackson, one of the first in this Country for tast;

borne a grat man by Nater, then the best of Lurning; . . .
the holl of the world can't exceed this . . . I have traveled
good deale, but ould steady men sayeth it is the first, that
it is the best in this Countery and other Countreys.

This appreciation was written some years after his arrival
at his new and final home and only after he had given the
idea of purchase considerable thought. He was cautious
enough first to rent the Jackson mansion from Captain
Thomas, who had purchased it from Jonathan Jackson,
when the Jackson and Tracy fortunes had reached a point
of embarrassment. The irony of Timothy Dexter's having
occupied first the Tracy and then the Jackson house has
never been lost on Newburyport. It is a matter, too, of
coincidental interest that all three of the dwellings, including Chester's, purchased by Dexter after his moving from
the Sign of the Glove, later became taverns.

Dexter's high opinion of his new property receives the
endorsement of Mr. Knapp, who expressed himself with
equal emphasis but with more virtuosity. "It was," he
writes, "a princely château, standing on the height of land
about a quarter of a mile from the river, commanding a
most beautiful and extensive view of the sea, the Isles of
Shoals and the far surrounding country. The grounds had
been laid out in the most approved European fashion by
intelligent artists from England and France. The house was
capacious and well finished and the outhouses tasteful and
commodious. A lovelier spot or a more airy mansion Lucullus could not have wished."

Lucullus himself might have been surprised could he
have seen the improvements that the new owner made on
this dignified estate, improvements of which Newburyport

was at the time ashamed. It is a pity they do not remain today, because they would be Newburyport's most visited monument and an eloquent commentary on Dexter and his age. For Timothy Dexter late in life was approaching his finest hour, as well as an intellectual level which may be called a flowering of genius. Something had happened to him during his stay in Chester. As we have seen, his rise to affluence had severely shaken his emotional stability, but the acceleration of change had not so far caught Newburyport's attention because, perhaps, Newburyport then as now sheltered more than a handful of highly individual citizens.

One Newburyport historian, in commenting on Dexter, comes right out with it. "Previous to this date the eccentricities of Timothy Dexter were not particularly prominent and had not attracted much public attention." The lion in the Dexter yard, the Dexter communications to the press, the ringing of bells to announce the death of Louis XVI were actions that could have been duplicated by other persons in an area to which showmen and acrobats made frequent visits and where once a coach carrying a bride and groom appeared, drawn by six white horses accompanied by outriders. The situation, however, was soon to change. The concatenation of circumstances in Chester had embarked Lord Dexter on a more conspicuous flight from reality. The beating he received had jarred him spiritually as well as physically. The rustic acclaim accorded him had caused him to lose his always unstable sense of proportion. His health, long subjected to unwise living, was on the decline. His temperament, always mercurial, was increasingly beyond prediction. His loneliness had grown

upon him with the realization that he was disliked by
wealthy Newburyporters and never would be invited inside their houses. But his imagination had never been so active. It appears to have been stimulated, in fact, by his in-
activity — and, parenthetically, he could not have been
disliked by everyone, for in the town election of 1798 he
was once more elected to the office he had held so long, Informer of Deer.

The most cogent example we have of this new Dexter is
the Jonathan Plummer poem of welcome, with its felicitous
footnotes. The ode was dedicated to Sir Timothy Dexter,
a mistake which shows the poet's unfamiliarity with the
peerage. What is more significant is that Jonathan Plummer
for the first time publicly refers to himself as poet laureate
to his lordship. This quick assumption of the title may also
reflect Dexter's change of manner. Plummer became Dexter's poet laureate in March 1797 and continued until his
patron's death in October 1806, and so he still remains in
Newburyport tradition. Here is the poem completed. It
reads:

> To Sir TIMOTHY DEXTER, *on his returning to Newbury-*
> *port, after residing a long time at Chester in New Hamp-*
> *shire; a congratulatory Ode: by Jonathan Plummer, Junr.,*
> *Poet Lauriet to his Lordship.*

> Your lordship's welcome back again —
>   Fair nymphs with sighs have mourn'd your staying
> So long from them and me your swain,
>   And wonder'd at such long delaying;
> But now you bless again our eyes,
> Our melting sorrow droops and dies.

The town of Chester to a Lord
   Must seem a desert dull and foggy,
A gloomy place — upon my word
   I think it dirty, wet, and boggy:
Far different from your Kingly seat,[2]
In good saint James his famous street

There all the arts and graces join
   To make you happy and contented:
There flowing wits and sparkling wine
   Will duly to you be presented —
Aye, raptures rare combinéd meet
To bless and crown saint James his street.

Your happy change I'll loudly sing,
   Your change to all the town transporting,
And while I make the valleys ring,
   I shall rejoice at your good fortune.
From Chester to saint James his street
Is quite a glorious retreat.

But I a suit of clothes must have
   To sing my joy in, and the best, sir:
A suit of red; not black and grave,
   Provided by the Earl of Chester.
To Todd the taylor send, I pray: —
Your Lordship's poet must be gay.

The sable suit is handsome yet;
   But not so proper to rejoice in,
As that which now you'll for me get,
   To tune my very joyful voice in.

[2] Kingly seat — The elegant house in saint James his park and street, which belonged some time since to Jonathan Jackson, Esq. [Plummer's note.]

In Europe I know not a King
Without a bard in red to sing.

You in this place have many friends,
  And all the Lawyers here are civil:
They know full well that envy tends
  To send its owners to the devil.
I think they will not beat you blind,
Because the Nymphs are to you kind.[3]

Your house [4] in Chester is not fit
  For a wise noble lord to dwell in —
In this you may display your wit:
  Aye, this I'm sure you will do well in.
I hope you'll shine gay as a lark
A glory to saint James his park.

Bless me! what wits and beauties there,
  With dazzling lustre gay are shining!
Nymphs whom to angels I compare,
  And wits who're not with envy pining:
Beaux who will never beat you blind
Because the Nymphs are to you kind.

Lo! what a place below the skies,[5]
  How stately, elegant, and splendid,
Is that boon earthly paradise,
  Where wit and beauty are so blended!

[3] Because the Nymphs &c. — It is strongly suspected that Lord Dexter was bruised half to death, by a lawyer in New Hampshire, partly on account of the ladies regard for him in that state. [Again Plummer's note.]

[4] The house is elegant; but only 2 stories high. [Still again, this is Plummer's note.]

[5] Lo! what a place, &c. — Newburyport in general, and saint James his park in particular. [Again, this burst of civic pride is Plummer's note.]

> You truly hit the proper mark
> By living in St. James his park.

> A man of sense should always live
>   Among the highest and the best, sir,
> And never pine away and grieve
>   Among the fighting folks at Chester:
> Then shine, rich lord, the gayest spark,
> The glory of saint James his park.

You will notice some slight confusions in this jingle. It would seem that our bard, on using the phrase "Saint James," was not wholly familiar with the habits of the British court, but this does not impair the elegance of the term. Whereas Dexter refers to himself as the "King of Chester," his swain calls him the "Earl of Chester," but I do not believe that either of them would have been greatly bothered by the discrepancy had it been pointed out. The versified preview of all the joys of which His Lordship would partake in his new palatial abode corresponds in many aspects with reality. The difficulties which Lord Dexter would experience are not mentioned, and rightly so, since pessimistic prophecy had no place in a paean of rejoicing. The effort, I believe, deserved the red suit for which Plummer asked, and so it is with regret that we must announce that Todd the tailor did not get the order. The circumstances are explained by Plummer himself in his reminiscences.

It happened [he tells us] that the Earl of Chester was ill of the gout about the time this ode made its appearance. This I imagine operated to my disadvantage in my obtaining the suit of red. The painful disease, in a great measure, destroyed

his Lordship's relish for poetry. Lady Dexter, too, cooperated with the gout in the business of withholding from
me the object of my wishes. She is not altogether so generous, so noble, so royal, as his Lordship, and when she rules
the house, those benevolent actions are not always done
which at other times adorn the place. I would not be understood to hint that she alone ever absolutely controls him;
but I cannot say that she and the gout together do not
sometimes get him under. I did not expect that any thing
would hinder him from cloathing his own poet; but alas!
I must confess I have not yet received the suit.

From the evidence that remains, Dexter, once more in
Newburyport facing his greatest hour, appears from the
very beginning of his stay to have exhibited a loss of physical mobility that contrasts dramatically with the eccentric
speed-up of his mind. Gout and other infirmities, that made
geriatrics a problem earlier than it is at present, curtailed
his visits to the docks and countinghouses in the vicinity of
Market Square. Something else also had changed in him.
He seemed aware of the painful truth that he no longer
belonged anywhere save in the new world that he was now
creating. Wealth had removed him from old friendships.
He was no longer living on State Street close to the center
of the town but further out on High Street in a region
much more rural. Farmers with their oxcarts plodded over
this thoroughfare, a rutted, unpaved street. The Dexter
palace was more of a country house than a town house,
with generous grounds, instead of the smaller yard that had
surrounded the Tracy mansion. From its wide frontage on
High Street its ample acreage, with flower and vegetable
gardens, a coach house, and stables, stretched down the

slope to the Common Pasture, with fine meadows, orchards and well-tended walks. There were hotbeds and cold frames, and there could have been a glasshouse or orangery. The extensive grounds and gardens were in better condition than any now existing in Newburyport. The lawns,

paths and planting about the house became one of Dexter's great preoccupations, and he spent so much time on them that he seldom moved from "Saint James his park." Instead of his going to see people, they came to him — not the gentry but the inquisitively vulgar, plus the malicious and mischievous, all of whom continue to form a segment of Newburyport's population.

Idlers in growing numbers paused to gape at the Dexter grounds. Total strangers began paying calls on the First Lord of America, now that he was an institution; and very often they were not disappointed by the sights they saw

or by Dexter's behavior. When he was in the right frame of
mind we hear that he was generous with his plums and
cherries and apples, as well as with his rum. In a genial
mood he was eager to display his house, grounds and stables.
He especially enjoyed entertaining young girls from the
country, of whose less sophisticated manners he was occasionally able to take advantage. If they were wise they
called on Mr. Dexter in numbers, when they romped with
him in a pastoral way through his groves and orchards in a
manner that would have pleased some Augustan Romans.
He also, according to Mr. Knapp, would go to great lengths
to set seductive traps for unwary nymphs. He was undis-
couraged by his Chester adventures. "The story," Knapp
tells us, "of his attempt at improper liberties with his female visitors soon became current," until finally those who
continued walking his grounds "were the less scrupulous of
their sex." With Dexter's weakness along these lines — one,
let us add, shared by other prominent persons from Biblical
ages to the present — his mind was often removed from
more practical matters. "When disappointed of his prey,"
Knapp writes, "he would rave about his house and curse his
family for joining in league against him. How wretched is
the life of a dotard, in the pursuit of what he calls pleasure!"

Dexter has left a remark that affords an excellent footnote to his biographer's heavy-handed moralizing. "Nater
gave me to doue good to my week brothers."

As a contrast, other and more intellectual though equally
convivial scenes began to take place in the Dexter house
and on the grounds, attended by citizens and mirth-search-
ing nymphs endowed with original ideas for entertainment.

An unidentifiable schoolteacher, referred to only as "John P ——," [6] was one of the leading spirits of the circle. He possessed more than the rudiments of a classical education as well as a smattering of astrology and an original taste for masques and rural routs. Plummer's importunings for a new suit eventually were given attention, and the schoolmaster's advice may have helped in its creation. It is difficult to reconstruct this garment now. Some witnesses recall it as being a sable cloak with silver stars which Plummer wore when he declaimed his poems and discourses in the Dexter garden. A more probable description indicates that the garment was a long black frock coat with stars on the collar and also on the front corners. Fringes were added wherever possible. The accessories were shoes with large buckles, a large cocked hat and a gold-headed cane. His lordship's poet must have looked gay enough, but we hear that he was embarrassed by the fringes, going so far as to tell his patron that it had been revealed to him in a dream that the wearing of fringes was a sin.

The crowning of Jonathan Plummer for his poetry may have occurred on High Street instead of on State, since the ode and the appearance of the agile schoolmaster afforded a more suitable background. Wherever it was, a tremendous group of nymphs and swains gathered to witness the ceremony, and when laurel leaves could not be found, parsley was substituted. The pressure of the crowd in its enthusiasm was so great that the exercises were interrupted. The fragile parsley crown was partially destroyed, but a nymph pinned

---

[6] The schoolmaster who once was a teacher of Mr. Knapp is described as an "original." A huge elm from the primeval forest stood in front of his schoolhouse. He encouraged his pupils in athletic feats. He taught them to swim, and, what was shocking to other teachers in Newburyport, he went swimming with them.

some flowers to a straw bonnet and used it as a substitute, thus completing a pageant unique in American letters.

Something new occurred nearly every day at the Dexter house. At one time a curious visitor might have seen Mr. Dexter giving away locks of his hair to the admiring youth of the town, and on one occasion his head was almost entirely clipped, but Knapp believes that he was wearing an old wig. And at another time it would have been possible to see Lord Dexter riding in a basket strapped to the back of a gigantic manservant or conversing about dreams and stars with the shabby but mystical seeress, Madam Hooper — she of the double row of teeth all the way around, who could handle a broadsword like a man, and who kept a hen as her familiar. If Dexter himself was not visible because of gout or the routine reactions resulting from a dissipated evening, inquisitive watchers could admire exterior improvements being made on the Jackson house. The proportions of the cupola and the eagle weather vane are exceptionally good. The eagle, always Dexter's pride, was executed by Joseph Wilson, a young Newburyport ship carver who had recently come to the town to ply his trade and whose house on Strong Street still shows exterior traces of his carving skill. The eagle was one of the first of many commissions that Dexter was to give the artist—a very able young man, as His Lordship himself tells us. "Show him a crows Neast, he can carve one—A fine fellow." If he never carved a crow's nest, other embellishments rapidly appeared on the house and grounds as the active mind of its peculiar owner darted from point to point.

Immense gilded balls were placed at the corners of the mansion roof and on portions of the roof's new railing. Work was in constant progress in the gardens, which had been too conventional for the Dexter taste. New and exotic trees and shrubs, according to old gossip, were being shipped to Newburyport from foreign lands on Dexter's order. If this is true, few of them survive. Some of the trees around the house, including a splendid specimen of linden and some large beeches, could have been planted by Lord Dexter, but most of the present trees belong to the post-Dexter era. The furnishings of the house also were undergoing elaboration. Consignments of veneered French furniture were uncrated. The hall and all the rooms were finally filled with gilded clocks that had the same appeal for Lord Dexter as they had for China's last wicked empress. Brocade curtains and fine Turkish carpets were arriving. Upholsterers and decorators were constantly busy. In short, Timothy Dexter was acting more like a parvenu than ever in his life before, but one doubts whether he would have cared if anyone had faced him with this fact. Someone, perhaps the schoolteacher again, advised him to buy paintings, as became a patron of the arts, and there is a story that he commissioned an agent to buy masterpieces abroad. The agent, it is said, made a very tolerable collection, which did not appeal to Dexter because of the antique appearance of the canvases. He turned them in for bright and garish modern works and was badly becozened and bejaped. This story has a somewhat improbable ring (except that Dexter's taste must have been execrable) because Federalist gentry as a rule did not go in for art collections.

The story of the Dexter library sounds much better.

"Clear Nature [he has stated] has been my schoolmaster, nothing borrowed by reading a very little. . . . Good common larning is the best; sum good books is best, well under stood." Nevertheless the rumor persists that he acquired a very fine "gentleman's" library from England, all leather bound, glittering with gold tooling, which guests could do with as they liked. Yet in spite of these appointments, his house manners had not improved. If he was not hard on the books, he was on the furniture and carpets, especially when engaged in writing. "My peopel," he says, "complane of bakker spittel." It was said that Dexter and his son Samuel, and any guests who were present, indiscriminately used the choicest apartments for both literary work and serious drinking, until books strewn on the floor and furniture were mingled with stains of spilled wine. Samuel Knapp may have had adequate reason to raise his eyes to heaven. "This mansion," he tells us, "once the abode of a wise and

elegant man now became a pest house and not unfrequently a bagnio."

There is one aspect of this eccentricity that may be worth pondering. It is curious that so many half-preserved legends should continue to exist about this man, when Newburyport of that period was facing its finest hour, and also a world that was fully as disturbed as our present one, not only torn by ideologies but by anarchy, piracy and war. There were plenty of other pressing events that should have eclipsed the activities of the newcomer on High Street. France was in the throes of abating anarchy and at the same time becoming as military a menace as a subsequent Nazi Germany. At any moment there might be war. The shipping of America was discriminated against by Great Britain and France and subjected to seizures, searches, and sequestrations. The Bey of Algiers was capturing American merchantmen in the Mediterranean and selling their crews into slavery, including many Newburyport sailors. Naval warfare was starting with the French in the West Indies, and Newburyport merchants were subscribing to build the sloop-of-war *Merrimack* to help protect shipping. The vessel was in the actual process of construction when Dexter moved to High Street. Yet in spite of the obstacles thrown in the way of commerce, profits for successful voyages were stupendous. It may have been this easy flow of money that made the extravagances of Dexter a caricature that everyone could enjoy. In fact his extravagance may have afforded a general sort of appeal to his generation that we no longer can wholly appreciate.

The broadening general interest that he was beginning to excite caused the *Impartial Herald* to open its columns to him in an increasingly hospitable manner; and either praise from his genial friends or a feeling of responsibility toward the public at large induced him to set more and more of his thoughts on paper in the form of advice and generalization. He evidently regarded these lucubrations as works of considerable importance during his sojourn at Saint James his park. The belief of his contemporaries that he was egocentrically taking every available opportunity to call himself to public attention, while partially accurate, may need further embroidery. He required an outlet for his pent-up feelings, which was supplied by the local press, and he was genuinely imbued with a growing desire to communicate, a desire caused by his increasing loneliness, and aggravated by senility. He honestly began to believe that his advice and his broad ideas were of real value to his fellow mortals, whom he so confidently salutes in his literature. When he writes, for instance, "Dont brak the

Chane, Renoue brotherly love — Never fade like my box in my garding," there is no doubting his wish to be of service.

His compulsion is a fortunate one for those of us who care to follow the final fantastic phases of his career. The pages of the *Impartial Herald,* from his return to New-buryport to his death, still demonstrate his entertainment value, for each of his contributions is a genuine outburst of feeling. Some reflect drunkenness, some depression, but whatever his mood, whether we find him advertising for sale on easy payment twenty-eight thousand feet, board measure, of yellow pine timber, or whether threatening to sell his Essex-Merrimack Bridge shares because he is short of funds, there is a sort of sparkling vivacity, and the thoughts that ran through his head, while reflecting an overstimulated mind, give a living picture of his character. There are also puzzles here that can never be unraveled, and one is constantly tempted to speculate on the circum-stances that induced him to write such communications as the one we quote below.

> Fellow mortals, why is so much money thrown away on mourning, and tails of women's gowns which drag on the ground about our streets a quarter of a yard. The chance is against us for a war, let us be saving money for it. . . . Fellow mortals think on these things — from your well wisher. T. D.

"By desire," the *Herald* adds, "the spelling in the above was corrected."

He wrote this while he was in the midst of improvements on his place, just a stray thought, casually jotted down.

We can thank this literary loquacity for giving us first-hand news of the misfortunes of poor Nancy Dexter, though we cannot guess exactly why Dexter should have made them public. Poor Nancy had come home from Connecticut. She was back in the palace under her father's protection and threatened with a divorce on ugly statutory grounds. He may have believed that his daughter needed his defense, and that his position demanded that he should make an announcement in the press.

> Lite is come from the East houe many wares my Clothes — swinglers — Abraham bone — a old coleage lant Coffed and all good men say Amen — but stop — as the big Roug is a good felow, go on Devil but dont bite me no more — nor dont beat brouse poure Nancy my dafter — for I am alive as yet.

The wretched situation of Nancy is confirmed by local history. After being expelled from bed and board by her mysterious bull-necked Connecticut intellectual, with his black curly hair, Nancy Dexter's simpering beauty vanished, and subsequently she was never able to pull herself together. It is Dexter who tells his public that her bodily and nervous suffering caused her wits to scatter when "likker" was inside her, and wits had never been her strong point.

> I be leave it [her father tells us] that knows the truth: the bloue he gave her on the side, she had to put plasters on her side neare three years — I be Leave if my father, the presedente knowe the holl trouth of A bs treatment of my dafter, from her mouth, the grat man would shed tears with greafe, and all peopel like wise; shoking is the A fare.

Only a hasty perusal of the files of the *Impartial Herald*
is needed to show that affairs in the Dexter household were
now surpassing the chaos that had existed in the Tracy
mansion. The confusions of the eagle and the cupola, improvements on the grounds, importations of books, French
furniture and *objets d'art* were complicated by the growing irascibilities of Mr. and Mrs. Dexter, the drunken fits of
Samuel, the spells of poor Nancy, and the extensive entertainment of visitors. The advice of Jonathan Plummer or
that of Mr. John P——, being always more mischievously
literary than practical, could have been of no great help,
but luckily Lord Dexter had other sources of assistance. In
the pages of Knapp there are mentions of other astrologers
besides the teacher who were around the house a good deal
and whose prognostications on Dexter's fortunate birth we
have already quoted. Yet they were not always so accurate
in foretelling the future as the ingenious Madam Hooper.
As Dexter's problems increased, this sinister, if entertaining, product of Newburyport appeared with great fre-
quency at Saint James his park.

The truth was Lord Dexter was depending more and
more on his entourage for both advice and diversion. Exactly as mischievous individuals had formerly broken into
the Tracy mansion, stealing bank notes and snuffboxes, so
the youth of Newburyport was now attracted to the spacious grounds, the fine fruit orchards and well-tended vegetable gardens of the High Street estate. When they began
raiding his melon patch, the astrologer on duty could not
find the culprit, but Madam Hooper knew who he was
and even discovered the melons hidden and ready to be sent
to market. However, if she was of occasional comfort in

hours of crisis, she was hardly the sort of person who could direct and run a household. A more practical individual was badly needed now that domestic details were moving beyond Madam Dexter's radius of capability. By coincidence a most capable woman, and no housekeeper either, was in Newburyport, prepared to meet this need.

She was the Lucy Lancaster mentioned earlier; and of all the group whom we find clustering about Lord Dexter, she stands, literally and figuratively, head and shoulders above the rest. "Black Luce" was a Negro woman, of "Patagonian" size, Knapp informs us. She was the daughter of the leader of the colored element in Boston, a man who had been imported to Massachusetts when young and who always said he was the son of an African chief taken in his first battle and sold into slavery. His master believed him, and his own people in Boston treated him with marked respect. On the annual occasion when the Boston Negroes paraded on Boston Common in a manner resembling the rituals still practiced by the Ancient and Honorable Artillery, Lucy's father was first marshal. He always rode the best horse in town and was attended by twelve footmen. Lucy Lancaster was keenly conscious of her lineage. By profession she was what one might call a practical nurse. She was immensely strong, well informed, with high courage and good judgment. It may displease the National Association for the Advancement of Colored People to learn that Lucy would allow no local Negro to enter her house, but this piece of Federalist racism can be excused because of her public-spirited generosity. In a yellow fever epidemic, which caused near panic in Newburyport in 1796, she gained the admiration of the town by her fearless visiting of the sick, as well as by her gentleness and skill. Her services were sought by the first families, and, in fact, she was often called "Lawyer Parsons" after the most respected citizen, Theophilus Parsons.

When there was an illness the Dexters called for her, and as time went on she grew to be almost the head of the ménage, able to settle many family quarrels and to exact implicit obedience from the servants. She could enter the

place at any hour and stay as long as she pleased. She could handle Samuel when attacked by the horrors, and if Nancy wandered off the grounds she was the one who could find her and lead her home. All the family, including Lord Dexter, respected her orders; and when Lucy was on duty she ran the establishment as efficiently as her grandfather had managed his African principality. Her judgment of Lord Dexter, as passed down to us, is the most sensible and unprejudiced estimate extant. Though temperamental, he was not at all a bad man, she said. In many respects he was intelligent, and he was also very honest, always scrupulously careful that workmen on the place were paid according to contract. His fits of temper and his more peculiar acts, she declared, were caused by lack of occupation. When he became nervous and restless, it was wise at all costs to keep him away from liquor, or trouble would ensue. Instead of drink, she advised that efforts should be made to interest him in some new project on the grounds, the garden, the outhouses or the fences. As soon as he could see his workmen improving the place, he would watch them happily in his large tasseled hat, with his cane, accompanied by his pig-like dog.

It is regrettable that the kind and efficient Lucy was not always at the Dexter house to control Dexter and his companions and to keep the "gost," as he now customarily referred to Madam Dexter, in a happy frame of mind. "My old head," Dexter tells us, "has wore out three boddeys." If it is biologically true that all the cells in a human being are replaced by new ones each seven years, he was less than right. But if his body was failing and covered with scars, the gray cells in his cranium were functioning more fantastically than ever, and his restiveness often contrived to destroy his self-control. It was such a condition that caused him to write the following communication to the *Impartial Herald* on July 3, 1798:

> Take Notice, I inform Men, Women, and Children not to trouble me with their pretended friendship in coming to beg my earnings in no shape whatever — nor to get my Fruit, for I have none to give away, and if they steal it they must suffer by the Law. Furthermore I mean to sift all Rogues and Vagabonds in and about Newburyport, for it is not a time to let lazy people live in their idleness: — if

they are poor, let them go to work, or they must be sent to some proper place — France or Guinea.

A well-wisher T. Dexter.

N.B. Please to understand me right — a few good friends that will come to see me or the old lady out of friendship — not for what they can get — my heart is with them — they are welcomed — come with true love with good hearts.

Amen

I don't swear, I affirm, I will not pay any more towards the Ship, as long as you Newburyport folks keep those black thieves on the back of the town, stealing my fence and my neighbors' both winter and summer. I mean to try to sell my House and Horses and Carriages and household Furniture at a moderate price. Payment made easy.

T. Dexter

Thus we perceive that the old maestro was at it again, pulling out of his bag of tricks that moldy threat of selling out and moving on to other fields. He started it on State Street. He repeated it in Chester, and he continued repeating himself in this manner almost to the day of his demise. In fact, we find him resorting to the threat so often that no one could eventually believe it, and perhaps he ceased to believe it himself, because he continued to make expensive and unprofitable improvements on his house and grounds.

At this point in his career, however, this familiar letter met with a gratifying reaction. Instead of the silence that had followed previous proclamations, this one was answered in verse some days later in the *Impartial Herald* by an anonymous writer. The poem is significant enough to quote in full, if only because it is documentary evidence of the impression that Lord Dexter had at last made on the community. Although his finest hour was just beginning, he was already accepted as what we would now call "a character." Since this was evidently what he desired, the following doggerel, which at least shows that Newburyport possessed its own sense of humor, surely made the gouty gentleman in the great white house with green trimmings, gold eagle, gold balls and minarets very proud and pleased.

> Attend, ye miscreants far and near —
> Great Dexter speaks — and all should hear: —
> E'en men and women, girls and Brats,
> Hogs, dogs, and puppies, Cats and Rats —
> Hear what (enraged) I say — and then
> Act like yourselves — or beasts or men!
> No more with canting looks pretend
> To call on me as my great friends
> "To beg my earnings" — justly due
> To Dexter's self, and not to you;
> My fruits, too precious, too refined
> To give away — I'm not so kind.
> And if you dare a cherry steal
> The vengeance of the law you'll feel.
> All rogues that here about resort
> Or lounge in streets of Newburyport
> I mean to sift — that lazy crew
> Should *work,* as I myself was wont to do.
> 'Tis not a time, you may believe,
> For idle folks to idle live
> They all should work or take their chance
> Of voyage to Guinea — or to *France!*
> But please to understand me right

True friends are welcome to my sight.
To them politely I'll display
My house, my plate, etcetera.
Or should they wish my *wife* to see
They're welcome both to her and me.
But then they must not — vile t'endure,
Attend — if motives are not pure —
If all they want is to obtain
Some pittance small from my domain.
But such whose hearts beat to the lay
Of love are welcome night or day.
I do not swear — although I'm mad
"But I affirm" (almost as bad)
That for the Federal Ship, though willing
I will not pay one single shilling
Unless the folks of Newburyport
Will check those blacks who now resort
Back of the town and thence
Make dreadful *havock* of my fence —
My house — my horses neat and trim,
(Fit only for the great Sir Tim)
I mean to sell — *My eagle too!*
And Carriages — I have but two —
My price is mod'rate, 'tis no whim,
For terms, apply to Great Sir Tim.

X V

The Rumor of His Death Was a Gross Exaggeration

FROM THE BEHAVIOR PATTERNS we have placed on exhibition it is obvious that age was advancing rather rapidly on Newburyport's Most Unforgettable Character. Granted that Lord Dexter, still in his middle fifties, was young according to present-day geriatrics, he had led a hard life, physically and emotionally. Mr. Dexter would have been delighted if he could have known that the ingestion of alcohol in moderation is now believed good for vascular difficulties. Even without being apprised of this modern therapy, he had learned by experiment that a drink did him good and that a second or third made him feel still better. Unhappily, he had never been told that smoking was bad for the arteries, nor had he or any other Federalist heard about cholesterol or the dangers arising from excessive ingestion of animal fats. The results of his indulgences were physiologically inevitable. The frustrations of senility hovered in growing numbers about Lord Dexter's head. They warped his character, but amazingly enough he was able to rise above most of them.

He achieved this because of a few gifts that age did

not take from him. He never lost his natural shrewdness. This often returned to him in time to save him from himself. Down to the very end he retained his trader's instinct. It is Mr. Knapp who tells us that Dexter in the last years of his life invested in Ohio lands which would have made a very handsome profit if the executor of his estate had

sold them at the proper time. Jonathan Plummer and John P—— and Madam Hooper might fool their rich client some of the time, but not all of the time. Also, neither age nor gout succeeded in slowing down our subject's imagination. The habit of being a Yankee hustler, so prevalent in his early life, did not desert him. There was no languor in his later days, none of the conventional lassitude that supposedly decorates the twilight years.

The final Dexterian trait that was never extinguished was his inordinate suggestibility that made him clay for any potter's wheel. In his incarnation as a man of wealth, he listened to all advice with the same credulous avidity

that he had in his days of speculation. If he had not listened
to advice, he would never have heard of astrology or of a
poet laureate. He was open to the influence of greater
minds, and it must have been some other mind than his
that conceived the idea of musicians playing in the cupola
beneath the eagle, but it may have been his own thinking
that made him, about this time, become preoccupied with
his approaching demise.

The first printed evidence informing us that Lord Dexter had built a tomb for himself on the grounds of his
estate appears in an advertisement inserted in the *Impartial Herald* and set up in the printer's own formal style.
It is another announcement informing the public that
Lord Dexter's house is up for sale, including furnishings,
plate, horses and carriages, all to be offered on easy terms.
But in it is this attention-arresting sentence:

> In one of the banks of the garden is an elegant new
> Tomb, on the top of which is erected the Temple of Reason,
> twelve feet square, eleven feet high, with a hundred and
> fifty-eight squares of glass in it.

This is the most explicit description of this latest project
of Lord Dexter's that now exists. A century of Newburyport rumor and also the Newburyport Board of Health
have done much to obliterate the outlines of the tomb and
to confuse the activities that surround it. The local authorities did not permit Lord Dexter to be buried in this mauso-
leum, and some subsequent owner of the property has done
away with both the tomb and temple. I once spent some
time on the Dexter grounds trying to find some trace of the
structure, but nothing, as far as I could discover, remains,

not even an indentation in the ground. In the advertisement its location is placed in one of the banks of the garden. Dexter's own description of its whereabouts is more indefinite. He says it is in the garden at the edge of the grass. But if the puzzle of the tomb can no longer be solved, one can still hazard a guess. There still exists a terrace to the left of the house as one faces it from High Street. It is the only logical location on the grounds for a commodious tomb, and if this actually was the site, the monument with the Temple of Reason, standing near the house and a little to the rear, would have been highly conspicuous.

In the year 1799 a large part of Lord Dexter's attention was centered on the construction of this last resting-place. His thoughts, it is said, were diverted to this project when one of his admirers pointed out to him that many great men had constructed their own tombs and mausoleums. On the other hand, Dexter may have conceived the idea of the tomb himself as other eccentrics have before and since. But the Temple of Reason on top of the tomb could only have been the suggestion of a friend.

Lord Dexter also gave exhaustive thought to his coffin, and the National Casket Company, had it existed then,

would have applauded his conclusion that the conventional
pine box of the period was not suitable. The coffin was made
by a local cabinetmaker out of selected mahogany. Lord
Dexter called at the shop frequently to oversee the work,
and when it was completed came himself with a man and a
wheelbarrow and saw his coffin safely home to High Street.
It is like him to take the public into his confidence and to
give us a description of these premature funeral arrangements.

Incidentally, before quoting Dexter's own words, this
may be a proper place also to quote an apologia by the
Newburyport *Impartial Herald* regarding the Dexter writings:

> Among all other newspaper correspondents lord Dexter
> is not the least to be read — if he is not the most perspicuous
> in his observations and profound in his remarks, he most
> certainly "makes the most fun" although it is some times
> difficult to determine what he would be at; however, one
> thing generally prepossesses the printer in favor of his con-
> tributions, — they are accompanied with substantial reason
> why they should appear, much like our advertisements.

No doubt the editor was also paid for this offering.

Nobel trimmings [Lord Tim tells us], uncommon Lock, so that I can take the kee inside and have fier works in the toume, pipes & tobaker & a speaking trumpet, and a bibel to read and sum good songs.

If it is hard to decide in this passage where the coffin ends and the tomb begins, legend informs us that Lord Dexter

rested often in his coffin and frequently took cat naps in his tomb, which was a cool, comfortable place in summer. Here is his most explicit announcement, stating once again that the house was up for sale, tomb and all, and attention is called to an uncompleted postscript that attests to one of Dexter's most peculiar acts:

Here will lie in this box the first Lord in Americake the first Lord Dexter made by the voice of hamsher state my brave fellows Affirmed it . . . fourder I have A grand toume in my garding at one of the gras sees and the tempel of Reason over the toume and my coffen made and all Readey In my hous panted with whit Lead in side and out side tuched with greane with brass trimmings Eight handels & a good Lock I have had one mock founrel it was so solmon and there was very much criing about three thousand spectators I say my hous is Eaquel to any mansion hous in twelve

hundred miles and now for Sale for seven hundred pounds
weight of dollars by me

TIMOTHY DEXTER

the A bove mock founel the grand pall holders or barers
Nams Lord East Lord West Lord North Lord South Lord
megul (Mogul) Lord Shambow the minister made the
prayer was Doctor Strong, thos saxtons — flimsee ones —
are (unavoidably omitted).[1]

The last two words add themselves to the Dexter riddle.
Did Dexter get tired and drop his pen, or did the printer
get tired, or was the remainder blasphemous? Enough, at
least, is left to establish a foundation of truth to the rumors
that still surround this unique event. Newburyport may be
full of newcomers, many of whom gaze upon the glories
of its past with indifference, but hardly a native who was
brought up there will not be glad to tell you of Lord Dexter's funeral rehearsal, whether or not you want to hear it,
and each version will be slightly different. For instance, in
Dexter's briefly adopted town of Chester a descendant of
the boys of Hampshire State told me last year that Mr.
Dexter kept his coffin in the hall of his house in Chester,
with an effigy of himself resting within it and that he beat
Mrs. Dexter for not weeping when she first saw this work
of art. This only goes to show how readily and eagerly facts
can be distorted. Mrs. Dexter was not beaten for this cause
in Chester, and if at all, it was in Newburyport. Also, if
Lord Dexter ever did lay a cane across her shoulders he very
likely received as good as he gave, in view of his own com-
plaints about the ghost. The only excuse for this digression
is to show that the shock of Dexter's mock funeral has not

[1] Printer's note.

subsided yet. As long as so much has been said, so long and so inaccurately, regarding this piece of horseplay at the Dexter mansion, it may not be out of place to attempt a narrative based on what we know of the scene and the facts.

The best time for an outdoor mock funeral in Newburyport would be when spirits would be high enough to cope with it. This would call for a sunny day, beyond the middle of June. Let us select this date arbitrarily and add that the time is past noon. The scent of early verdure from trees, lawns and herbaceous borders was still fresh with the final unfoldings of a New England spring, and nothing as yet was weary from the heat of summer. There was a peace past all understanding on High Street then — no trucks, no motors, no stench of gasoline exhaust. Yet despite the bright sunshine Lord Dexter's house was a place of mourning. Crepe enfolded the knocker of the great front door. Crowds were gathered on the street, peering through the palings of the handsome new fence, or wandering about the grounds to examine the new box borders of the formal garden and to gape at the gilt globes, at Mr. Wilson's eagle, or at the green trimmings of the house that now gave it a harlequin quality of which the mansion's former owner would not have approved.

The grounds were open to the public, and there was automatic hospitality in a house of mourning. There was rum punch in the dining room and funeral delicacies, and more rum and ale for visitors outside. Everyone as a matter of course eventually filed through the great front hall to view the effigy of Lord Dexter resting in his coffin ready for his tomb. The chief mourners, when they were not refreshing themselves, stood by the remains. Lord North was of course the unpopular prime minister of George III, and obviously Lords South, East and West were derived from him. Lord Shambow had stove blacking on his face or was a faithful colored retainer, and Lord Mogul wore a turban.

The musicians who had played in the cupola performed the funeral march. The coffin, attended by the lords and other mourners, was carried out the rear door toward the tomb, where an excellent crowd had gathered; but hardly three thousand, as Lord Dexter has stated, since the population of Newburyport was then not much over six. In spite of his not being mentioned, we can guess who delivered the funeral eulogy — Jonathan Plummer, of course. It is said that he was an excellent and moving speaker. In fact, in later years when some professional elocutionists visiting Newburyport heard Jonathan Plummer declaim, they said that he would have been one of the best if he had not used the nasally whining dramatics that he had picked up in his youth from an echelon of the clergy. When he extolled the virtues and generosities of his patron, Lord Dexter, there is no doubt at all that great numbers of the crowd groaned and wept because of mass hysteria, plus an undue consumption of liquor. The prayer by Dr. Strong, assisted by the flimsy sextons, may have been carrying things too far for such an occasion, but tears still flowed.

It would not have been proper, of course, for Lord Dexter to mingle with the crowd when the tomb doors beneath the Temple of Reason were finally closed. Instead, to keep the dramatic proprieties, he witnessed the scene from an upper window of the mansion, and was so deeply moved by the manifestations of grief that he could not refrain from weeping himself. When Mrs. Dexter, who was with him, did not follow his example, it is said he beat her.[2] This hearsay is only a fillip that beautifies a myth. It became a tale to be told and retold by children who were present, who were to live on past the middle of the nineteenth century. It was a day that was remembered long after Lords North, South, East and West, not to mention Shambow and the Mogul, had passed to their rewards. It is a pity that the first Lord of America was not allowed to lie in his tomb as he desired. Instead he accompanied greater men than he to the Old Hill Burying Ground near Bartlett's Mall, where the slope below the cemetery is now adorned with a caption in white stones, "Welcome to Newburyport."

"I must say something," we find Dexter writing in what can generously be termed an apology for his life, "or I should say Nothing — therefore make sum Noise in the world." This may explain why he consented to the horrid parody of a solemn event, but one must look further to understand why Newburyport, with its deep religious conventions, tolerated the travesty of his mock funeral. The explanation must lie partly in the differences between the "whiners" and the "grunters" and the more worldly merchant class, with its new manners and sophistications. Also, a special sort of tolerance always exists in a seaport town. Newburyport may have been devoid of "canaille," but its ship captains, its sailors and its *émigrés* from France and

---

[2] Another version of the mock funeral states that invitations were sent to leading citizens to attend the obsequies and that many came genuinely believing that Lord Dexter had passed away. This same version indicates that Lord Dexter was in the kitchen when he beat his wife and subsequently appeared in the dining room to partake of his funeral feast.

Guadeloupe were inured to much worse spectacles than a jolly pageant.

But the real reason for local patience, finally, must be attributed to Dexter himself. As Lucy Lancaster has testified, he was not a bad man when he was not drunk or ill. Normally he was good-natured and glad to be amused. Also he had one virtue always appreciated in a commercial community — he paid his debts promptly and never welshed on a bad bargain. An anecdote still exists concerning his keen anxiety to pay. Once when there was illness in the household a minister was summoned who refused to take a fee for his parochial services. The refusal so infuriated Dexter that he forced the money on the divine by pointing a horse pistol at him. The habit of rushing for a firearm grew on him in his later years.

His position, as he has reminded us, placed a variety of social obligations on him, and he made no effort to conceal the truth that he was well-to-do. He was a constant target for begging and for charity when he appeared on the public street or on his own grounds. It is said that his gifts brought him no respect, but they did create an aura of good will. We would surely have heard if Lord Dexter had been niggardly or tight-fisted or if a hungry individual could not get a meal at the Dexter kitchen or a silver piece from the gentleman himself when visible. Newburyporters of that distant day did not shoot Santa Claus any more than they do at present. When he was in a happy mood he would give away fruit and flowers, even to the nymphs, without asking for a *quid pro quo*.

Yesterday [the *Impartial Herald* announces only a few months after the trial burial] a valuable bell, "The gift of

Timothy Dexter Esq., to the 2nd Presbyterian Society of Newburyport," was fixed in the steeple of the house of worship of that Society. The liberality and public spirit of the donor in this and many other instances reflect much honor on him. His generosity has been directed by a discriminating judgment. It may hereafter become proverbial to say "generous as DEXTER."

The irony in the paragraph is not wholly ill-natured. His desire to have his name attached to his gifts is not unusual, as any harassed fund-raiser will agree. The fact still remains that Dexter was by way of being a public benefactor. Until the edifice burned, a memorandum hung in Saint Paul's Church stating that Mr. Dexter had given that religious body a sum of one hundred pounds toward the improvement of the building. He also made an offer to the town, similar to the one he had made to Chester, to pave High Street, which was then in a deplorable condition, if it were named Dexter Street. When the offer was refused he filled, at his own expense, a large hollow in the same street near his house. In other words, he was not the person that one would want to run out of any town. In fact he had already done more for his town than many of its solider citizens. And now he was to perform a unique and imaginative feat that was to link his name indelibly with Newburyport, and in a smaller way with the ephemeral historical period in which he lived

It is quite possible that parts of the Dexter fantasy may have seemed almost pedestrian to his contemporaries. No doubt much of what we consider impossible in that past was once readily accepted before its whole way of life was erased. Change has seldom been so violent as it is today, and life patterns in Newburyport have so completely changed in the past fifty years as to render any decade previous to World War II incredible.

By way of illustration I venture to offer a further piece of personal reminiscence of a rather ordinary nature which now assumes an almost neolithic shape.

In the winter of 1910 when my mother and I were visiting my aunts in their country house outside of Newburyport, my mother took an early morning train to Boston. She was driven by my aunts' hired man, Walter Grant, to the Haverhill-Newburyport trolley line, which then ran into Newburyport along Storey Avenue and High Street. She took the Newburyport car at the trolley turn-out about a mile away from home at a point opposite the old fair grounds, in a region once known as the Plains, because of the level and somewhat barren aspect of that part of Newburyport's countryside. It was snowing hard when she left that morning. There was also a previous fall of snow, but the roads had been plowed a day or two before, and thus there seemed very little chance of being snowed in that day. My mother would return on the trolley that would reach the Plains at seven o'clock that evening, and since Walter Grant only worked by the day I said that I would hitch up the horse and meet her, an ordinary enough procedure. I had recently turned seventeen, but I was not even especially impressed by the responsibility. I had also told Walter Grant that I would milk the two cows if he wished to go home early.

The barn in back of my aunts' house had been built in 1902, after the old one had burned down. Thus it was only eight years old that winter evening, a modern functional structure as unremarkable as a two-car garage might be at present. It housed two cows and a heifer, since there was no regular milk delivery so far out of town. In another section was the carriage horse named Pete, standing in a straight stall near the chutes for oats and bran that were stored upstairs in bins beside the hayloft. There was also a harness room, redolent of polished leather, heated by a small coal stove, and finally the carriage room with a buggy, a two-seated buckboard and a light sleigh known as a cutter and a heavier one called a pung. There were, incidentally, three pigs in the barn cellar. Pete the horse, patient, coarse-bred and lazy, was our only means of locomotion.

It had been snowing hard all day, and by late afternoon the wind had begun to blow hard from the northeast, indicating stormy weather and more snow. I can still remember the order and comfort of the barn when I went in there to harness Pete — carrying a kerosene lantern, for of course there was no electricity. I can also remember the steamy atmosphere and the odor of manure and the stirrings of the dozing animals.

Due to millennia of close association there existed in those days a tolerance and understanding between a utility horse and man that is now rapidly disappearing, a very different relationship from the one that now exists in a hunting or racing stable. Pete made no objection to being backed out of his stall or to being harnessed except to shake his head suspiciously at the bit until he found it was warm, and he did walk with unnecessary deliberation into the carriage room. He understood that he was useful and, in consequence, required respect. He was even helpful about backing between the shafts of the pung. I brought out a moth-eaten buffalo robe and the heaviest horseblanket. When I opened the barn door, it made a hollow, solemn sound which one seldom hears today. The horse and sleigh stood quietly in the driving snow while I closed the door again and tied the lantern to the dash. Its warm light shone on the barn for a moment, making it a part of a Currier and Ives winter scene. Nothing seemed more permanent or part of that present than the barn. It is curious to recall a visit I paid to the old barn last autumn. Part of its foundation had sagged and some of its sill had rotted. The building was deserted except for some rusted screens, broken storm windows and a ghostly buggy and a sleigh. It no longer served any useful purpose whatsoever. It was not worth the cost of renewing its sill or its foundation; it was as useless as a commercial sailing vessel.

The snow had drifted and it was deeper than I had thought. The snowfall was also turning into sleet, so that the horse's plodding steps and the sleigh runners began to make a crackling, tearing sound. We reached the Plains ten minutes before the trolley's estimated time of arrival. The wind was blowing harder there, and the sleet was painful. I put the blanket over Pete and turned his rear to the wind. Across the road the fence, barns and exhibition halls of the old fairgrounds were still standing, but I believe the fair itself — or "the cattle show" as my great-aunt called it — had been discontinued several years before. I could think, as I waited for the trolley, of how much the fair had taught me about the world for which I was beginning to be trained. I had seen my first balloon ascension there. The balloonist had hung by his knees from a trapeze and had drunk a bottle of tonic water upside down. I had seen my first harness race there; I had once won a canary bird for fifteen cents on a Wheel of Fortune. I had also seen my first shell game and had my first glimpse of three-card monte behind the trotting stables. These activities had moved elsewhere, but the buildings still remained dark against the snow.

The trolley was half an hour late and the going was harder getting home than going out. On several occasions, my mother took the reins while I walked ahead of Pete with the lantern to pick out the road, which was becoming obliterated by the drifts. We arrived back safely, but we were snowed in by morning. Pete and I were equally pleased to be back in the barn again. He stood happily relaxed while I rubbed him down and put a dry blanket on him and gave him an extra measure of oats.

The one reason for describing this pedestrian and everyday incident is that nearly every aspect of it has disappeared forever. Pete and the sleigh and the buffalo robe are gone, and so too is the rural electric car line. The very ground occupied by that ancient institution, the cattle show, has vanished. An underpass, a throughway and a cloverleaf have taken its place. It is hard even for me, who was once a part of that scene, to realize now that any of it once had use or form or substance.

By the same token, Lord Timothy Dexter may have been a rather ordinary figure in his time. Pronounced character divergences may have been more common then.

"I Wants to Make My Enemys Grin"

THE MEMORY OF Lord Dexter and his works would not be so vivid as it is if a publisher had not been so enterprising as to bring out an engraving of Lord Dexter's house and grounds in 1810, four years after the owner's demise. This aquatint has always been a treasured item in Newburyport and among other collectors of Americana. Luckily for the Dexter legend, but also because curiosity regarding the late citizen was already becoming intense, a lithographic copy was published between 1838 and 1850. This lithograph had a still wider distribution. Thirty years ago it hung in the hallways of many High Street houses and could be obtained with reasonable promptness at local and Boston antique shops. I was startled the other day to learn from Mr. Goodspeed, Boston's dealer in old books and Americana, that the lithograph, like the aquatint, has almost disappeared from the market. It is a tribute to the bizarre qualities of Lord Dexter's mind that this should be the case, and also to the other-worldness of the picture itself.

The print is a detailed elevation of the house and grounds of the Dexter property as they existed in His Lordship's lifetime. The scene is very different from any descriptions

A View of the mansion of the Late Lord Timothy Dexter. Newburyport 1810

that have been attempted hitherto in this book. For, commencing with the year 1801, Timothy Dexter translated his estate from a residential property into a great outdoor museum, fraught with confused symbolic significance. This all becomes apparent from an examination of the print, and here a magnifying glass is helpful, for a close scrutiny is rewarding. One can see that the formal picket fence of the Jackson era has been altered so that it sweeps in a wide arc of welcome almost to the mansion's front door. A high arch has been erected before this door, on which stand the three figures of the Presidents of the United States: General Washington in the center, flanked by Messrs. Adams and Jefferson. There are other arches to

right and left, that support figures of lions and soldiers.
Then among these main decorations, rising above small
trees and shrubbery, appear a profusion of tall columns,
each one a base for some other figure, here an Indian, there
a goddess or a famous statesman. These figures, you will
notice, are grouped more or less symmetrically about the
house and cover the spacious grounds to its rear, until they
are lost in the dimness of perspective. The house itself looks
much as we have already described it, with its cupola and
its eagle and ornamental balustrade and spheres. The windows of its first and second stories, though in the print,
look higher and narrower than the windows extant in the
house today. Mr. Howells, in *The Architectural Heritage*

of the Merrimack, advances the theory that the tall windows were not a Dexterian alteration but a piece of artistic
license. Though composition affords a good excuse for this
inaccuracy, this appears to be almost the only error existing
in this realistic picture, and we can forgive the artist, since
the house is only a background for the figures, not com-
plemented but submerged by their numbers.

High Street in the foreground presents a scene characteristic of that pastoral epoch. A horseman, a farmer with a
yoke of oxen, a few pedestrians, as well as the occupants
of a two-wheeled carriage, are all staring at the display.
And we may be permitted to gape ourselves after a space
of a hundred and fifty years and wonder whether this
grotesquerie ever existed in actual fact. There is no doubt
that it did, because the picture is confirmed by documentary evidence.

In the year 1801, approximately two years after the construction of his tomb and Temple of Reason, Mr. Dexter
evolved, assuredly with the help of a handful of his better-
educated admirers, a plan for constructing for the benefit
of the world at large a museum containing the life-sized
figures of men and women famous in mythology and history. This was a tall order, but it was a challenge that fitted
perfectly Dexter's temperament. We can see it as the projection of his old drive for recognition, a parallel of the
lion, the coach with the cream-colored horses, the crowning
of the poet laureate, and the funeral; but here there is an
ambition that outstrips previous concepts; and the result
was something more than notorious. Dexter once said of
himself that he was as active as those darning needles that
were forever flying back and forth over his garden. Cer-

tainly the museum was a very unstable project, the design and purpose of which changed from week to week, whenever a new idea was supplied him by Mr. Plummer, by the schoolmaster, or by Madam Hooper or Lord East or West.

Several of Lord Dexter's more thoughtful contemporaries, in reviewing this supreme piece of exhibitionism, have held it as the final proof of a mental disorder. They point to what is obvious — the extravagance, and the intellectual confusion. It is difficult not to agree that Mr. Dexter was very confused, but, as in the matter of the warming pans and the mittens, there is unexpected lucidity in his actions. It can be that his plan was part of a commercial scheme. It has been mentioned that he was a heavy investor in that modern project, the Essex-Merrimack toll bridge. The bridge was doing well, but the Newburyport, the Salisbury, the Carr's Island and the Amesbury ferries were still competing. Dexter, in his anxiety to improve High Street, displayed an intense desire to get more traffic moving along this thoroughfare, which was the way to his Essex-Merrimack Bridge. If he could make his house and grounds a wonder that would attract travelers journeying north, it would increase bridge tolls and defray the expenses of his decorations. He always possessed, in his most depressed moments, the instincts of a showman. P. T. Barnum would have understood him, because they both shared the desire to create the Greatest Show on Earth.

In the year 1801, only five years before his death, this bedeviled man (whose thoughts in reality often turned to the devil) was in greater need of diversion than ever before in his career. His quarrels with Madam Dexter were more violent. We have alluded to a document written by him in

1805 mentioning a contract drawn up by Theophilus Parsons, in which Madam Dexter seemingly agreed to quit the State in payment of four hundredweight of silver. The details are not clear, but Dexter late in his life complained of his marriage and said he was seeking a rich widow. Samuel Dexter had become more threatening in his demands for money. Nancy's wits were not improving, nor were Mr. Dexter's own nerves.

There is evidence that Dexter originally intended the figures about his house and grounds to be carved in marble, and the projected collection of famous persons would no doubt have truly been in marble except, as Dexter admits, he found he did not have the cash for work done in this medium. Instead he turned to the young man who was to become his most willing collaborator. We have already met him — Joseph Wilson, the ship's carver, who did the eagle weathervane. The day of embellishment on ships was far from over, and the Merrimack Valley was one of the leading, if not the largest, shipbuilding centers in the country. Wilson was outstanding in his profession, and his work for Lord Dexter, though now almost entirely obliterated, is still a tribute to his artistic skill and ingenuity. There are echoes of His Lordship's conversations and arguments with this carver of figureheads, who was more artist than artisan. Wilson must have been a student of history, too, to have executed such a collection of characters and animals. His work, Mr. Dexter says, was much liked "by our great men." One day while the carver was working on the place, Mr. Dexter confides to us that, feeling funny, he thought he would ask the young man where he was born. Mr. Wilson replied with a remark, difficult to interpret in the Dexter text, to the effect that he was born in no town but on the water. "I says you beat me," Dexter tells us, "and so wee lafed and it shuck of the spleane. . . . I shold had all marbel if any bodey could to me the prise so I have sent for 8 busts for kings and grat men and 1 Lion & 2 gray hounds I hope to hear in foue Days. . . ."

The price must have been beyond his means, because he stuck to Wilson, but the transition from marble to wood did not diminish the scope of the undertaking.

The impulses that made him move forward with the museum were varied. We have discussed the profit motive. There is another one more dominant — the human desire to stun people who misunderstood him or disliked him, by the sheer weight of his achievement. This theme is implicit in *A Pickle for the Knowing Ones,* if it possesses a theme at all, and his preoccupation with the great museum forms some of the work's best passages.

> I wants [he writes] to make my Enemys grin, in time, Like a Cat over A hot pudding, and goe away, and hang there heads Down Like a Dogg bin After sheep.

It is conceivable that before the idea of heaping rebuke on his enemies struck him, he had not thought of such an extensive operation. In his earliest announcement to the press of his plan he lists only a limited number of carvings, although these show a variety great enough for the *Impartial Herald* to give it a prominent position. At first the wooden personages were to be as follows:

> The 3 presidents, Doctor Franklin John hen Cock, and Mr. hamelton and Rouffous king and John Jea — 2 grenadars on the top of the hous, 4 Lions below; 1 Eagel *is* on

the Coupulow, one Lamb to lay down with one of the Lions
— one younecorne, one Dogg, Addam and Eave in the
Garden — one horse. The houll is not concluded as yet —
Dexter's Mouseum.

This item aroused public interest and also caused some
confusion as to exactly what it was Lord Dexter intended
to do. The public did not understand until later that the
figures were not a piece of disjointed fantasy. They learned
only in subsequent explanations that the lion and the lamb
were to symbolize international accord and that the three
Presidents were to stand upon an arch. At the moment the
patron was thinking out loud and was not yet committed
to any fixed idea. Thus a few days after, he was obliged to
set the public right by a notice, suitably italicized.

> Squire Dexter has intimated he did not intend the para-
> graph in our paper respecting his Museum for publication
> — he had not actually determined on all the subjects men-
> tioned, but he says "I *will* have George Washington, John
> Adams, Thomas Jefferson, Benjamin Franklin, John Han-
> cock, and John Jay, and after all above mentioned is fin-
> ished *I will if I please*, have Adam and Eve in my garden."

Finally the word seeped out that the project was to be a
museum dedicated to the memory of the Father of His
Country, George Washington, lately deceased, and the ex-
hibit was further intended to show a respect for all great
characters, ancient or modern; and also, Dexter set a time
limit on it.

> I will shoue the world one of the Grate Wonders of the
> world, in 15 months, if No man murders me in Dors or out
> of Dors. . . . Forder, hear me good Lord, I am going to
> Let our shildren know — Now to see, good Lord, what has

bin in the world grate wase back, to our own forefathers,
Not old Plimeth, but stop — to Addom & Eave — to sho
45 figers, two leged and fore leged, becos we cant doue well
without fore Leged; in the first plase they are our fude.

If these excerpts seem bewildering to a hasty reader, the
complete prospectus appearing at intervals in *A Pickle for
the Knowing Ones* is still more so. There were to be four
lions to defend the great and mighty men, a lion for each
point of the compass. The general plan was also to illustrate
the unity of nations and the concord of the earth. There
were also to be a series of opposing abstractions — good and
evil, peace and war, love and hate, and the devil himself
was to have his place in this three-dimensional pandemonium, including his cloven hoof, but he was to be so nicely
concealed that he would not frighten inquisitive women.

Gossip in Newburyport could not encompass what Dexter intended; but by the end of October 1801 the general
plan was so close to approaching crystallization that its
author evidently felt that the time had arrived for a full-
dress, carefully balanced announcement. In order to make
things completely clear, he called on his schoolmaster or his
poet or his printer to help him with the composition. The
result is an elegant journalistic announcement which is the
completest prospectus we have of the museum, overambi-
tious but still not a bad forecast of the final result.

Timothy Dexter, Esq., of Newburyport, is now erecting
a museum which will (when completed) exceed in elegance
and grandeur anything of the kind in the United States to
consist of the following marble Figures viz:

Adam and Eve in their fig leaf dresses of the present white
marble and finished in the highest style. Noah, dressed in

the style and fashion of Antediluvian time. Abraham and
Sarah, Abraham in a patriarchal style; Sarah represented as
a very handsome woman, dressed in an elegant dress suitable to the times she lived in. Joseph, his head, hands, etc.
of white marble, his drapery of the most beautiful varie-
gated marble that can be purchased. Moses, the leader of
the Israelites from Egypt to the land of Canaan, represented
as a youth in a Shepherd's dress with a sling in his hand.
Solomon represented as a young monarch dressed in the most
superb and magnificent eastern style with his crown, scep-
tre, and the other insignia of his station. Hirum represented as an elderly monarch arrayed with all the habili-
ments of masonry and majesty. The goddess Venus of the
finest white marble, polished and finished in the highest
style. Three of the apostles viz — St. Paul, St. John and St.
Peter. The immortal Washington, father and savior of his
country, represented in Complete American uniform, with
his hat on, leaning the right hand upon the hilt of his sword,
with the point upon the ground, his left hand resting upon
his hip. John Adams, late worthy president of the United
States, represented standing in an easy graceful posture
with his face looking a little to the left. Thomas Jefferson
the present President of the United States represented in a
similar posture to John Adams, except his face looking a
little to the right.

(The Presidents stand upon a platform, supported by
two Corinthian Columns with an arch sprung from each
column under the entablature upon which they stand.)

Dr. Benjamin Franklin, the Philosopher and Statesman.
John Haveloch, late governing Massachusetts. John Jay,
late minister to the Court of Great Britain. Doctor Dwight,
president of Yale College. Aaron Burr, vice president of the
United States. Caleb Strong, governor of Massachusetts.

John J. Gilman, governor of New Hampshire. Rufus King, minister plenipotentiary to the Court of St. James. Jonathan Jackson, Esq.; the great Indian Chief Cornplanter, represented in complete Indian dress with his Bow, Arrows, Tomahawk, moccasins, etc. Toussaint L'Ouverture, governor of St. Domingo. George III, King of Great Britain. The late William Pitt, Earl of Chatham. Lord Nelson Baron of the Nile, etc. Louis XVI, late king of France. Bonaparte, first Consul of France. Charles IV, king of Spain. Alexander I, Emperor of Russia. The king of Sweden. The king of Denmark. The king of Prussia. The Emperor of Germany. The grand signior of Constantinople. The Emperor of China, the great Mogul.

The above figures are to be as large as life, each standing upon a block of marble 2 feet square and 6 inches thick. One marble lion standing with his fore and hind feet upon two blocks of marble.

Two handsome English grayhounds of gray marble. Two Boys of white marble 3½ feet in height standing upon suitable marble blocks.

It was still marble, not yet ready to be turned into wood for purposes of economy. It would be impossible, I am afraid, for an analyst to derive from this catalogue of beasts, men and goddesses any subconscious symbolism that could throw light on the Dexter psyche, because Lord Dexter never wrote the piece. He may have possessed a veto power, but his desire for the greatest show on earth had pushed him to an intellectual level with which he was not familiar. And yet one may draw a few significant deductions from this communication. One is that whoever wrote it must have had a good time doing so, because it betrays

a tongue-in-the-cheek mischief more kindly than malicious. Its author was a man of the world with cosmopolitan
tastes above those of Plummer. An impressive sidelight is
cast upon this Newburyport society which could produce
a person so well read or traveled. Federalist Newburyport
was full of travelers then, in that period which saw American merchant shipping in nearly every port in the world.
Our author was not only well educated but he may have
been to Italy, where he saw at first hand some of the statues
of the later Roman Empire, with their togas of porphyry
and green and yellow marbles.

There is one other fact worthy of attention. President
Dwight of Yale College appears in the list of great men
under consideration. He could only have been included on
the insistence of Mr. Dexter, who did not offer a similar
tribute to the president of Harvard. In spite of Nancy's
disastrous marriage and her tragic years in New Haven,
Dexter remained a Yale enthusiast, with a respect for
learned men. In the midst of his most violent diatribe
against his educated son-in-law, he pauses to interject the
charitable statement that after all he was a good fellow.
During Nancy's earlier nuptial days, he paid the young
couple what must have been a successful visit. He attended
a Yale commencement, where he saw President Dwight at
a distance, if he did not encounter him personally.

The scribe of our High Street patron (our fun-loving
schoolmaster or some genteelly crammed law clerk or supercargo) did not desert his aging amateur when marble
changed to wood, and when the statues turned to images
and when the versatile Wilson appeared with his carving
tools.

The autumn of 1801 was approaching, and with it another New England winter. The time was near when shipwrights moved indoors from the yards to make the paneling, the mantels, the moldings and cornices of the houses of Newburyport. In the slack days of winter Joseph Wilson could only have been pleased by the commission; but also he could not help falling in love with the project and sharing his patron's enthusiasm. Scant though it may be, there is enough of the Dexter commission extant to prove it. There is the eagle so often mentioned. There is the statue of William Pitt, comical and full of life, after nearly all the misfortunes that could befall a figure except extinction by fire or loss at sea or dismemberment by vandals. There is also a single arm, now preserved by the Newburyport Historical Society, the oversized member of an heroic figure, which may have belonged to one of the three Presidents on the central arch. The wooden lacework at the wrist is intricately elegant. Only a man who was both amused by his problem and proud of his achievement could possibly have done such carvings. He had the added advantage of the assistance, when needed, of the best painters and carpenters in America. There will never again be such artisans in Newburyport.

"money," Dexter tells his public, "wont gitt thos figers so fast as I wish."

Obviously the work could not all have been completed within the fifteen months' time limit that was set. In fact the project was never finished and kept undergoing changes throughout the life of the director. Yet long before the fifteen months were up extraordinary sights revealed themselves on High Street. In front of the mansion appeared thirteen pillars, one for each state of the union. A "Royal Arch" seventeen feet in height arose before the front door, surmounted, according to promise, by our first three Presidents. We still can feel the contagion of the Dexter enthusiasm, for, besides overseeing the museum, Dexter was simultaneously engaged in serious writing.

> To mankind at large [he wrote in his mansion with his golden pen], the time is come at last, the grate day of Regoising. What is that? Why I will tell you; Those three Kings is Raised, on the first Royal Arch in the World — almost not quite; but very hie up — or so they are a good mark to be scene; so the womans Like to see the frount, & all peopel loves to see them; and the Quakers will Com & peape slyly & feele glad & say, houe thee doue, frind . . . the God of Nater has done very much for our present king; they are all very good. I want them to live forever, and I be leave they will.

He was disturbed to discover that the figures were finished in blank white, conceivably in an attempt to imitate marble. Their pallor was neither suitable nor agreeable to his taste, but the services of a painter familiar with ships' figureheads were immediately available. In no time this decorator was up on the arch busy with his paints. The figure of Thomas Jefferson had been carved holding in one hand a scroll. Dexter's unknown adviser must have been away, or else the patron might not have made the error of asserting that Mr. Jefferson was holding the Constitution of the United States, which Dexter stated Mr. Jefferson had written. The painter said that Mr. Jefferson was the author of the Declaration of Independence, and this was what should be lettered on the scroll. And the painter started, stubbornly, on the lettering without taking into account the Dexter temper. He only had time to paint DEC before his employer rushed into the house for his pistol, which he discharged upward toward the arch. In consequence, for nearly the next half century Jefferson stood before the mansion grasping the Constitution — not the Declaration of Independence.

There is no record of exactly how many figures were placed in the Dexter garden, and no one can give names to all of them. The lithograph of the Dexter place affords the best key, but its list is not complete. Our other authority is Mr. Knapp, who saw the figures as a boy and whose book was written while the three presidents still occupied their arch. Knapp places the number of figures at "upwards of forty," enough to make a compact crowd in spite of the mansion's wide street frontage. They were all brightly painted and gilded, making a spectacle whose garishness has lingered in many memories. There were some exceptionally fine individual pieces, Knapp recalls.

The best of the lot, in his recollection, were four lions, two couchant and two passant, which attracted more notice from persons of taste than all the rest of the exhibition except the Presidential arch. The lions were open-mouthed and fierce. We can wonder where Wilson found the models and whether Dexter thought of his State Street lion when he ordered them. This overwhelming number of images received careful maintenance. With the exception of the Presidents and the guardian lions, they do not seem to have been arranged in any planned historic or logical order. Indian chiefs, philosophers and generals, scholars and politicians rubbed shoulders with goddesses of fame and reason and representations of maternal piety. Furthermore their names were often painted out and new ones substituted at the whim of their owner, who took great pleasure in wandering among the columns. One of his favorites was Napoleon Bonaparte, the only member of his wooden company to whom Lord Dexter invariably touched his hat. It it hard to understand why contemporary descriptions of this show are so difficult to find. There may be some existing in still-to-be-discovered diaries and letters.

An allusion to the figures appears in a dissertation by Dr. Oliver Wendell Holmes, whose interest in Lord Dexter was shared by his son, Mr. Justice Holmes. The Doctor could have seen the whole garden of figures in his childhood, but probably not. He was only about six years old when the September gale of 1815 overthrew most of the museum and blew his best breeches off the clothesline. It is the Doctor who offers us a curious tale of the image of Lord Dexter himself, which we neglected to say was placed well up front, bearing the caption "First in the East." Dr. Holmes asserts that there were two pedestals for two Dexters near the fence, one bearing the title, "I am First in the East" and the other the caption, "I am First in the West." One wonders where the Doctor got the story. Knapp speaks of only one statue of Dexter, labeled "I am the greatest man in the East." This again shows how readily Newburyport can garble facts, but the phrase, "First in the East" was first used at about this time as a reference to Dexter, and I personally suspect it was the profligate John P——— who coined it. The Dexter statue is gone long ago, to the shame of Newburyport. Its caption, though, still exists beneath a rare and famous engraving of Lord Dexter. It reads as follows: "I am the first in the East, the first in the West, and the greatest Philosopher in the Western World."

Knapp makes an arresting speculation regarding the cost of the images, which he thinks may have amounted to twice as much as the whole Jackson estate when Dexter purchased it. "The arch and figures of the Presidents were expensive, two thousand dollars or more; the lions, without the columns on which they stood, were carved at two hundred dollars a piece. The other thirty-six columns, with their images, must have cost two hundred dollars each — taking in the lettering and gilding, the whole could not have fallen short of fifteen thousand dollars." I do not know how Knapp arrived at such categorical figures, which add up to an extravagant sum at a time before our country's currency was the debased paper that it is at present. Personally I doubt whether Dexter, whose head for business was harder than his head for rum, would have consented to so lavish an outlay. The costs, I believe, were hearsay or supplied by Lord Dexter himself.

This theory is not demolished by the following sad but revealing announcement. Our poor friend is again offering his house for sale:

Mr. Dexter's Seat for Sale

I say one great bargain for a great man, if you will buy my house (and all that stands out of doors) I am in such a state of health I must sell my Pallace under the worth to go to the springs and one thing more my life is at a risk. Pay a part and good security for the rest; all the guts, plate, and books, horses and carriages, &c. A large amount of plate, it will show for itself. I will finish the museum 87 figures, four arches; 17 figures front and rear next the house; some scattering ones in the rear, eight acres and 107 rods of land, cuts 14 load of fodder; very good orchard. I have no family only robbers; I want to be still, not in my tomb I have one store house to sell on broadway, 2 dolors for 3 if my house, Pallace &c. is worth above 25000 Dolors give me less for I am afraid of my life, of being killed by my son; this is the truth.

TIMOTHY DEXTER.

Money, as a local moralist could have said, is not everything. We can feel sorry for our hero's tribulations and for his physical failures while simultaneously observing that the advertisement sounds like a modern New York fire sale. Dexter was still enough in trade to own a warehouse — the first we have heard of it. He was willing to double the number of figures as a sales inducement. He asks twenty-five thousand dollars for everything, in a tentative manner, knowing that not for an instant would he get the full price. This would scarcely indicate that he had paid anything like fifteen thousand dollars for these figures, and let us hope that the advertisement, like those that preceded it, was another passing whim of our sorely tried friend. Before turning to a happier subject, the great ode that was written to Lord Dexter by his poet, let us answer the often asked and intelligent question: Whatever became of all of this collection of figures? The answer is a sad reflection on Dexter's contemporaries and on the generation that succeeded him.

The museum was well preserved at the time of his death, after which the house and grounds came under the control of his executor, the same man who failed to sell the Ohio real estate in time. It never occurred to this gentleman, or to anyone else then living, that this fantastical collection

might have an eventual value. No money was expended on repairs of the images. The columns began to lean, the paint to peel. The great Indian Chief Cornplanter was the first to fall. Instead of putting him back in place, the grounds-keeper moved him to the vegetable garden for a scarecrow. When the hurricane of 1815 overthrew all of the company except the Presidents, instead of setting the figures up again, the executor sold them at auction. The prices mentioned are piteous. The goddess of Fame fetched the most. The image of William Pitt, the only known survivor of the whole *galère*, went for a dollar, and an ecclesiastic labeled "traveling preacher" sold for fifty cents. The town was apparently glad to be rid of the wooden parade, which had been viewed in serious circles with more mortification than interest and had been long considered an eyesore.

Mr. Howells, in his *Architectural Heritage of the Merri-*

mack, tells another tale. After the hurricane, a local citizen was commissioned to haul the figures away and to split them up so that they would not be sold, and there is a story still extant in the family of the womenfolk of the household being afraid to go to the woodshed at night because of the jumble of arms and legs. The auction tale should be believed, since Knapp himself may have witnessed it, and so may the other tale, if the latter refers to the Presidential arch. No matter what the circumstances were, it is strange indeed that only one authenticated figure and one arm and the hand of another remain extant. (I was once offered a wooden lamb by a Boston antiquary, which was said to have been on the Dexter place, but it looked more like a butcher's sign than a Wilson carving.)

The figure of William Pitt is now in the same category as the whooping crane. He is shown in the engraving of the palace, an incontrovertible proof of his validity. For some time he belonged to the Little family in Brookline, and Mr. Howells has obtained a splendid photograph of him, a solid, determined British type on whom one can gaze and then readily imagine what the Dexter place must have been like, with forty-odd other figures to accompany him. He is now, I believe, in the Smithsonian in Washington, the worse for wear for having stood long outdoors and for having been filled with concrete where he had been rotted by the weather.

While Dexter's museum cannot be called the capstone of the Dexter pyramid, it ranks among his finest achievements. Incidentally, it did more than these or the tomb to solidify his position. The museum marked the town's acceptance of him, and thus it became a monument of Chris-

tian tolerance as well as an educational institution. Everyone who passed the palace was obliged to recognize that its owner had attained the distinction of being not quite like other people, and yet of not being bereft of his wits. When one examined the pictured figures, one became aware of an insubstantial quality about this lonely man that raised him above the other original characters who abounded within the town's narrow limits. He was a step above Madam Hooper, though not so well educated. He had neither the wit nor the intelligence, the background nor the sophistication of his ablest adviser, our astrological schoolmaster, but he had greater stature and initiative. He lacked the oratorical and the literary adroitness of his own poet laureate, but he had a literary style of his own. He was as offbeat as any of his admirers, but at the same time he was more of a man than the lot of them. This realization was impinging at last upon the consciousness of Newburyport.

The ode that Jonathan Plummer wrote for him after the completion of the museum expresses quite accurately this sentiment. At the very least it is a summation of the Dexter activities in Dexter's finest hour. It is, incidentally, too, Jonathan Plummer's finest work. One is saddened to learn that Jonathan Plummer, who lived for some time after his patron's departure and who was once an omnivorous reader, finally gave up the perusal of great works of poetry. He did so because of the shame and discouragement that beset so many writers when confronted by the classics. He had thought, until he read these works, that he was the greatest poet of his time. It tortured him to find that he was not. But let us, by turning to his ode, judge for ourselves whether Jonathan Plummer was correct in his self-criti-

cism. The ode, according to rumor, was printed as a typical
Plummer broadside, and sold from his basket in Market
Square, where it was well received. It must have been, since
its lines have survived a century and a half of Newburyport
spring cleaning.

> Lord Dexter is a man of fame,
> Most celebrated is his name;
> More precious far than gold that's pure,
> Lord Dexter shines forevermore.
>
> His noble house, it shines more bright
> Than Lebanon's most pleasant height;
> Never was one who stepped therein
> Who wanted to come out again.
>
> His house is fill'd with sweet perfumes,
> Rich furniture doth fill his rooms;
> Inside and out it is adorn'd,
> And on the top an eagle's form'd.
>
> His house is white and trimm'd with green,
> For many miles it may be seen;
> It shines as bright as any star,
> The fame of it has spread afar.
>
> Lord Dexter, though, whose name alone
> Shines brighter than king George's throne;
> Thy name shall stand in books of fame,
> And princes shall his name proclaim.
>
> Lord Dexter hath a coach beside,
> In pomp and splendor he doth ride;
> The horses champ the silver bitt,
> And throw the foam around their feet.

The images around him stand,
For they were made by his command,
Looking to see Lord Dexter come,
With fixed eyes they see him home.

Four lions stand to guard the door,
With mouths wide open to devour
All enemies who dare oppose
Lord Dexter or his shady groves.

Lord Dexter, like king Solomon,
Hath gold and silver by the ton,
And bells to churches he hath given,
To worship the great king of heaven.

His mighty deeds they are so great,
He's honor'd both in church and state,
And when he comes all must give way,
To let Lord Dexter bear the sway.

When Dexter dies all things shall droop,
Lord East, Lord West, Lord North shall stoop,
And then Lord South with pomp shall come,
And bear his body to the tomb.

His tomb most charming to behold,
A thousand sweets it doth unfold;
When Dexter dies shall willows weep,
And mourning friends shall fill the street.

May Washington forever stand;
May Jefferson, by God's command,
Support the right of all mankind,
John Adams not a whit behind.

America, with all your host,
Lord Dexter in a bumper toast;
May he enjoy his life in peace,
And when he's dead his name not cease.

In heaven may he always reign,
For there's no sorry, sin, nor pain;
Unto the world I leave the rest,
For to pronounce Lord Dexter blest.

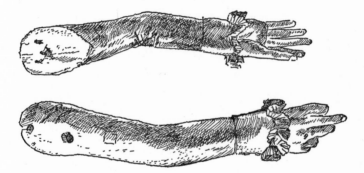

X V I I

Lord Dexter's Odd Volume

WHILE MR. WILSON's mallet and chisel made the chips fly from the emerging forms of the palace figures, life in the Dexter ménage moved on with the same totterings and gyrations that have characterized it throughout our history. The death of Madam Hooper caused him to take up with a more famous seeress, Moll Pitcher — a difficult matter, since she lived twenty-eight miles away and was averse to making house calls. On Dexter's first visit to her, in spite of his disguising himself, she astounded him by retailing all his past history. Madam Hooper had helped solve the theft of the Dexter melons, and Moll Pitcher continued the good work. Because of charms and night watchmen, Newburyport boys became afraid to steal the plums and apples.

Dexter, during his more peaceful moments in the palace, was developing so great an interest in clocks and watches that all the rooms became filled with them to an extent that made it necessary to employ a clockmaker to wind and set them. It delighted His Lordship to follow this expert as he went the rounds, and once Lord Dexter surprised him by making a philosophical remark. He said that he wished mankind could be wound up and controlled as readily as

clocks. Mr. Dexter also brought a further projection of this thought into a conversation with a caller. When one of his favorite subjects came up — that of local ministers — he wished that these men would cease their quarreling. If they could only be handled like clocks, he could arrange it so that they did not tick so loudly.

His fits of temper grew more uncontrolled. On some days he was delighted at the public interest in his wooden figures, whereas on others he violently resented curiosity. Finally he flew into a rage at a pedestrian who peered through the picket fence and fired at him with a pistol.

This seems to be the only time that our friend ever came in full-dress contact with the law. He drove to the Ipswich jail in his own coach, delighted with the idea that he was the first man to go to jail behind his own horses, but he was allowed to go home again after payment of a fine.

While all these things transpired, Lord Dexter was indoors more than usual. He was finding a growing solace in what may be termed creative writing, and his increased interest displays itself in the number and length of his contributions to the *Herald*. His longest one, published about this time, was a detailed letter to the General Court of Massachusetts on the subject of building bridges across the Merrimack River. From it one can gather that Dexter was averse to having any other bridges across the Merrimack except the Essex-Merrimack Bridge. He was alarmed that the General Court was planning another. The communication comprised a column of fine type, consisting of one- and two-syllable words, all of them misspelled, each usually in a different manner from the other. With the exception of three numbered paragraphs, there was not a single punctuation mark or capital.

The most noteworthy result of the effort is that it elicited a poem by a Newburyport writer, under the pen name of "Rusticus," purporting to be the answer of the General Court of Massachusetts.

> My Lord, of royal, silken Robe,
> We hear that you own half the globe
> And though your suit to us preferred
> Is outrée, here and there a word
> May such a Lord have all that's good
> And lambs and Lions when of wood;

Give him coaches, give him horses,
Fortune make up Samuel's losses,
Young flesh give him — every pleasure,
Stone rings, pictures without measure;
Brandy, give good punch and cider,
Gold-lac'd waistcoats stretched still wider,
Nectar'd oceans let him drink
But, Gods withhold — a pen and ink!

The world would have been a sadder place, and the Dexter memory more ephemeral than it is today, had the prayer of Rusticus been answered. Instead, Timothy Dexter, while figure after figure appeared on his grounds, was working on his *Pickle for the Knowing Ones.* We have seen, beginning with his formal advertisement of moosehide and blubber, how this malady of composition so prevalent among other nervous and unfulfilled types grew on him through his most fruitful years. Once he had exhibited diffidence when he had approached the local printers and had been apologetic for his untutored style. As early as the year 1798 he called publicly for the help of "Coleage Lant" people to assist in putting his ideas in order, because, as he confided, he knew, in spite of his limited powers of self-expression, that he did possess a lot of good ideas. Although we know from the way his sentences were brushed and furbished on various occasions that there were a few in town who did heed his plea, the main part of the work on which he was now embarking was wholly his own. His grammar and his spelling were already part of a tradition, with which printers may have taken liberties in order to increase its comicality, but still the Dexter product has a hallmark that is not susceptible of parody.

There is no way of telling exactly what made him want to write a book, but the result is still phenomenal. With a limited education and with no fixed idea of what he wished to say, between the autumn of 1801 and before the year 1802 had expired Lord Dexter succeeded in producing a printed work. Judging from the beginning, he may have planned it as an informative explanation of the museum and the figures that might be sold or given to the general public, but if this was his intention, it soon got out of hand. This book of Timothy Dexter's, exceptional by any unit of measure, was published in Salem in the year 1802, and not in Newburyport. Its title seems too witty to have been the author's, but it expresses perfectly the spirit and the contents: *A Pickle for the Knowing Ones; or, Plain Truths in a Homespun Dress*. The contents discuss so many aspects of its author's career that we have quoted from it freely throughout this text. Thus we are familiar with its character; yet it is still hard to describe the general nature of the Dexter opus.

Roughly it may be placed in the category of anthology, in that parts of it are a collection of previous statements to the press, and the rest is in general an assortment of announcements intended for public consumption which end nowhere in particular; but this is not a complete definition. There is something as elusive in *A Pickle for the Knowing Ones* as in the whole Dexter libido. It might be better to say that the *Pickle* is a mirror, held before the contradictions of its author's febrile mind. This does not imply that it is a human document in the dreariest sense of the phrase, because it is much more. Its unselfconsciousness makes it one of the most astonishing exhibitions of character achieved in the world of letters.

Exactly as its contents indicate, it is a pickle of words, misspelled, miscapitalized, and put together without punctuation; but a careful perusal will show that it is not meaningless. On the contrary, each page is crammed with bits of extraneous information that are scrambled to fit its author's mood. If it takes broken eggs to make an omelet, it is almost impossible to count the eggs of thought that Lord Dexter broke in composing his masterpiece. His sentences tumble over themselves in his eagerness for self-expression. Seldom have so many extraneous ideas been included in so little space. For example in its pages are Dexter's full plans for his museum, including its metaphysical significance. The *Pickle*, besides, contains his views on world politics (including a brief outline for a parliament of nations), a dissertation on his becoming a lord, a first-person revelation of how he made his money, some thoughts on the folly of

Newburyport's divorcing itself from the larger township of Newbury, notes and anecdotes on religious intolerance, a dissertation on the character of the devil, a description of his marital difficulties, thoughts on good fellowship and the usefulness of laughter, an account of the beating he received at the hands of the Chester lawyer, a criticism of his son-in-law, a vignette of a Yale commencement, more thoughts on human nature, and still more on the geographical location of Newburyport and the proper method of planning future highways and bridges. Each sentence is as explosive as a grain of popcorn, and the explosions occur in such quick succession as to be nearly simultaneous.

The excerpts quoted in these pages cannot do *A Pickle for the Knowing Ones* full justice. It is necessary to view them all together to understand why this book has given Lord Dexter a degree of literary immortality. Take the *Pickle* at any point, and a sentence or so chosen at random is enough to recreate Lord Dexter as well as to give the illusion that he is actually speaking.

> I will let you know the sekret hou you may see the Devel: stand on your head before a Loucking glass: take a bibel into your bousum, fast 40 owers and look in the Loucking glass; there is no Devel if you do not see the Ould fellow, but I affirm you will see that ould Devel.

Or turn another page.

> Man is the best annemal and the worst: all men are more or less the Devel, but there is site of ods — sum halfe sum three-quarters.
> The preasts fixes there goods six days, then they open

shop on sundays to sell there goods; sum sets them of better than others; when a man is so week he wont do for a Lawyer make a preast of him for week things to go with week things, the blind to lead the blind.

No matter what Dexter Rites [he also adds], it Dus to make the Ladyes laff at the tea table.

At the most unexpected moments there emerges an awareness of self that kept America's great eccentric on a legally even keel.

It is said when the book was published—privately printed, by the way — that Dexter's circle of admirers gave it praise that would have turned his head if it had not been turned already. They told him that this philosophical work was comparable to the best of Shakespeare and Milton. It would be unfair to his memory to say that *A Pickle for the Knowing Ones* is literature in an academic sense, but it does have some of the attributes of literature. It has a style that raises it above the level of its thought content. It has the unselfconscious naturalness of a first-rate work of art. Its illusion of reality is often perfect. It reflects the mood of its author, and its obscurist qualities may deserve the study of a modern school. Finally it has a vitality which fashion has not effaced. It still makes delightful reading, if you do not read too much at once. This all can be said for the *Pickle* without perjury. The *Pickle*, in spite of its detractors, has succeeded in standing on its own literary feet. With very few lapses, it has been in print for the last one hundred and fifty years, a remarkable record when so many better books have been forgotten.

In view of these characteristics, it may seem odd that the

Pickle was scornfully received by its contemporary public, and that among the critics, at least, it did not cause the ladies and gentlemen to laugh over their tea. The *Impartial Herald*, which for so many years had been hospitable to Dexter's contributions, dismissed his effort as follows:

> We observe advertised in a Salem paper, a thing just published entitled *A Pickle for the Knowing Ones; or, Plain Truths in a Homespun Dress,* by Timothy Dexter, Esq., of Newburyport. This will be a valuable acquisition to the lovers of knowledge and polite literature.

Overelaborate satire, a weakness of the *Impartial Herald* when it mentioned the name of Dexter, blinded its editors to the truth that the *Pickle* as a whole was a better satire than any achieved by that journal. It still remains a satire on the manners and morals of one of the most ephemeral and impossible eras in our history; but then, few people living in a given age have the perspective that enables them to judge what part of it may be hilarious to future generations. "Mankind," as Dexter has written, "is mankind."

His fellow mortals, being what they were, began reading the *Pickle* in spite of its frigid reception. It was given away liberally to visitors at the mansion during the next few years, and copies were passed from hand to hand, until it had a good circulation and better word-of-mouth advertising. It evoked a letter from Philadelphia regarding the *Pickle*'s style and punctuation. New England school children, according to rumor, were required to write compositions on the book's literary folly and the vanities of its incoherent author.

The *National Aegis* gave it greater space than the *Herald* in an "Evening Speculation," and, I am sorry to say, handled our friend with greater harshness.

For what purpose are riches given to some men unless to display in more glowing colours the disgusting deformities of their characters? There are many who would pass current in the throng without being distinguished for any positive vices or ridiculous foibles were they not brought into notice by the glare and glitter of wealth. . . . Timothy Dexter in our own country . . . exhibits an instance — This man, had he continued in that situation to which he appeared to have been destined by his birth, would never have been conspicuous for his foibles, or ridiculous for his folly. Had fortune been satisfied that he should have remained a leather dresser through life, he might have tanned and curried with the reputation of an industrious mechanic and a useful citizen.

A speculation lucky for his *purse* and *unlucky* for his memory, took him from his *work shop* and seated him down in a *palace*. The gilded trappings and glittering ornaments of his house serve only to render more lucid and ludicrous the folly, the ignorance and the contemptible vanity of the owner. His incoherent and unintelligible jargon furnish subjects of laughter for his guests: his whimsical taste and capricious temper furnish subjects of speculation to those who are eager to analyze the wild eccentricities of the human Character! That pride which is ever inseparable from folly, keeps his tongue and his pen in perpetual motion, that his name may be abroad and his memory may not be forgotten. . . . Lest there should be no record to hand his name to posterity, he occasionally calls in the aid of the press, to assist him in proclaiming his folly to the world. The public papers bear witness that though "a fool may be brayed in a mortar, he will not depart from his folly" and

in his *Pickle for the knowing ones* he has effectually *preserved the full grown fruits* of his nonsense."

His ruling passion [writes a third contemporary] appeared to be popularity and one would suppose he rather
chose to render his name "infamously famous than not
famous at all." His writings stand as a monument for the
truth of this remark, for those who have read his *Pickle
for the Knowing Ones,* a jumble of letters promiscuously
gathered together, find it difficult to determine whether to
most laugh at the consummate folly, or despise the vul-
garity and profanity of the writer.

It has remained for the severe Dexter critic, William
Cleaves Todd, to point out that the *Pickle* often contains a
background of common sense. We must go beyond the
middle of the century to the golden age of Boston letters
before we discover another defender of the Dexter work,
a kindly advocate, even if his tongue is in his cheek. In one
of his *Autocrat* essays, Dr. Holmes has delivered a disquisi-
tion on Lord Timothy Dexter. It is disconcerting to find
that his paragraphs at present are more dated than those of
the first lord of America, when Dr. Holmes uses Dexter
and his writing as a rebuke to a poetic parvenu, Walt Whitman. One wonders, if we were to compare the *Pickle* with
the poetic patterns of e. e. cummings, whether we might
be treading on equally dangerous ground. Speaking of Dexter as an author, Dr. Holmes gives the following appraisal:

As an inventor of a new American style, he goes far
beyond Mr. Whitman, who to be sure, cares little for the
dictionary, and makes his own rules of rhythm, so far as
there is any rhythm in his sentences. But Lord Timothy

spells to suit himself, and in place of employing punctuation as it is commonly used, prints a separate page of periods, colons, semicolons, commas, with notes of interrogation and of admiration, with which the reader is requested to 'peper and solt' the book as he pleases.

I am afraid that Mr. Emerson and Mr. Whitman must yield the claim of declaring American literary independence to Lord Timothy Dexter, who not only taught his countrymen that they need not go to the Herald's College to authenticate their titles of nobility, but also that they were at perfect liberty to spell just as they liked, and to write without troubling themselves about stops of any kind.

It is only fair to allow the author himself the last word in this battle of critics, and Mr. Dexter has availed himself of the privilege, using his favorite sounding board, our old *Impartial Herald:*

> Mister Printers — of N Port, I thank thee to put thous skraps into your paper I being one of your Customers and I will pa you for it — A littel mousement to mankind at Large — A Littel sortment to poussel mankind for gassing A about Nater & things of Noue DisCoverys of men and things. I — I — me T Dexter of N Port Desires Any man or men on the gloube to Exseeds me as to what I have rote in my Littel book; and what I can Rite Consarning Nater and the sole and the frame of man. . . . I am the old plane Tim to see any felosofer in the world Ime
>
> TIMOTHY DEXTER

We have left until the end of this discussion the most challenging detail presented by *A Pickle for the Knowing Ones.* This one aspect, in fact, has made the Dexter work known to thousands who have never read it. After the publication of the first edition in the year 1802, two other known editions, with only slight changes, appeared during the author's lifetime. But not until the more elaborate edition of 1838 was printed (in Newburyport, this time) do we encounter what is frequently considered the greatest gem of Dexter humor.

In the appendix to this carefully edited and annotated printing suddenly appears the following:

> fouder mister printer the Nowing ones complane of my book the fust edition had no stops I put in a Nuf here and thay may peper and solt it as they plese

```
,,,,,,,,,,,,,,,,,,,,,,,,,,,,,,,,,,,,,,,,,,,,,,,,,,,,,,,,,,,,,,,,,,,,,,,,,,,,,,,,
,,,,,,,,,,,,,,,,,,,,,,,,,,,,,,,,,,,,,,,,,,,,,,,,,,,,,,,,,,,,,,,,,,,,,,,,,,,,,,,
.................................................................................
,,,,,,,,,,,,,,,,,,,,,,,,,,,,,,,,,,,,,,,,,,,,,,,,,,,,,,,,,,,,,,,,,,,,,,,,,,,,,,,
:::::::::::::::::::::::::::::::::::::::::::::::::::::::::::::::::::::::::::::::::::
...................................!!!!!!!!!!!!!!!!!!........................
.................................. !!!!!!!!! .............................
.................................!!!!!! ..................................
................................ ! .....................................
,,,,,,,,,,,,,,,,,,,,,,,,,,,,,,,,,,,,,,,,,,,,,,,,,,,,,, ,,,,,,,,,,,,,,,,,,,,,,,
............ ??????????????????????????????????? ............
```

This footnote has been repeated and paraphrased from Dr. Holmes on through a century, until it has become a better-known part of Dexteriana than his mercantile successes.

But where is the second edition containing this long-lived quip? This question has no present answer, for modern eyes have yet to see the edition in which this note first allegedly appeared — if there ever was such a printing.

We have to thank a Newburyport writer for a thorough study of this subject — Edmund Pearson, whose *Studies in*

Murder, macabre in theory but not in practice, are on their way to becoming a classic. Mr. Pearson was a loyal son, always, of Newburyport, devoted to its atmosphere and history. While connected with the New York Public Library he prepared for that institution a brochure on the various editions of the *Pickle,* which was published in the early nineteen-twenties. He could only throw light on the mystery of the unknown edition without solving it.

Was this note appended by the editor of this 1838 edition, who, from his explanations and headings, was obviously delighted with the intricacies of the Dexter prose? Like Mr. Pearson, I am inclined to doubt it, because the statement is too characteristic of Lord Dexter to have been manufactured offhand.

The best argument, I believe, that an undiscovered second edition, or something approximating it, once existed lies in the Knapp biography. Knapp's Life was first published in 1838, the same year as this important *Pickle* printing, but the manuscript itself must have been completed earlier. In his text Knapp states that he was unable to find a copy of Dexter's work after the "most diligent search," and then he lapses into a soliloquy on Dexter's alleged hopes that his work would prove immortal. Not being able to obtain a copy, Knapp is obliged to describe the Dexter book from memory. Without discriminating between editions, or mentioning a second, he alludes to the punctuation marks, saying that Dexter "puts them all in the last page, requesting the reader to place them where he pleased." He also states that the *Pickle* had a cut of Dexter and his little dog upon the cover, which must have been taken from the engraving made of him in 1805. No early known edition of

the *Pickle* has this picture. This would indicate that Knapp
had in mind some vanished edition, and we might agree
except for the vagueness of the Knapp recollection. But it
is still hard to believe that he saw the edition of 1838 at the
time he wrote the Life.

Mr. Pearson submitted the problem to three men "as
learned in early American bibliography as any living"—
Messrs. Wilberforce Eames, Charles Evans, and George
Parker Winship. "I find them," Mr. Pearson writes, "all
agreed in thinking that the note was probably printed by
his [Dexter's] authority and in his lifetime but in some
form not easily discoverable today. Mr. Eames suggests a
missing edition of the *Pickle;* Mr. Evans, a broadside; Mr.
Winship, a looseleaf to be inserted in the pamphlet." There
is one other possibility— the note may have first appeared
in a Dexter communication to a Newburyport or Salem
editor. If it is in the *Impartial Herald,* I missed it when I
last perused the files, and I have never attempted to pursue
this clue as far as Salem.

This is enough of Dexter as a writer. It is time to return
to the end of his career, but before doing so, let us add that
when Mr. Pearson made his study no fewer than nine editions of *A Pickle for the Knowing Ones* were in existence,
and it has been reprinted twice subsequently.[1] An inter-

[1] Mr. Pearson lists the following editions of *A Pickle for the Knowing Ones,* and
there have been at least two other printings since, raising the total to eleven or twelve.
  1802. Salem. 24 pages.
  1805. Newburyport. 32 pages.
  1805. n.p. (Salem?). 36 pages. Title page says: Second Edition.
  1838. Boston. 42 pages The Peter Quince edition, with punctuation marks and
      note to printer, stated here to come from "Dexter's Second Edition." Dexter
      died in 1806, about 32 years before this edition appeared.
  1847. Newburyport. 24 pages. Expurgated and rearranged; with punctuation intro-
      duced into the text by the editor.

ested reader can purchase the latest at Newburyport's Historical Society.

His Lordship has now made his last bid for recognition. The clocks in the mansion were ticking, but the clock inside Timothy Dexter needed more than mortal winding. It was running fitfully, and its ticking grew sadly slow.

1848. Newburyport, 32 pages. Title page says: Fourth Edition.

1858. Boston. The reprint included in the 1858 edition (the 3rd) of Samuel L. Knapp's "Life of Lord Timothy Dexter," pages 123–153.

1881. Boston. 36 pages. Reprint of 1838 edition.

1916. Newburyport. 36 pages. Reprint of 1838 edition.

X V I I I

Gateway to Fantasy

AT THE SEASON of year when the crickets begin chirping, time itself often gives the impression of stopping in Newburyport, reminding one of a pause in the brisk unrolling of a film. This phenomenon, allowing everyone to see everything very clearly, without distraction, existed in the last years of Dexter more markedly than in ours. From the cupola of the palace, a spot now visited seldom, if ever, by the lord of the manor, the Merrimack was blue and silver in the sun, and the dunes of Plum Island, that shifting bulwark that protected the town from the ocean, were as gold as ever when the sun's rays were at a proper angle. The light of late summer had an autumnal clarity that occasionally made everything as peaceful as the surface of a millpond. The shipping in the harbor was more intricate and beautiful than it had been earlier. The hulls of the ships, the brigs, the hermaphrodites and the schooners, now to be seen only in the shop of a local maker of ship's models, had a variety of color not to be equaled by the later clipper ships. New dwellings were rising on High Street. The spire of the church of the First Religious Society on Pleasant Street had appeared when Dexter's museum was in the making. The museum itself was in excellent condition, with every figure painted, crowding the grounds more thickly than the statues in the acres of an elaborate French château. The lawns and gardens, tended and improved under Lord Dexter's supervision, had never looked better, and the orchards seldom more tempting to the covetous eyes of youth on High or Low Streets. They were still protected by watchmen and by mystical incantation. The green and

white house itself rose in a miragelike lack of realism above its lawns, its images and its exotic trees and shrubbery. The whole place had never looked better, but the word was passing through Newburyport that the creator of this Federalist Disneyland was not all he used to be.

This gossip was carried by workmen and servants and by the faithful group that still attended the palace. But passers-by looking through the fence could still see the master, inspecting his domain, gazing at his own effigy and saluting that of Napoleon, whose star was not yet on the wane. In spite of such reassuring glimpses, word was circulating that Timothy Dexter, whose life since he had made his fortune had been one long flight from reality, was now retreating further. He had traveled a great way from his Malden boyhood and thence down the old shore road to

Newburyport, to mansions and speculations and patents of nobility.

He had been through the War of the Revolution. He had seen the privateers and their prizes. He had seen the Tracys and Jacksons lose their fortunes. He had seen the town change from a small seaport into one of the greatest shipbuilding centers in the country, with prospects of becoming a metropolis. He had struggled with a recalcitrant wife and children and with all the temptations of leisure. The gigantic Lucy Lancaster, whose services were more in demand, and others familiar with the household, said that Mr. Dexter harbored doubts about himself as he grew feeble; and sometimes there was a lull, though temporary, in his verbal war with his son and Madam Dexter. He had done enough, and more than enough. He had amply repaid his town in charity, in trade, and wages, as well as in taxes, for the shelter it had given him; and in the years of twilight there was some recompense.

When he appeared downtown with his cane and jewelry, many addressed him as His Lordship, and the press now referred to him openly as Lord Dexter. People were beginning to realize that he was more of a local ornament than a disgrace. The stories of him were already being adorned by local humor and exaggeration. Parents were beginning to point him out to their children as something rich and strange that should be remembered. Timothy Dexter, after the publication of *A Pickle for the Knowing Ones,* while still alive, was in the process of becoming a myth. Travelers from Portsmouth, Salem and further points came to view the images and to interview their owner. The younger and more brazen walked beneath the Presidential arch and knocked on the front door. When received, they introduced themselves as foreign visting nobles, and Lord Dexter was not disconcerted. They discussed the merits of his book, asking abstruse questions which their host often attempted to answer. On one occasion, when hospitality was very generous, the visitors insisted on placing Lord Dexter and his chair on the center of his own table, crowning him, as he had crowned his poet. His character was finally so widely recognized that James Akin did Dexter's full-length portrait, which he advertised for sale as "Wonderful and Philosophic." It has been called by those who remembered Dexter an excellent likeness. This curiosity, good cheer and encouragement did not have the reviving effects that might have been expected. Lord Timothy's answers grew rambling of an evening and he was uncertain after a very little drink.

The ills that the total abstainer predicts for the heavy drinker were finally falling to Dexter's lot. It was an age when heavy drinking was often a badge of gentility. No one minded much when prominent citizens were helped upstairs to bed; but even Newburyport had been shocked by Dexter's behavior in his cups. Yet, ironically enough, one favorable comment has been made regarding his drinking habits. It is said that in his worst days, when alcoholic addiction held him hardest in its grip, Lord Dexter had none of the habitual drunkard's coarseness of taste. He continued to insist on the very best brandy obtainable and on the choicest vintage wines, instead of carelessly drinking raw and unwholesome spirits. This constant demand for the best, Knapp believes, was what kept him so long alive.

Though failing physically, his mind was as alert as ever,

and his habits were not changed, including his old desire
to buy and sell. He chartered at least one vessel in his last
years, and brought in a final foreign cargo, as is proved by
his advertisement of it, which is with us still, including his
favorite phrases: "For Sale Cheap," "Assortment," "lowest
rate for Cash."

For Sale Cheap
By Timothy Dexter
A handsome Assortment of English
and other
Goods
Consisting of

27 Groce Buttons, different kinds, 50 doz shawls, number
pieces Calicoes, Dimothies, handsome assortment of watch
chains, Ribbons, Bandannas, Elegant Straw Mats, Pewter
Canns, Pictures and Vinegar by wholesale and retail

Muslin Handkerchiefs

600 cwt Assorted Pewter Ware

800 yards Flannel, Cotton Hose

1300 Spanish Otter Skins suitable for Napping Hats

1000 wt. Candles 250 wt. Tallow wholesale or retail

All or part of the above will be sold at
lowest rate for Cash.

As late as 1805 he wrote a recapitulation of his grievances
against Madam Dexter, extending over a period of thirteen
years, and said that he was in hopes of marrying a widow.
When a member of Madam Dexter's family attempted to
give some orders in the household, Dexter once again had
recourse to his pistol, but no damage resulted. Other behavior patterns also continued. He continued to worry over
his financial resources. He still persisted in his communica-

tions to the press. The Houghton Library at Harvard possesses a peculiar Dexter item. It is a sheet smaller than a piece of typewriting paper on which a philosophic thought is printed, to the effect that men are much like animals, some resembling cats, some cattle, some wolves. It was a broadside that was intended as a give-away, or to be included with the *Pickle*. The date is 1805.

He still objected to the high cost of mourning garments. He called on men of learning to inform him whether there was any truth in the assertion that angels had wings, or whether men or horses were ever known to have possessed these appendages, and suggested leaving it all to the judgment of certain eminent men including "bonnepart." It is not necessary to continue the list of this old man's suggestions, because this is nearly the last one that he ever advanced to the world. He asked these questions in the year 1806, and in that same year Lord Timothy Dexter was in a better position than some to know the answer. He died on the 25th of October. His green and white coffin, with its lock and handles, was ready, and the key was in his pocket.

Knapp, in describing Dexter's last days, implies that a period of grace descended upon him, coupled with a deep regret for his frivolous behavior. So anxious was he to repair as best he could his omissions that he called on the best legal advice to draw a sound and sensible will. There may have been remorse, but in this last regard our biographer is incorrect again. Lord Dexter's will was drawn in 1799, and let us applaud his good sense in never changing it.

Mrs. E. Vale Smith, in her *History of Newburyport*,

gives him a terse and grim final summation: "He died un-
regretted, (as he had lived without the respect of the community)." This assumption, we hope, is too sweeping, but
it does appear that in the community his passing evoked
a sigh more of relief than of sorrow. He had been in the
depths, full fathom five, for so long that many persons
must have feared that, had he lived more than the fifty-
nine years allotted him, he might have turned into something stranger than he was already. His impact on the community may be measured by the size of his obituary, which
appeared in the *Herald* three days later. It was a neat blend-
ing of charity and criticism, composed in measured terms.

"He lived," the notice reads, "perhaps one of the most
eccentric men of his time"—an unduly cautious statement. "His singularities and peculiar notions were universally proverbial"—meaning that at his death he was

already a public figure. "The qualities of his mind were of that indefinite cast which forms an exception to every other character recorded in history, or known in the present age, and 'none but himself could be his parallel.' " This is not a bad summation, besides being an admission that a remarkable man had left Newburyport forever. "But among the motley groups of his qualities, it would be injustice to say he possessed no good ones — he certainly did. No one will impeach his honesty, and his numerous acts of liberality are in the recollection of all, while one of the items of his last will will be gratefully remembered."

The item must have been his bequest to the town of Newburyport, of which more later. The writer then speaks with embarrassment of the warming pans and of the deceased's commercial ability, and says that the Dexter house "exhibited more the appearance of a museum of artificial curiosities than the dwelling of a family." The conclusion of this rather perfunctory article contains its unkindest cut. "His principles of religion, (if they could be called principles) were equally odd: a blind philosophy peculiar to himself led him to believe in the system of transmigration at some times; at others he expressed those closely connected with deism; but it is not a matter of surprise that one so totally illiterate should have no settled or rational principles. His reason left him two days before his death, but he has gone to render an account of his life to a just and merciful Judge."

To venture a conservative guess, this piece was written by one of the town's several ministers, who had called on Lord Dexter in a helpful way and who was correct in being confused by his theology. The hesitation shown here in

fixing the final destination of Dexter's soul is contradicted
by another.

He had one stanch supporter who was not afraid to
honor the end of his career. Jonathan Plummer, his laureate,
who would never again wear the star-spangled livery and
who was disappointed at not being mentioned in the Dexter
will, allowed loyalty to conquer hurt feelings. He composed several broadsides on Lord Dexter, the best of which
is entitled "Something New." It begins with various bits of
information regarding the Dexter career, and concludes
with a funeral sermon. Here the laureate expresses a belief
that Lord Dexter's many acts of charity would so over-
balance his faults, when he appeared before the Throne,
that he would finally take his place in "the glorious company of Abraham, Isaac, and Jacob" — to which Mr. Pearson adds this comment:

"The imagination halts at the picture of Timothy Dexter making one of this *partie carrée,* but Plummer's theology is perhaps as good as that of the pedant who prepared
the notice for the Newburyport *Herald.*"

While underlining the Dexter eccentricity and originality, it should be noted that nowhere in the obituary is there
a hint that Dexter was feeble-minded. On the contrary,
his business judgment was respected, and his will shows
the care he could apply, when obliged, to practical matters. It is a model of clarity, and generosity. In spite of his
battles with the ghost and Samuel, they were liberally provided for, and so were his daughter, and his granddaughter,
the child of Nancy and Mr. Bishop, who, we are told, was
well brought up by her father. Also two of his brothers are
mentioned.

There is one clause of especial interest. Lord Dexter left
to a schoolmaster named Joseph Somerby two of his shares
in the Essex-Merrimack Bridge, his best silver can, his turtle-shell pinchbeck watch (the one he lost on State Street),
three of his best silver spoons, and one pair of gold sleeve-
buttons. This is the most personal of all his bequests, a conspicuous display of friendship that arouses curiosity as to
why the name of Joseph Somerby was never previously
mentioned. I believe, until investigation contradicts me,
that Joseph Somerby must have been the schoolmaster-
astrologer mentioned by Samuel Knapp. If so, the bequest
indicates the extent of his influence over Dexter as well as
the latter's affection. There is only one thing wrong about
this theory. John P———, according to Knapp, prophesied
that his own death would not occur until the sun was blot-
ted from the heavens. Oddly enough, he did die "in a miserable mansion" during a total eclipse of the sun on June 16,
1806, thus predeceasing Dexter by some months. Timothy
Dexter left to the town of Malden, his birthplace, three
hundred dollars for the purchase of one of his favorite gifts,
a bell for the meetinghouse, and the sum of two thousand
dollars, the income of which was to accumulate for a century. The interest was then to be appropriated annually
"for the support of the gospel in said town of Malden." To
the town of Newburyport he also gave two thousand dollars, the income of which was to be applied annually to
the support of the poor outside the almshouse.

It has been said and never refuted that Timothy Dexter
was the first individual in the history of Newburyport, a
town whose importance to the United States at that time
may be compared to that of Boston today, to leave a be-

quest for any purpose to its inhabitants. If so, his course of charity has been liberally followed by others.

There remains of the erratic Dexter career only one aspect that demands consideration, and this is perhaps the most outstanding of all the Dexter problems; and one that asks once more the question that arises at every turn of the man's superficial and spiritually useless life. What was it that he actually did that has made him deserving of any sort of memory? At the risk of being unkind to one who can no longer answer back, let us make an inventory of his accomplishments, starting with that of his estate.

Here the propensity for exaggeration had reached a staggering proportion. When the figures of the estate of Timothy Dexter, Esq., were made public, the smallness of the total made it difficult to believe.

House and land on High Street	$12,000.00
110 Shares in the Essex Merrimack Bridge	15,400.00
Two Shares in Chester N.H. Turnpike	100.00
Furniture, Crockery and silverware, Horses and carriages, clothing, and promissory notes, &c., &c.,	7,527.39
	$35,027.39

The purchasing power of the dollar was vastly greater then than at present, and the estate may have been valued low for tax purposes, but at its best the figure is an anti-climax. The Dexter fortune, so inflated by rumor, was modest when placed against the acquisitions of the Jackson and Tracy families, and small compared with the estate of several of Timothy Dexter's Newburyport contemporaries.

If we wish to give the largest latitude and take the Dexter fortune at its zenith before the profligacies of Samuel and the rapacities of Abraham Bishop and commercial losses may have reduced it, it could hardly have been more than seventy thousand dollars — not a large sum then for New-buryport. Where was the gold and silver by the ton? It was a figure of collective imagination, stimulated by an old man's love of exhibitionism.

But let us go down the list. What about Dexter's trading reputation? What of the cornered market in corset stays? The coals to Newcastle? The cats? The mittens? And those warming pans? Half of these are fantasy, and truth about the remainder lies behind a cloud of reasonable doubt. What about the tomb and the Temple of Reason? François Villon could tell you where they are — gone with the snows of yesterday. Incidentally, when the figures were sold at auction the image of Lord Dexter could find no bidder what-soever. What of *A Pickle for the Knowing Ones?* In spite of its originality and hilarity, it must finally be termed a literary curiosity. The one fragment of it that has com-mended it to generations is the salt-and-pepper note about the punctuation marks, and this itself has no proper ac-creditation. What of all the Dexter stories, the funeral, the wife beating, and Jonathan Plummer's cloak with stars? They are overblown pieces of fantasy, too, designed more for popular diversion than serious information.

Finally, what of Lord Dexter himself? At best he was a vulgar old man whose servants complained of his habit of spitting tobacco in the house. His temper was capricious. He suffered from senile concupiscence, he was ill-educated, and he was vulgar when drunk or sober. He suffered also

from an inflated ego. He obeyed the most absurd suggestions of his flatterers. As he said himself, it was better to
make some sort of noise than none at all. It might be charitable to add some of his few good traits to the list, but even
so, the minus total still would be appalling. Timothy Dexter
would still be obstreperous. By no stretch of the imagination could he have been what we now call "lovable." What
did he have, then, that has made him persist, at least in the
annals of Americana, when wiser, abler and better men
in Newburyport and elsewhere have marched into oblivion?

His memory assuredly does not live only because he was a
peculiarly flamboyant eccentric. The world, particularly
the Dexter world, has been filled with eccentrics. Their
antics have been recorded in many volumes, and in only
one respect is our hero different from the rest of this off-
the-record group with which he is generally classified. All
the others whose careers I, at least, have ever encountered
have lived in such peculiar ways that it is impossible to
identify them with their times except in the most superficial manner. By changing their dress it would be possible
to move them from century to century, so they would all
of them be capable of happily exhibiting their oddities in
any historical environment; but this is not true of Lord
Timothy Dexter of Newburyport. His life was so closely
integrated with his era that he is a caricature of it more
than merely a sportive personality.

In the beginning of this book I have tried to recreate
some aspects of Federalist Newburyport — unsuccessfully,
because no past can ever return. There is no use weeping
over things that are gone. They can never be retrieved in
their ancient combinations. Newburyport was a much

greater town in Dexter's time than it is now a city. It was more cosmopolitan and cultivated. Conceivably the mass education of the place may now be higher, but the education of its leading citizens in Dexter's day was more cultivated and thorough than anything that can now be obtained. Its inhabitants were more skilled in more crafts and more diligent in their work and worship. The food was better and more varied. There were good taverns, good wines and liquors. Life was easier, at least in the higher echelons. We can balance this with the shortness of the life span, the discomfort of cold rooms, the prevalence of epidemics, and birth and infant mortality. Nevertheless, the Newburyport of Dexter's day had as much or more than any other American community could then offer. The same cannot be said of it at present, nor of any of its prototypes along the New England seaboard.

The shipbuilding and the commerce of Newburyport grew in the Dexter era because of America's commercial prosperity, stimulated by European wars. It was a commerce of inexpensive, light-draft vessels, offering huge profits and negligible losses. The Dexter age was one of chance that encouraged speculation. There was a boom-town atmosphere along the New England coast beneath its Georgian veneer. It was a time of generous spending and prosperity for every segment of society — an era that was ephemeral. The ports for shallow-draft vessels were already on their way to obsolescence, with the beginning of the Jeffersonian Embargo. Newburyport's shipbuilding was doomed as soon as the forests of its hinterland were eliminated.

But it was a great time while it lasted, a day of gold-laced waistcoats, of finely painted coaches and chaises, of over-dressed, overpolite, overpretentious ladies and gentlemen. It was a time when many people became newly rich, and tried, not very successfully, to imitate the manners of London and Paris. It was, in some respects, a period of pretentious elegance, as well as one of hypocritical virtue; and its spirit is reflected in the writings of its day. Looking at the town and the people in this light, it is not hard to see that Timothy Dexter represented not only its prosperity but also all of it that was ludicrous. He did not intend consciously to be this representation. The role was thrust upon him through no fault of his, except that his character was ideal. He could never have dreamed of being the Dexter of the legend. It is Newburyport's fault, not his, that he has been more than a local figure for a hundred and fifty years. He is the result of the combined operation of Newburyport, as surely as his figures were carved by Joseph Wilson. His own generation helped in his creation, but it was abetted by succeeding ones.

The Dexter figure, primarily designed by a few wits among his own associates and by others on the wharves and in the town countinghouses, has been embellished, and beautified by the town's collective humor, which was often surprisingly original. This work has been going on for many, many years, until Lord Timothy Dexter has been changed from a difficult old man into a communal work of art.

Despite all efforts to eradicate it, there is an element so human and so expansive in his memory that it embraces the whole time in which he lived. All the appurtenances of an ancient maritime supremacy are Timothy Dexter's now.

Timothy Dexter, Died Oct 26, 1806
Elizabeth Dexter, Died, July 3, 1809

It is strange but it is true that the name of an irresponsible man is now remembered beyond all his richer and more virtuous brother merchants. Up from the shadows comes Timothy Dexter of Newburyport to represent them all and to stand for all their forgotten words. The profusion of the age, its uncertainty, its license, its bright colors all lie with him.

A simple stone with an urn engraved upon it, initialed "T. D.," marks the resting place in Newburyport of all that was mortal of this man. Madam Dexter died in 1809, Samuel three months later, and they lie beside the head of their house on the hill above Frog Pond. Nancy lived on, a pitiful sight, maintained as a paying guest in the palace of her father, which was leased to an enterprising innkeeper. She died in 1851, surviving by a year the Presidents on the arch. There are now no direct descendants of Lord Timothy Dexter left.

There is a kindly epitaph on the stone that marks his grave.

In Memory of
Mr. Timothy Dexter
who died October 23d
a. d. 1806
Aetatis 60
He gave liberal Donations
For the support of the Gospel
For the benefit of the Poor
And for other benevolent purposes

"Mr." they called him, not a glittering title but one of more social significance than it possesses at present. It is a pity that the stonecutter did not add: "His town made him the First in the East." But it was too early for anyone to foretell this future.

The End

JAN 1 3 '61

JAN 2 4 '61

SEP 1 4 '61

FEB 2 4 '62

MAR 2 7 '62

AUG 2 4 '62

AUG 1 2 '62

PRINTED IN U.

LEE COUNTY LIBRARY SYSTEM

3 3262 00021 4558

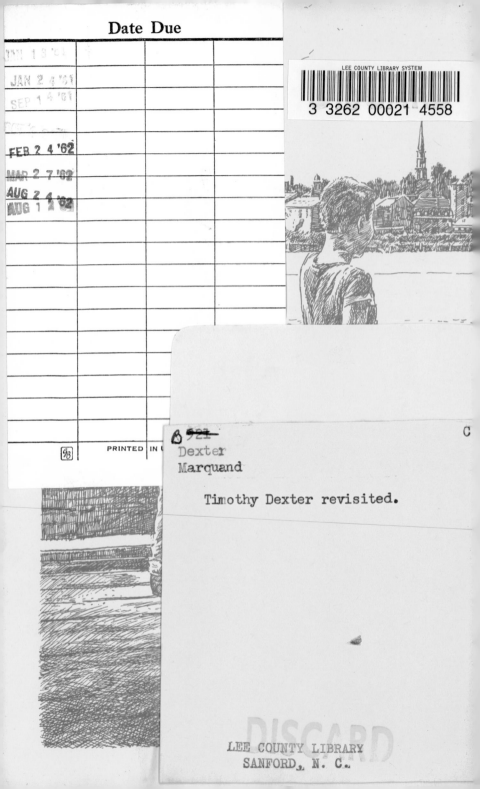

B 921
Dexter
Marquand

Timothy Dexter revisited.

C

DISCARD

LEE COUNTY LIBRARY
SANFORD, N. C.